11/16

God Bless America

God Bless America

The Surprising History of an Iconic Song

Sheryl Kaskowitz

OXFORD
UNIVERSITY PRESS

OXFORD
UNIVERSITY PRESS

Oxford University Press is a department of the University of Oxford.
It furthers the University's objective of excellence in research,
scholarship, and education by publishing worldwide.

Oxford   New York
Auckland   Cape Town   Dar es Salaam   Hong Kong   Karachi
Kuala Lumpur   Madrid   Melbourne   Mexico City   Nairobi
New Delhi   Shanghai   Taipei   Toronto

With offices in
Argentina   Austria   Brazil   Chile   Czech Republic   France   Greece
Guatemala   Hungary   Italy   Japan   Poland   Portugal   Singapore
South Korea   Switzerland   Thailand   Turkey   Ukraine   Vietnam

Oxford is a registered trade mark of Oxford University Press
in the UK and certain other countries.

Published in the United States of America by
Oxford University Press
198 Madison Avenue, New York, NY 10016

Library of Congress Cataloging-in-Publication Data
Kaskowitz, Sheryl.
God bless America : the surprising history of an iconic song / Sheryl Kaskowitz.
    pages   cm
Includes bibliographical references and index.
ISBN 978-0-19-991977-2 (hardcover : alk. paper)
1. Berlin, Irving, 1888–1989. God bless America. I. Title.
ML410.B499K37   2013
782.42′1599—dc23   2012046073

Publication of this book was supported by grants from the H. Earle Johnson Fund of the
Society for American Music and the AMS 75 PAYS Endowment of the American Musicological Society,
funded in part by the National Endowment for the Humanities and the Andrew W. Mellon Foundation.

1 3 5 7 9 8 6 4 2

Printed in the United States of America
on acid-free paper

To Ben, Ezra, and Elliott

CONTENTS

ACKNOWLEDGMENTS

Many thanks to everyone at Oxford University Press, including my editor, Norm Hirschy, whose unfailing support and wise advice guided this project into being; the production editor, Joellyn Ausanka, for her thoughtful oversight; Lisbeth Redfield for her attention to manuscript details; Mary Sutherland for copyediting; Sue Marchman for a comprehensive index; and the anonymous manuscript readers who provided insightful comments. I am also grateful to everyone who made time within their busy lives to help with my research, including the many former members of Congress who participated in my survey and the 1,849 people who participated in my online survey. Special thanks go to Mary Ellin Barrett for her support and encouragement, and to Bert Fink at the Rodgers & Hammerstein Organization for his generosity in sharing his time and materials with me. Thanks also to Victoria Traube, Robin Walton, Sarah Outhwaite, Karen Smith, and Sebastian Fabal at the Rodgers & Hammerstein Organization. I am also grateful to Richard Hayes at the Kate Smith Commemorative Society for his help identifying photos and recordings and for his support of this project from the beginning. Thanks to Caroline Park for her help reformatting musical examples, and to Karim Delgado and Wally Gobetz for the use of their photographs.

Many executives and staff within professional baseball provided critical assistance to my research. Thanks to Tim Gunkel, Vito Vitiello, and Greg Romano at the New York Mets; Marty Ray and Dan Lyons at the Boston Red Sox; Bryan Srabian, Maria Jacinto, and Jon Miller at the San Francisco Giants; Stanley and Josh Getzler (former team owners), John Davison, and Michael D'Ambroise at the Staten Island Yankees; Jeff Bradley at the Pawtucket Red Sox; and Rich Levin, Heather Flock, and Mike Teevan at Major League Baseball headquarters. Thanks also to Sgt. Elizabeth Quinones for sharing her Shea Stadium performance and her perspective on the song with me.

I owe a multitude of thanks to Kay Kaufman Shelemay and Carol Oja for their support, advice, and mentorship. I am also grateful to Nancy Cott and Jeff Magee for their helpful comments on early chapter drafts and to other scholars who provided support in various ways, including Daphne Brooks,

Mark Clague, Virginia Danielson, Greg Epstein, David Hall, Claudia Macdonald, Ingrid Monson, Melinda Russell, Jonathan Sarna, Judith Tick, Denise Von Glahn, and the participants in Harvard's 2006–2007 Warren Center Seminar on "Cultural Reverberations of War." Thanks to Joyce Antler and everyone in the American Studies program at Brandeis University, and to the staff of the Harvard music department for their friendship, logistical support, and encouragement.

I am grateful for the assistance I received from librarians and research directors: Sarah Adams, Andy Wilson, and the rest of the staff at Harvard's Edna Kuhn Loeb Music Library; Mark Eden Horowitz and Ray White at the Music Division of the Library of Congress; George Boziwick and Sara Velez at the New York Public Library; Sean Noel, Ryan Hendrickson, and Jennifer Pino at the Howard Gotlieb Archival Research Center at Boston University; and Tim Wiles at the A. Bartlett Giamatti Research Center at the National Baseball Hall of Fame.

Financial support that made this book possible came from generous publication subventions from the Society for American Music and the American Musicological Society. Early work on this book was funded by research fellowships from the Charles Warren Center for Studies in American History, the Harvard Graduate Society, and the Harvard Graduate School of Arts and Sciences.

Thanks also to my colleagues and friends for keeping me sane throughout this long process—to Ayden Adler, Emily Abrams Ansari, Ryan Bañagale, Andrea Bohlman, Corinna Campbell, Elizabeth Craft, Marc Gidal, Glenda Goodman, Katherine Lee, Drew Massey, Lara Pellegrinelli, Katie Pratt, Meredith Schweig, and others who provided feedback and friendship at Harvard and beyond. Also in the "keeping-me-sane" department, special thanks go to Erin Barnett, Krista Enos, Lisl Hampton, and Emily Straus. And thanks to my community of friends in Providence, especially Kiri Miller, James Baumgartner, Tobia Imbier, Kelby Maher, Jessica Glatzer Murphy, Matt Murphy, Anna Solomon, Britt Page, and Rachel Kulick. Thanks should also go to my old friends Alex Moggridge and Zed Starkovich for sharing their opinions about "God Bless America" with me through the years. I also want to acknowledge Kathlyn Fujikawa, the late Daniel Moe, and the past and present members of the women's vocal ensemble Solstice, from whom I learned the true power of communal singing.

I would like to extend a big thanks to my family for their love and support: Shira Shore, David Kaskowitz, Louis Kaskowitz, Susan Kahn, Mimi Sommer, Bill Shore, Rebecca Shore, Alexa Kaskowitz, Dave Sommer, Matt Diaz, Norah Shaykin, Rebecca Shaykin, Gabriel Shaykin, and Leonard Shaykin.

Finally, this book is dedicated, with love, to my boys. To Ezra, who was born when I began researching this book, and whose sweet curiosity and intelligence help keep me honest. To Elliott, who was born a week before the manuscript draft was due, and whose smiling wonder at the world helps me keep things in perspective. And to Ben—not only because he helped with research, read it, proofread it, and designed the cover, but because his friendship, advice, humor, patience, partnership, and unwavering support are what truly made it possible.

ABOUT THE COMPANION WEBSITE

www.oup.com/us/godblessamerica

Username: Music5

Password: Book1745

Oxford has created a password-protected website to accompany this book. It includes streaming audio of recordings referenced in the book, links to videos of relevant performances, and detailed information from the author's online survey. It also provides an opportunity for readers to share their own experiences with "God Bless America" by participating in the author's survey.

God Bless America

Introduction

Something More Than a Song

And now it's going to be my very great privilege to sing you a song that's never been sung before by anybody. . . . It's something more than a song—I feel it's one of the most beautiful compositions ever written, a song that will never die. The author: Mr. Irving Berlin. The title: "God Bless America."
    —Kate Smith, introducing the song's radio debut, 10 November 1938

I don't remember when I first learned "God Bless America." Maybe it was in fourth-grade chorus—I can almost picture its lyrics in our songbook, somewhere between "Don't Fence Me In" and "This Land Is Your Land." But it may have been earlier. It is one of those songs that I just know.

I do remember when I first became aware of the song's symbolic power. It was 1991, and my high school choir was rehearsing for that year's Broadway revue, part of which was dedicated to songs by Irving Berlin. As the finale to the show's first half, we were set to perform a medley of Berlin's songs, ending triumphantly with "God Bless America." As we rehearsed that winter—during the final months of the first Iraq War—a friend of mine complained that he didn't think we should sing the song, that it represented blind patriotism and support for the administration and the war. I myself had no such associations with it, but as choir president, I decided to bring my friend's concerns to our choir director. She told me that "God Bless America" was one of Berlin's most beloved and well-known songs, and that it needed to be included in our tribute to the composer—end of discussion. When we performed it that spring, neither my friend nor I can remember if he staged an angry protest by walking off of the stage, if he stood silently, or grumbled his way through it. The experience has joined my first encounter with the song, both now faded from memory.

I gave "God Bless America" very little thought until ten years later, when I sat glued to the television along with millions of others on 11 September 2001 and watched members of Congress sing it tearfully on the steps of the Capitol. I thought about it again a few weeks later, when I stood and sang it along with the rest of the crowd during the seventh-inning stretch at a San Francisco Giants game.

I have always loved the seventh-inning stretch, when the stands are transformed into an impromptu choir, standing together to sing that anthem of fan allegiance, "Take Me Out to the Ball Game." And so I was struck by this new addition to my beloved baseball sing-along—moved by the crowd's enthusiastic response in the fall of 2001, intrigued as the song appeared to once again take up the mantle of support for a second Bush administration and its own war in Iraq, fascinated as the song became a lasting part of the baseball ritual long after 9/11. My high-school experience with "God Bless America" made me aware of the song's complicated power, and I wanted to understand the meanings underlying these moments of communal singing. How did this simple melody come to inhabit our collective American consciousness, and how might its meanings have shifted over time?

This book tells the surprising story of "God Bless America." It begins with the song's early history, from its composition in 1918 by Irving Berlin and its premiere performance by Kate Smith in 1938 to its reception, uses, and shifting meanings from the years preceding the United States' entry into World War II to its sudden popularity in the aftermath of the 9/11 attacks. Moving to the present day, it explores the song's recent use within professional baseball as a case study to understand the song's varied functions and meanings in contemporary American life.

Whether you love "God Bless America" or shudder when you hear the opening bars, the song's history reveals fascinating stories about American culture—shifting ideas about the role of composer and performer in popular music, about intervention and war, assimilation and acceptance of outsiders, the rise of the ideological Right, rifts between generations, and definitions of Americanness itself. At the same time, tracing the song's uses illuminates the role of secular communal singing in American public life. Such singing represents unique moments when music is interwoven into everyday life—not as a performance to be appreciated but as a mode of civic participation, a vehicle for the forging and contesting of community ties.

PREHISTORY: THE "HOME SONG," TIN PAN ALLEY, AND
THE UNOFFICIAL ANTHEM

Where did "God Bless America" come from? In a 1940 interview, Irving Berlin described his song in these terms: "It's a ballad of home. It's not a song about a flag, or liberty, or something like that. It's a song about home. Instead of the home being a little cottage, it's America."[1] Berlin here links the lineage of "God Bless America" to two popular song traditions: the *home song* genre within Victorian parlor song, and the Tin Pan Alley ballad. The song's last line, "my home sweet home" quotes directly from the song that spawned the Victorian home song: "Home, Sweet Home," written in 1823 by the British composer Henry Bishop with lyrics by American expatriate John Howard Payne.[2] In 1851, the success of the home song was furthered by the popularity of Stephen Foster's "Old Folks at Home," which fused the home song with the minstrel song, transplanting the nostalgic longing for home expressed in earlier Victorian songs to the plantation setting of minstrelsy. Although highly problematic in their romanticism of slavery, these plantation songs allowed white audiences to identify with the imagined homesickness of the song's black protagonist, as the American music scholar Richard Crawford notes: "Many white Americans, including Easterners gone west and rural folk newly arrived in cities, looked behind the black mask and stage dialect of 'Old Folks at Home' and heard some of their own melancholy feelings expressed."[3] Irving Berlin first followed Foster's lead in a song published in 1912, "I Want To Be in Dixie," a rare early collaboration in which he served only as lyricist; Ted Snyder wrote the music.[4] And Berlin continued to plumb the home-song genre in subsequent early songs such as "I Want to Go Back to Michigan (Down on the Farm)" (1914), "Homeward Bound" (1915), "Home Again Blues" (1920), and "Homesick" (1922)—not to mention his most famous home song of all: "White Christmas."[5]

"God Bless America" can be understood as a belated product of the nineteenth-century Victorian parlor song on a more general level. Charles Hamm explains in his study of Irving Berlin's early songs that the music of the Victorian era was designed to uphold American Victorian values, including "faith in God and eternal life," "cheerful obedience to authority," and "appreciation of the beauties of nature."[6] Hamm points out that one typical anthology had as its subtitle "The Music of Home, Country, and Heaven"[7]—a formula that "God Bless America" follows precisely.

Chronologically, "God Bless America" emerges from the Tin Pan Alley era, a popular song tradition that Irving Berlin has come to epitomize.[8] As popular tunes that captured the patriotic spirit of their era, George M. Cohan's patriotic songs, such as "I'm a Yankee Doodle Dandy" (1904),

"You're a Grand Old Flag" (1906), and "Over There" (1917) appear to be logical predecessors to "God Bless America."[9] But the tone of these patriotic Tin Pan Alley songs—described by Hamm as "brash, noisy, aggressively patriotic, oriented to the present, usually devoid of sentimentality"—seems at odds with the more serious "God Bless America."[10]

Within this world of Tin Pan Alley, "God Bless America" was often described as a *ballad*,[11] a term that the popular music writer Arnold Shaw later gave this all-encompassing (and tautological) description: "a loose term covering one of the three major classes of popular songs: 1) novelty songs, 2) rhythm tune, 3) ballad."[12] But Shaw is much more definitive when it comes to a ballad's content: "Its subject-matter is romantic love. Its mood is sentimental, devotional, and/or romantic."[13] Using this definition, "God Bless America" can be understood as rooted within the Tin Pan Alley ballad tradition—a love song from Berlin to his adopted country.

Beyond the realm of nineteenth- and twentieth-century popular music, "God Bless America" has also become part of a repertoire of unofficial national anthems. In his study of music and European nationalism, Philip Bohlman defines such songs as serving the same functions of a national anthem without the formal authorization to represent the country abroad.[14] Bohlman specifically points to the post-9/11 popularity of "God Bless America" as one example of the power of these unofficial anthems, noting that they "may demonstrate even greater national unisonality than their official cousins, perhaps because they have more immediate historical or modern relevance, or even because they are easier to perform or to sing as a collective."[15] This use of the term "unisonality" here draws on Benedict Anderson's discussion of national anthems' role in defining the boundaries of a national community:

> No matter how banal the words and mediocre the tunes, there is in this singing an experience of simultaneity. At precisely such moments, people wholly unknown to each other utter the same verses to the same melody. The image: unisonance. Singing the Marseillaise, Waltzing Matilda, and Indonesia Raya provide occasions for unisonality, for the echoed physical realization of the imagined community. How selfless this unisonance feels! If we are aware that others are singing these songs precisely when and as we are, we have no idea who they may be, or even where, out of earshot, they are singing. Nothing connects us all but imagined sound.[16]

Within Europe, Bohlman observes that unofficial anthems "usually contain particularly powerful historical narratives, which invests them with a common narrative of nationalism," and this is certainly true in the case of an American song like "My Country 'Tis of Thee," derived as it is from the English national anthem "God Save the King."[17] But many American national songs—such as "America the Beautiful," "This Land Is Your Land," and "God Bless America"—focus not on past conflicts but on the beauty of the country's natural landscape, drawing the attention inward rather than to past adversaries.[18] In fact, the power of such songs may also derive from the fact that unlike national anthems, unofficial anthems are not necessarily well known outside of the country's borders, thus representing a shared American song repertoire that itself strengthens the idea of a national community. And the fact that these kinds of songs are not official affirmations of state power can give them a populist, almost grassroots sense of intimacy and solidarity. But as this book will show, unofficial anthems like "God Bless America" can easily be appropriated by the state and imbued with the same kind of ceremonial power as sanctioned national anthems.

CHAPTER OVERVIEW

The story of "God Bless America" begins in 1918, when Irving Berlin first sketched the song for use in an all-soldier musical revue, then leaps forward to 1938, when Kate Smith premiered it on her radio show. Chapter 1 explores the stories and myths surrounding the song's origins, introduces the main characters, and goes behind the scenes to expose the struggle between Irving Berlin and Smith's manager Ted Collins for control of the song and its legacy. The purpose is not only to understand the historical context surrounding the song's creation and first performances, but to examine the underlying tensions between composer and performer in American popular music.

Chapter 2 turns to the early compositional and interpretive decisions that shaped the song into the anthem we know today. The changes that Berlin made in 1938 served to distance the song from its Tin Pan Alley roots and also reflect shifting opinions about intervention in the looming war in Europe. An analysis of recordings of Kate Smith's early performances illustrates how interpretative and orchestration choices contributed to the song's connection to war and its disassociation with popular music to become an unofficial anthem.

Chapter 3 highlights the early reception of "God Bless America" during the period leading up to the United States' entry into World War II, considering how the song's popularity was a response to the public mood of anxiety and fear in response to the Depression at home and escalating war abroad. Of course, there was dissent against the song from the beginning— from those on the left who felt it glossed over the country's problems with simple jingoism and religiosity, to an anti-Semitic and xenophobic backlash against it because of its composer's ethnic identity as a Jewish immigrant.

Chapter 4 focuses on the shifting meanings of "God Bless America" within the seventy years since its debut, tracing associations that have increasingly tilted toward the ideological Right. It follows this rightward shift along three principal themes: (1) ethnicity and race, beginning with early associations with cultural tolerance and religious pluralism; (2) protest, which illustrates how the song's conservative connections were forged and solidified during the social upheaval of the 1960s; and (3) political uses of the song and phrase, which demonstrate not only a rightward ideological shift but also a general move away from communal singing in public life.

Chapter 5 explores the profusion of post-9/11 uses of "God Bless America," beginning with the spontaneous congressional performance on the steps of the Capitol that anointed the song as a vehicle for public mourning. Drawing on surveys and interviews with former members of Congress, I attempt to discover the origins of that poignant sing-along, exploring the nature of memory, commemoration, and the role of communal singing along the way. The chapter examines the reasons behind the newfound embrace of the song before turning to a discussion of its coercive power, as it was used to convey support for the War on Terror in a post-9/11 world.

Chapter 6 looks at professional baseball—where "God Bless America" continues to be a part of the game—in order to understand the song's function within contemporary public life more than ten years after 9/11. Drawing on interviews, observations, and responses from an online survey on attitudes about the song, the chapter examines differences in the song's role at a small sample of major- and minor-league ballparks to highlight tensions between local, vernacular commemoration and a top-down, official nationalism. It also explores recent responses to the song's inclusion, showing that "God Bless America" has now become what the anthropologist Victor Turner has dubbed a "multivocal symbol," invoking different meanings for different people in the stands.[19] Sincere commemoration, support for the troops, forced patriotism, and other associations coexist in this newly invented tradition within the ritualized pageantry of baseball.

Themes of public memory, memory distortion, and remembrance run throughout this story. The very notion of tracing a song's shifting meanings depends upon the power of memory, as layers of past associations inform and complicate each subsequent experience with the song. The distortion of these memories—intentional or otherwise—contributes to the creation of the song's origin myths, which themselves mutate over time in the retelling.

And of course, communal singing as a form of commemoration—like "God Bless America" after 9/11—intersects with the idea of remembrance and public memory, as the singing itself serves as a marker to remember past events.

Connected to memory, another important theme running through this book is nostalgia. Because there was a twenty-year delay between the song's original composition and its first performance, "God Bless America" has always been thought of as an "old" song, imbued from the start with nostalgia for a lost past. In the 1960s, the song carried nostalgia for a World War II–era sense of patriotism and unity for an older generation that was dismayed at the social discord and upheaval of the period. Today, some conservatives sing the song with nostalgia for the Reagan years. And on a more general level, communal singing itself is a nostalgic endeavor, a grown-up reenactment of the uninhibited sing-alongs of elementary school and summer camp.

METHODOLOGY

This book is inherently interdisciplinary, connecting to ethnomusicology, historical musicology, history, and American Studies. But it is rooted in what has come to be called "historical ethnomusicology," using a combination of archival and ethnographic research methods in order to gather information from the present to reconstruct the past, as well as information from the past to deepen an understanding of the present.[20] To understand the song from the perspective of both the past and the present, a wide range of research methods was required, including archival and online research, interviews, observations, and print and online surveys.

In addition, this book makes use of an exhaustive survey of references to both the song and the phrase "God Bless America" in the *New York Times*, which included 1,774 references between 1885 and 2009. This online search yielded an extraordinary amount of data on the changing uses and functions of the song over time. Figure I.1 reveals two distinct peaks in the number of references to the song and phrase—first in 1940, just before the United States entered World War II, then in 2001, in the wake of the 9/11 attacks. In many ways, these two periods serve as bookends to the song's history, when it was imbued with a particularly powerful symbolism as a result of global events.

This kind of "microhistory" research could not have happened without the searchable databases of newspapers available online, and thus technology has enabled a different kind of history to be written. Of course,

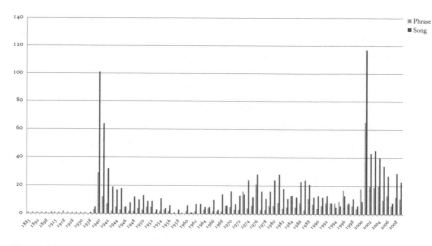

Figure I.1
References to "God Bless America" in the *New York Times*, 1885–2009.

many of these references to "God Bless America" were not central to the main point of an article; they often represent details that a journalist happened to observe and mention. These reporters must be understood as active participants in this history, not only as cultural observers but as propagators of stories and associations surrounding the song that played a role in shaping its meaning.

Of course, there are limitations and drawbacks to this reliance on the *New York Times*. In its favor, it is considered a national newspaper of record as well as serving as the local paper at the main site of the terrorist attacks in 2001. But not all voices are represented there. It captures a particular point of view—East Coast, often cosmopolitan, urban, elite, white—which relates to larger issues surrounding this book's focus on the dominant majority.

By studying "God Bless America," this book foregrounds what Mark Slobin has dubbed the "superculture": "The usual, the accepted, the statistically lopsided, the commercially successful, the statuatory, the regulated, the most visible."[21] Although ethnomusicologists traditionally examine the music of subcultures and minorities, there is value in looking at the musical practices of the mainstream. Defending her own study of mainstream commercial radio, the historian Michelle Hilmes argues that "dominant forms also take shape as sites of cultural tension and conflict."[22]

"God Bless America" does represent the white mainstream, but as Hilmes points out, even the bland, dominant center holds a surprising amount of complexity. For example, contemporary listeners might be unaware that the song was a target for anti-Semitism and xenophobia during its early years because it was composed by Irving Berlin, a Jewish immigrant. Kate Smith, the song's principal performer, appears to be a clear representation of white middle-brow culture, but even this image is more complex than it may seem. Although she cultivated a wholesome, "folksy" image as a radio and TV personality, Smith began her career in the 1920s as a "coon shouter," a label with roots in vaudeville and minstrelsy, which refers to female performers (often large-sized, usually white) who sang blues and torch songs and danced in styles like the Charleston, genres associated with African Americans.[23] And the medium of radio itself—where "God Bless America" was first made popular—can serve to elide racial assumptions by "transcending the visual," as Hilmes writes, "How could one be sure a person belonged to his or her purported racial or ethnic group over the radio?"[24] Such blurring of racial boundaries is demonstrated in a 1941 letter to the children's club of the African American *Chicago Defender*: "Down here in Newport, Ark., I listen to the radio programs quite often. Is Kate Smith white or colored? I have heard that she is white. Since I have never seen her or many radio artists, it has become hard for me to tell."[25]

This book is a hybrid. It is not just about memory and nostalgia, or popular song, or Irving Berlin, or Kate Smith, or music and commerce, or the rise of the Christian Right, or music and baseball. It is about all of these elements together, seen through the lens of one song over time. And while revealing the history, reception, meanings, and uses of "God Bless America," it also tells a story about communal singing as a form of collective music-making in American public life.

CHAPTER 1

✧⌒✧

As the Storm Clouds Gather

Origin Myths and Hidden Battles

The reason "God Bless America" caught on is that it happens to have a universal appeal. Any song that has that is bound to be a success; and let me tell you right here that while song-plugging may help a good song, it never put over a poor one.
—Irving Berlin, July 1940[1]

When Kate Smith first practiced "God Bless America" with [her manager Ted] Collins and Tony Gale, her instrumental arranger, the words were simply typed, the notes of the melody scribbled on a lead sheet. Gale polished it up and wrote the orchestration. When it went on the air it was neither the song Berlin had written at Camp Upton nor the one he had sung for Collins.
—*Look*, December 1940[2]

The "God Bless America" that we know today was forged from both collaboration and contestation between its composer, Irving Berlin, and Kate Smith, the performer who first brought the song before the public. Both stars contributed to the song's initial popularity, but behind the scenes they battled for a sense of control and ownership over a song that was quickly embraced by the public as an alternate anthem.

Such tensions between composer and performer are a long-standing phenomenon within American popular music. Richard Crawford has made a categorical distinction between "composer's music," in which the authority for the song's performance rests with the composer's notated score, and "performer's music," which emphasizes making the music accessible to audiences, with the score serving as a guide for interpretation.[3] But Tin Pan

Alley songs challenge the idea that these two categories can be so clearly demarcated. On the one hand, a song's success was dependent on "song pluggers" responsible for performing new tunes and convincing high-profile entertainers to include them in their repertoires, and the rise of radio and the recording industry in the 1920s meant that people were increasingly likely to know songs as a result of performances rather than from a printed score.[4] Yet the ongoing importance of sheet music sales within the economics of the music industry ensured that the role of the score—and the composer—retained some importance.

Although many popular songs become inextricably linked to a performer while the composer remains virtually anonymous, in the case of "God Bless America," with a famous composer and an equally well-known performer, it is unclear where the authority for the song's performance ultimately rests. According to the law, Berlin was the rightful "owner" of the song as the copyright holder, and he stood to gain the most financially. And as publisher and producer of his own music, Berlin was always fiercely protective of his copyrighted creative output.[5] In the early days of Tin Pan Alley, it had been standard practice to cut in performers as authors in return for plugging a song on the air, thus making them eligible to receive royalties, but ASCAP banned that practice in 1931.[6] In her study of jazz and the civil rights movement, Ingrid Monson notes that until changes were made to copyright law in 1972, the system heavily favored songwriters and publishers over performers, since mechanical and broadcast royalties were much higher than performer royalties or earnings from recordings.[7]

Of course, these issues of copyright usually remain behind the scenes. From the perspective of the general public, Smith had the sonic power of radio and the phonograph on her side, so that "God Bless America" would become linked to her voice in the minds of millions of listeners across the country. It was not at all clear who would ultimately win this battle for control, which began with the story behind the song itself.

IN THE BEGINNING: AN OVERVIEW

The origin story of "God Bless America" has by now passed into the realm of folklore and myth, with multiple variations of the same basic plot.[8] Berlin himself acknowledged the folkloric qualities of the stories behind the song as he wrote in a 1940 letter, "It is the privilege of everyone who had anything to do with the success of 'God Bless America' to give their own version of their connection with it."[9] In his study of the song "White Christmas," Jody Rosen called Berlin "his own best hagiographer" who learned the "value of legend-building and tall tales" from many successful years on Tin Pan Alley and Broadway.[10] Kate Smith also knew the power of a good story in shaping her own folksy persona—for example, she claimed the small town of Greenville, Virginia, as her birthplace, but she was actually born in urban Washington, DC.[11]

The song's origin story begins in 1918, when Irving Berlin was drafted as an army private—yet even this date is not always agreed upon. Many press stories about the song's history report that it was composed in 1917, but Berlin scholars note that he did not in fact begin his military service until May 1918, a few months after he officially became a US citizen.[12] (Berlin had immigrated with his family to the United States from Russia as a young boy, but did not file citizenship papers until the year he turned thirty.) The source of the 1917 story appears to be a press release issued from Berlin's office in June 1940, which identified Berlin's original version as written in 1917.[13] It is impossible to know if this was simply a minor error made through the fog of memory after twenty years, or a subtle positioning of Berlin's military service as longer than the eight months he actually spent in uniform. Although Berlin completed a draft registration card in June 1917, as mandated by the Selective Service Act of 1917, he would have been considered an "alien" and exempted from service before becoming natural-ized in February 1918.[14] This "alien status" was an aspect of Berlin's biogra-phy that later became a target for an anti-Semitic and xenophobic backlash against "God Bless America" (see chap. 3). Moving the date of his military service to 1917, the first year of the draft, erased any questions about Berlin's status as a true American, creating a cleaner origin story for "God Bless America."

While stationed at Camp Upton in Yaphank, New York, Berlin was asked to write a soldier show as a fund-raiser for a community house to be built at the camp. The revue, called *Yip, Yip, Yaphank*, opened on 19 August 1918 at New York's Century Theatre with an all-soldier cast. It included a black-face number ("Mandy"), satirical spoofs of army life (including the now well-known "Oh, How I Hate To Get Up in the Morning"), and boisterous, Ziegfeld follies–style dance numbers featuring male soldiers in drag that one reviewer characterized as "one long laugh."[15] Berlin originally wrote "God Bless America" as the show's finale but decided not to include it. In-stead, he ended the show with the upbeat "We're On Our Way to France," after which the cast marched down the aisles and out of the theater into the New York streets.[16]

Many different reasons have been cited for the decision to remove "God Bless America" from *Yip, Yip, Yaphank*. Harry Ruby, Berlin's pianist and transcriber at Camp Upton, claimed that Berlin cut it after Ruby complained

Figure 1.1
Irving Berlin during World War I. Photograph courtesy of Rodgers & Hammerstein: an Imagem Company, on behalf of the Estate of Irving Berlin.

that there were already too many patriotic songs being written during that period, while two of Berlin's biographers said it happened because the song's solemn tone did not match the irreverence of the upbeat revue.[17] Berlin himself felt the song was "too obviously patriotic for soldiers to sing," saying elsewhere that it was "like carrying coals to Newcastle" or "gilding the lily" to have men in uniform performing such an obviously patriotic tune.[18] For Berlin, it seems that soldiers amply demonstrated their patriotism through military service; patriotic songs were strictly for civilians, a home-front proxy for serving one's country overseas. As he later wrote about touring the Pacific with *This Is the Army*, his World War II update of *Yip, Yip, Yaphank*: "[G]roups of soldiers from all over the world would gather around, and they did not sing 'The Star-Spangled Banner,' 'America,' or 'God Bless America,' but they did sing 'Give My Regards to Broadway.' To them it meant coming home."[19]

Whatever the reason, in 1918 Berlin filed "God Bless America" in his trunk of rejected songs, where it lay until a confluence of events led to its rediscovery twenty years later. Berlin went to London in September 1938 for the British premiere of *Alexander's Ragtime Band*, and he returned home worried about the growing tensions in Europe. He tried writing a new song to express his feelings of gratitude for the United States, but he was not satisfied with his attempts, which had titles like "Let's Talk About Liberty" and "Thanks, America."[20] Berlin found these songs to be too literal, "like making a speech to music."[21] A consummate hit-maker, Irving Berlin knew that a song with such an obvious message stood little chance of catching on, as he proclaimed in an August 1940 interview: "A song to become popular should not establish any new ideas—it must be a means of expression for sentiments already in vogue."[22]

Meanwhile, Kate Smith and her manager, Ted Collins, approached Berlin looking for a patriotic song for Smith to sing on the Armistice Day show of *The Kate Smith Hour* that November.[23] The sequence of these events varies in different tellings of this story, but at some point in September or October 1938, Berlin rediscovered his old song, made changes to it, and gave it to Kate Smith to premiere on her show, which aired on the eve of Armistice Day, 10 November 1938.[24] Collins and Berlin agreed that radio performances would be restricted to Kate Smith, in order to protect the song's dignity and longevity.[25]

According to one journalist, the song was an immediate sensation after its first performance, setting the phones ringing in Berlin's offices as people from across the country called with requests for the printed sheet music.[26] As the story goes, Berlin himself was so pleased with Smith's performance that he changed his plans for the evening and took a taxi to Smith's studio in Times Square to watch her rebroadcast for the West Coast at midnight.[27] Beginning the next morning, telephone calls, letters, and wires "started pouring in praising the song and asking for more."[28] But media critic Ben Gross recalled that early performances of the song "failed to make much of an impression," and Ted Collins later told a reporter that Smith and Berlin were both unimpressed with the first performance, with Collins claiming sole responsibility for the song's continued performances: "I had to fight for it. I insisted that she keep it on the program."[29]

Smith went on to sing "God Bless America" nearly every week from November 1938 until the broadcaster's ASCAP boycott in January 1941 prohibited its performance.[30] Her recording of the song was released by Victor in March 1939 and reached the Billboard charts for four weeks that April (peaking at number ten), then took off again in July 1940, reaching number five and remaining on the charts for eleven weeks.[31] Victor's success prompted other labels to follow suit, issuing new versions by artists like

Bing Crosby, Barry Wood, and Leopold Stokowski's All-American Youth Orchestra.[32] Berlin published the sheet music in February 1939, and by December of that year, more than 500,000 copies had been sold.[33] But perhaps more critical to the song's longevity than this commercial success was its embrace as an unofficial anthem at public gatherings in the years following its premiere—sung in schools, churches, civic meetings, concerts, sporting events, and elsewhere. As a gesture of goodwill, in July 1940 Berlin established the God Bless America Fund, through which all royalties from the song were to be donated to the Boy Scouts and Girl Scouts of America.

Some facets of this creation story are verifiable, and others have passed into the unconfirmable realm of popular lore. But the stories themselves were shaped by a behind-the-scenes struggle for control of the song. Once it became clear that the song's popularity was not a short-lived fad but a product of a deep resonance with the public during this period, each side worked to construct a creation story that put either the performer or the composer at the center.

CAST OF CHARACTERS: IRVING BERLIN, KATE SMITH, AND THE MEDIATORS BEHIND THE SCENES

The year 1938, when "God Bless America" received its radio premiere, was a high point in the careers of both Irving Berlin and Kate Smith. After many years as a broadcasting and recording star, Smith's hour-long variety show debuted on CBS in September 1937, and her daytime commentary program, *Kate Smith Speaks* kicked off in the spring of 1938.[34] By this time, Berlin had established himself as one of the most successful songwriters of his day, and that same period saw the release of three new movie musicals with scores by Berlin: *On the Avenue* (1937), *Alexander's Ragtime Band* (1938), and *Carefree* (1938).[35]

In addition to the main celebrity players in this story, there are a number of mediating characters who played important roles in shaping the song and its legacy. Saul Bornstein, Irving Berlin's business partner at the time, often served as a go-between in Berlin's correspondence, representing his business interests and writing letters on his behalf on the many occasions that Berlin was away from his New York office. Tony Gale, Kate Smith's pianist and arranger, had an enormous influence on the sonic identity of "God Bless America" when Smith first performed it, as did Smith's bandleader Jack Miller.[36] But no one played a larger mediating role between performer and composer than Ted Collins, Kate Smith's manager, often likened to Svengali in his control over his star.[37]

Figure 1.2
Jack Miller, Ted Collins (*seated*), and Kate Smith, ca. 1929. Photograph courtesy of the Kate Smith Collection, Howard Gotlieb Archival Research Center at Boston University.

As a result of Smith's subordinated relationship to Collins, her own perspective is virtually absent from this narrative, perhaps paradoxically so given that her fame as a recording and radio star rested on the sound of her voice. In some respects, Smith's lack of agency fits within the model of the music industry put forward by David Suisman, who argues that the early music business centered not on performers but on a "commercial class of music makers" who made things happen.[38] But Smith and Collins represent an extreme case. As one newspaper columnist described in October 1938, "She never makes a decision, she never does anything without asking Ted Collins."[39] Smith herself later wrote, "Without Ted there would have been no Kate Smith—the Kate Smith the public has known for almost 30 years. . . . I knew I could trust him to do what was best for us."[40]

Collins became Smith's manager in 1930, when he was an A&R man for Columbia and she was performing as the unhappy brunt of "fat girl" jokes in *Flying High*, a Broadway musical starring Bert Lahr.[41] Collins launched Smith's radio career, wrote the scripts for her shows, handled all press and business contacts and all financial aspects of her career.[42] Even on her daytime talk show, Smith spoke words that Collins had written for her. In her

Figure 1.3
Kate Smith and Ted Collins, ca. 1940. Photograph by Charmante Studio, courtesy of the Kate Smith Collection, Howard Gotlieb Archival Research Center at Boston University.

1960 autobiography, Smith described how her image of old-fashioned womanhood on that show was "brilliantly projected by Ted. . . . Whenever we discussed a topic for the noon program, he always managed to put into words the exact point of view I had in my own mind."[43]

As vexing as this unequal relationship may be for contemporary readers, Smith appears to have enjoyed her arrangement with Collins, and further, she often advocated a subordinated role for women. In one example, a 1943 newspaper article reported that Collins filled the role of newscaster on her show because Smith "sincerely believes that straight news reporting on radio is a man's job."[44] Smith glorified the role of woman as homemaker and mother in her written and radio commentaries—some of which were, of course, likely written by Collins.

Yet there is something fundamentally contradictory in this stance, since Smith herself was a successful, independent, single woman who used her radio show as a platform to promote civic engagement, and during World War II she was responsible for the most successful war bond drive in history.[45] Smith managed this contradiction by arguing that women must make a choice between career and motherhood.[46] In fact, there are some striking passages in Smith's 1938 autobiography in which she seems to advocate for women's empowerment, though usually within the confines of the home, as she wrote, "While I have never been accused of being an ardent feminist, the happenings of the past few years have strengthened my belief in the tremendous influence for good which can be exerted by the keen, intelligent women of today, not only in the home, but in the political, industrial, and civil life of our nation."[47]

In many ways, Smith was the Martha Stewart and Oprah Winfrey of her era, though her main task appears to have been to emphasize traditional gender roles, as she later wrote: "I spoke to women of their importance as homemakers and mothers and stressed the values of ordinary tasks well done everyday. . . . I wanted to be an anchor of wholesome wisdom on which women felt they could depend."[48] She shared recipes and household tips and held populist contests celebrating the stories of everyday Americans— "most heroic," "most typical American boy," and an *American Idol*–like talent quest to find new radio stars—all featuring balloting by her listeners to choose the winners.[49] And although some certainly disliked her folksy persona, she was wildly popular in her day.[50] In the summer of 1938, a few months before she first performed "God Bless America," a national survey by the Character Research Institute of Washington University reported that "Kate Smith and Babe Ruth ranked higher as outstanding personalities than any scientists and men of letters."[51]

Ted Collins does not emerge from history as appealing a character as his star. Smith's biographer Richard Hayes diplomatically describes him as "a person who was either liked or disliked intensely."[52] In a study of Smith's less-than-successful transition to television in the 1950s, Marsha Francis Cassidy wrote, "The historical record suggests that Smith alone experienced the placid side of Collins's personality. In the opinion of his business associates, Collins's behavior was consistently abrasive and uncooperative."[53] Hayes quotes some of Collins's former associates who mince no words to describe him as "a son of a bitch" and "a bastard," a womanizing drinker who mistreated his staff and played mean-spirited practical jokes on his friends.[54] Collins also reportedly prevented Smith from maintaining any other close relationships.[55] And yet, Smith always described Collins as the one responsible for her success, and always spoke of him and their friendship in glowing terms.[56] As troubling as it may be to outsiders, their partnership appears to have been mutually beneficial.

Ted Collins must be understood as a critical mediator between performer and composer in the story of "God Bless America." Although I found

Figure 1.4
Kate Smith, ca. 1932. Photograph courtesy of the Kate Smith Collection, Howard Gotlieb Archival Research Center at Boston University.

volumes of correspondence between Collins, Berlin, and Bornstein, I found no relevant letters from Smith herself, in either the Irving Berlin or the Kate Smith collections where I did research. Smith's voice can be found only in forceful contralto form, and her own intentions read through her vocal performance. As Collins reportedly told Smith when he became her manager, "You do the singing and I'll fight the battles."[57]

COMPOSER V. PERFORMER: "GOD BLESS AMERICA" AS BATTLEGROUND

In the behind-the-scenes struggle for control between the song's composer and its principal performer, all aspects of "God Bless America" became contested areas—when it was written, whom it was written for, the reason for its popularity, who had the right to perform it, and where its profits would go. This conflict was played out in correspondence and through the press, revealing an underlying struggle for ownership of the song and its legacy.

One main source of tension was the question of Kate Smith's role in the song's creation. During her daytime radio talk show on the day of the song's premiere, Smith described how she had asked Berlin for "a new hymn of praise and love and allegiance to America."[58] Smith said that Berlin "worked day after day, night after night, until at last his task was completed. The other day he sent me his masterpiece, and along with it this little note: 'Dear Kate: here it is—I did the best I could, and it expresses the way I feel.'"[59] Here, Smith makes no mention of the song's earlier incarnation during World War I, and it may be that Berlin did not feel a need to share the song's history with her and Collins when he first gave it to them. However, as the song gained in popularity, Berlin showed an increasing interest in making its provenance known.

A version of Smith's spoken introduction became part of an article with her byline that appeared in *Pic* magazine in October 1940 (among other places).

Figure 1.5
Ted Collins, Irving Berlin, and Kate Smith, after the radio premiere of "God Bless America" in 1938. Photograph courtesy of the Kate Smith Collection, Howard Gotlieb Archival Research Center at Boston University.

But in the printed version the note that Berlin wrote to Smith had been transformed; it now read: "Dear Kate: This song is yours and yours alone. I have written so many for everyone to sing but this one I give to you."[60] In response to the *Pic* article, Berlin wrote to Smith's publicist in protest: "The simple facts are—I wrote a song entitled 'God Bless America,' Kate Smith introduced it with great success and it was restricted to her exclusively for a long time."[61] Berlin focused his complaint on the fact that he was misquoted, acknowledging the multiple versions of the song's genesis but protesting, "I feel I should not be quoted as having written a letter which I never wrote."[62] He was obviously unhappy with the content of the article as well, which positioned Smith as a central figure in the crafting of the song, rather than as the performer who first brought it to life.

The question of whether Berlin wrote "God Bless America" with Smith in mind would continue throughout that period and beyond. When introducing the song before its first performance, Smith had said, "And now it's going to be my very great privilege to sing you a song that's never been sung before by anybody, and that was written especially for me by one of the greatest composers in the music field today."[63] Early newspaper and magazine stories about the song (likely generated by press releases from Collins's office) echoed this assertion that "God Bless America" was written "especially," "expressly," or "exclusively" for Smith, with no mention of its earlier history as part of *Yip, Yip, Yaphank*.[64]

In July 1940, a press release from Berlin's office announced that Berlin composed the song during World War I, effectively challenging the idea that the song was written especially for Smith.[65] On a copy of this press release in Collins's files in the Irving Berlin Collection, the line "Berlin composed the song in 1917" is underlined; next to it, a handwritten note reads, "? This kills our story of how it came to be written—in 1938!—Jane."[66] This note (likely from Smith's personal secretary Jane Tompkins) is an interesting acknowledgement of the fact that the song's history is made up of multiple competing stories, created to shape the public's understanding of "God Bless America" as inextricably linked to either Kate Smith or Irving Berlin. In a handwritten note to Berlin, Collins expressed doubt about these early origins, an indication that either Berlin had kept the source of the song to himself when he showed it to Smith and Collins in 1938, or that Collins had forgotten about it. Collins wrote, "If the storm clouds were gathering in 1917 (or were they)? Some people think there was a hell of a war going on then."[67] Here Collins casts doubt on Berlin's story of the song's origins by questioning the relevance of the verse's first line ("As the storm clouds gather far across the sea") in light of its World War I origins. (In fact, Berlin did not write the song's verse until the fall of 1938.) Such struggles for ownership and authority indicate that there was an awareness of the song's significance among all involved, setting off a high-stakes battle for the right to be associated with "God Bless America" in the public consciousness.

Perhaps one of the central areas of contention revolved around the stated reasons behind the song's overwhelming popularity, whether it was a result of Smith's treatment of the song or qualities inherent in the song itself. A December 1940 profile in *Look* magazine focused on Smith, beginning with a full-page photograph of the singer captioned, "Kate Smith, who put 'God Bless America' across."[68] But Berlin was particularly incensed by a caption for a photograph of Smith, Collins, and their instrumental arranger Tony Gale, which implied that Berlin gave Smith a mere sketch of the song ("the words were simply typed, the notes of the melody scribbled on a lead sheet") and that Gale "polished it up" in his orchestration, so that when it went on the air, "it was neither the song Berlin had written at Camp Upton nor the one he had sung for Collins."[69] Given the opportunity to review proofs before the article was published, Berlin wrote to Collins, complaining

Figure 1.6
Ted Collins and Irving Berlin. Photograph courtesy of the Kate Smith Collection, Howard Gotlieb Archival Research Center at Boston University.

that this statement "was incorrect and really libelous. It was so contrary to the facts that I could not believe that you had authorized such a state-ment."[70] Collins claimed that he did not approve this caption, though the magazine apologized for the error by maintaining that they were "misin-formed as to collaboration on 'God Bless America.'"[71] Regardless of where the caption originated, the effect was to minimize Berlin's claim of author-ship of the song and give additional credit to Kate Smith and her staff for the final product. The caption was corrected before publication, but due to a mechanical error, some copies included the original caption implying that the song was a collaboration rather than the sole creative product of Irving Berlin. This caption defied an unspoken rule that orchestrators work behind the scenes and tend not to be given credit for a song's success, though Tony Gale certainly had a hand in shaping Berlin's song for public consumption.[72]

A few months earlier, Smith's publicist had written to Berlin, "You asked me one time what it was that might be upsetting Mr. Collins. As one gen-tleman to another, I imagine such an article as this would upset anyone."[73] Included with the letter was a copy of the New York Times Magazine's profile of Berlin from July 1940, with the following passage underlined:

> "The reason 'God Bless America' caught on," [Berlin] continued, "is that it hap-pens to have a universal appeal. Any song that has that is bound to be a success; and let me tell you right here that while song-plugging may help a good song, it never put over a poor one."[74]

Collin's publicist objected that this statement implied that Smith did not play a role in plugging the song, writing, "I think you will agree that it has become a great song because of the treatment given it by Kate Smith." In response, Berlin wrote that he saw nothing in the article that should upset anyone.[75]

Here, the tensions between the role of composer and performer are explicitly evoked, with Smith's camp complaining that Berlin did not give her performances enough credit for the song's success. Smith's spoken in-troduction before the song's premiere certainly sounds like plugging, as she announced the new song written "by one of the greatest composers in the music field today. It's something more than a song—I feel it's one of the most beautiful compositions ever written, a song that will never die."[76] But for Berlin, who had by this point been a Tin Pan Alley songwriter for more than thirty years, the term "plugging" had an industry-specific meaning, a technique of saturating the market with a song in order to make it a hit, in which "every plug helped and any plug was better than none at all."[77]

By this Tin Pan Alley definition, the fact that performances were restricted to Kate Smith meant that the song was not truly "plugged."

Smith's exclusive right to perform the song became an additional source of strife on many fronts: within Berlin's organization, between Berlin and Collins, and between Berlin and those wanting permission to broadcast the song. According to Berlin, it was he who first suggested that early radio performances should be restricted to Smith.[78] In February 1939, Saul Bornstein and Collins came to an agreement that Smith would have exclusive rights to broadcast the song for eight weeks. Bornstein wrote to Berlin that he had been refusing permissions for others to broadcast "God Bless America," arguing, "if we ever open the door and turn it loose it will be played all over the lot for about four or five weeks like a popular song and then be dead."[79] A few days later, Bornstein confessed that though he thought the restriction to Smith wise, he also worried that they would be seen as "unpatriotic" by those who were refused permission. Berlin replied that while he understood the importance of living up to his agreement with Collins, he disagreed with refusing other broadcast versions:

> I think it is wrong to withhold any permission, either commercial or sustaining, that is given for patriotic purposes. After all, isn't that why I wrote the song? . . . I certainly hope the blanket refusal will be lifted. Not alone is it unpatriotic, but you will create a feeling of animosity toward the song, me personally, and the firm generally.[80]

Berlin then gave permission for the *Texaco Star Theatre* radio show to perform the song on Washington's Birthday; the show's producer sent a telegram to inform Bornstein of his arrangement with Berlin, writing that "you have no right to keep this song off air on occasion of Washington's Birthday," and that "Washington himself would turn over in his grave if he knew all the fuss you people are making."[81] Bornstein sent a telegram to Berlin responding that he had to adhere to his understanding with Collins; despite what he satirized as a "national need for twenty-four hour 'God Bless America' service," Bornstein would not break his word.[82] The eight-week restriction was upheld, and all sides seemed content; as Bornstein wrote to Berlin at the end of March: "The song was the right one and the restriction to Kate Smith up to the present time has been wise and if it is not kicked around it should be an outstanding patriotic song for a long, long, time to come."[83]

When the eight weeks were up, Berlin wired Bornstein that they could no longer withhold requests for important patriotic occasions, and Bornstein balked, wiring Berlin, "I am not going to antagonize Kate Smith."[84]

He continued, "If it were not for her the song might have been a popular song hit and dead by now or you may not have had it published. While I realize the song should be made available to all suitable programs I am not going to fight with the one who made it and with such dignity and credit." Here, again, is the question of whether Berlin or Smith could claim the most responsibility for the song's success. Predictably, Berlin fought back, writing to Bornstein: "I don't agree with you at all that if she hadn't sung it the song wouldn't have been just as big a hit as it is today. I appreciate how much Kate Smith has done for it, but they must appreciate also what the song has done for Kate Smith."[85] He addressed the issue of ownership directly, saying, "after all, this is my song," and concluding, "I don't want to go back to New York in an atmosphere where Ted Collins is going to take the attitude of being part-owner in 'God Bless America' because I am going to be *awfully tough* about it."[86]

But Bornstein appears to have been right about the response from the Smith/Collins camp. Once Collins heard that the song would be made available to other performers, he sent a furious telegram releasing Bornstein and Berlin from all agreements regarding the song, saying that he was "all through with 'God Bless America.'"[87] In response to Berlin's complaints of being criticized for withholding the song, Collins himself took full credit for the song's transcendence of its pop music roots, writing, "Do you realize that today because and only because of my directing the proper and dignified presentations of your song you are being mentioned reverently in over nine hundred public schools throughout this country as a great patriot?"

Collins's telegram turned Berlin into a diplomat, and that night, 5 April 1939, he and Collins spoke over the phone.[88] Obviously, no transcript of their conversation exists, but there is a draft of a letter in Berlin's files that is a measured response to Collins's wire. It seems likely that the letter (with handwritten changes and no signature) was never sent, but it does serve as a guide to Berlin's thinking; it is worth quoting at length:

> I have no desire to do anything that will undo the good work that you and Kate have done for "God Bless America." Nor do I underestimate how much good this song can do for me, so it was quite unnecessary for you to point it out to me in your wire. I could point out how much good this song has done so far and can continue to do for Kate Smith, but all this is too obvious Ted, and, I think, beside the point. I didn't know it was your intention to have the song restricted indefinitely and surely you must realize the position I am placed in to have to refuse its performance for legitimate and dignified patriotic occasions.
>
> I think you are hasty when you say you and Kate Smith are through with "God Bless America," and certainly want to do everything I can to make you

change your mind. I don't think it is a mistake to make the song available for patriotic occasions. Nor do I think anyone of us can afford to turn our patriotism on and off because we don't agree. I am completely unselfish where "God Bless America" is concerned. I don't want to make any money out of it, nor do I want to be ballyhooed as a great patriot. I would be more than repaid if the song proved to have the quality of something more than just a popular song.

I earnestly urge you to reconsider your decision and have Kate Smith continue to do the song as part of her broadcast and you can rest assured that I will be very careful not to grant any permission that would in any way hurt the song.[89]

Berlin's sincere fondness for the song comes through vividly in this letter, as well as a sense of the song's fragility (promising that he will be "very careful" not to "hurt" it in anyway). He also acknowledges Smith's role in bringing the song to the public, without minimizing his own.

Whatever was said in their phone conversation, Berlin's diplomacy seems to have successfully assuaged Collins. The official policy for the song then became:

"God Bless America" is restricted to educational, religious, patriotic and charitable non-commercial programs, with the exception of Kate Smith who introduced the song November 11, 1938, and with the further exception that it can be done on National Holidays such as Columbus Day, Washington's Birthday, etc., providing the spirit of the composition is retained.[90]

In September 1940, Berlin's office requested that this modified restriction to Kate Smith be lifted, since the song had "become part of our national music life."[91] Despite the strain they seem to have imposed on the relations between the Berlin and Smith camps, these restrictions do appear to have done their job, preventing "God Bless America" from "flaming out" as an ephemeral pop song and allowing it to enter into American musical life in a fundamental way.

More behind-the-scenes battles raged over Berlin's plan to donate his royalties from the song to charity.[92] Berlin had made his intentions clear from the beginning, but he and Collins disagreed about how the plan should be carried out. Collins, likely hoping to seize more positive publicity and public goodwill surrounding the song, wanted to announce Berlin's donation on the air as soon as possible. Beginning in February 1939, he pressed Berlin on several occasions to choose a patriotic organization—he suggested the hospital fund of the American Legion for War Veterans— so that Smith could make an official announcement on her radio show.[93] Berlin was more cautious, though. He wanted to choose the benefiting organization carefully and first wanted to know what the royalties would be; in a letter to Bornstein regarding this issue, Berlin wrote, "The motive must not be misunderstood, nor do I want to make a big fuss about a small amount."[94]

This issue was one of the factors that led Collins to write the angry telegram disavowing Smith's affiliation with the song, telling Berlin that he had made a "big mistake" in not allowing Smith to announce the royalty donation on her radio show.[95] Berlin explained his position in response, writing:

> That first day in my office I told you I would be glad to donate my royalties to some worthy American cause. Immediately after then it appeared in a couple of columns and in the past two months I have been approached by at least three patriotic organizations, all worthy, asking for part of that money saying that they were entitled to it. . . . I would be glad to have Kate Smith make the announcement but wanted to wait until I return so we could all discuss it first and do it in such a way that wouldn't leave me open not alone to criticism but to many headaches afterwards.[96]

Berlin evokes the practical aspect of not making a public announcement to avoid being hassled by deserving patriotic organizations requesting money. But the ever-present issue of "ownership" was also a factor here. For example, in March 1939, Collins had wanted to send autographed copies of "God Bless America" to congressmen and state governors, with a letter from Smith asking them to "cooperate with us in carrying the message of America through this song."[97] In addition to claiming that the song was written by Berlin "especially for me," the sample letter from Smith also said, "I might add that neither Mr. Berlin or myself has any interest, beyond a patriotic one, in this song. All profits accruing from its sale are to be turned over to organized charity." Both Bornstein and Berlin took exception to this; Bornstein worried that the letter implied that Smith "has some rights in the song and that her profits as well as yours are being donated to charity."[98] Berlin responded angrily to Bornstein in a terse telegram from California:

> Not alone do I object to her saying song was written especially for her but I strongly resent the idea of her giving away my money without my having something to say about it. Appreciate how much she has done for song but regret Collins has seen fit take my property in his own hands without consulting me. How about Kate Smith donating part of her salary to some worthy patriotic cause along with me?[99]

Berlin makes an important point: though it was Collins and Smith who were emphasizing the fact that the royalties were being donated to charity, Smith actually had no claim to the song's royalties; her earnings came from her radio show salary.

From Berlin's perspective, then, Collins was trying to capitalize on the good publicity of donating royalties without actually making any financial sacrifices. Berlin complained that though he himself did not want to make money from the song, "it can very easily turn into a profitable commercial proposition for Kate Smith, who is giving away nothing, and getting the kind of publicity she has never had before."[100] While this may have been the case, it is also likely that Collins wanted to announce the donation publicly in order to counter criticism that he, Berlin, and Smith were making an unfair profit on the patriotism of others, an especially unsavory prospect during a time of economic depression and looming war.

Despite Collins's impatience, Berlin waited until July 1940 to announce the establishment of the God Bless America Fund, through which all royalties from the song would be distributed to the Boy Scouts and Girl Scouts of America, rather than one of the organizations that Collins had advocated. Berlin chose to make his announcement about the fund through a press release—rather than on Smith's radio show—and Collins was bitter about being left out of the loop. Collins appears to have written "Can't we get on the Trustee Board?" on a copy of the press release in his files, and he wrote back sarcastically to Berlin, "Congratulations on a fine Board of Trustees. They all worked very hard to promote 'God Bless America.'"[101] Collins obviously felt snubbed; although the song was still restricted to Kate Smith for radio performances, she and Collins were kept out of the new inner circle of control represented by the God Bless America Fund.

This rancor—which was surprisingly prevalent behind the scenes during the song's early years—stems as much from a cultural clash between urban sophistication and small-town folksiness as from any specific interest in the song. Berlin was associated with the glamorous vision of the musical spectacle, an escapist dream of luxury during the Depression years.[102] And as Berlin's biographer Philip Furia points out, during the 1920s the composer became associated with the Algonquin Round Table, a group of intellectuals in New York (including Edna Ferber, Dorothy Parker, and F. Scott Fitzgerald), which was part of a "revolution" that pitted the "cosmopolitan world of New York against the values of small-town America."[103] The fact that Collins felt snubbed by not being asked to serve on the God Bless America Fund board of trustees can be linked directly to this cultural rift, since the person appointed fund chairman was the journalist Herbert

Bayard Swope, a central player within the sophisticated New York "in-crowd" who was said to be the basis for Fitzgerald's Jay Gatsby.[104]

Smith was not a part of this elite world, and her radio show focused on the issues faced by ordinary folks, appealing directly to the part of America scorned by the New York elite. One small-town paper described her as "warm-hearted, generous, kindly and essentially wholesome. She is simple and unpretentious, 'folksy,' is probably the word she'd choose."[105] As a re-sult, Smith was a natural target for sophisticated, urban critics, as illus-trated in a 1934 profile of the singer by Joseph Mitchell in the *New Yorker*. Founded by Harold Ross, another member of the Algonquin Round Table, the *New Yorker* was created to represent the voice of the cosmopolitan and specifically "not for the little old lady in Dubuque."[106] Mitchell's piece is marked by a condescending tone, as in the way he describes Smith's "throaty contralto, which sentimentalizes even the most concupiscent torch song," and her "folksy manner (in which the word 'something,' for example, be-comes 'sumpin')."[107] Other observations—that Smith hated Broadway, pre-ferred staying home or visiting suburban movie houses, and that "she hardly ever reads"—seem calculated to disgust and amuse the *New Yorker*'s target audience of urban sophisticates.

In his biography, Furia wonders how "shy, hard-working, and uncynical Berlin" would have fit in with the scoffing Algonquin group,[108] and in fact Berlin and Smith both complicate this binary that pits the values of urban New York City against small-town America. Although he lived among the cosmopolitan upper class in Manhattan, Berlin's music appealed to the masses, and he himself could not afford—and perhaps did not want—to look down on them. Kate Smith lived in a penthouse on Park Avenue while cultivating her homey, down-to-earth persona. Perhaps "God Bless America" allowed them to meet each other—and their audiences—somewhere in the middle.

Ironically, a song meant to unify the country during this prewar period was itself marked by discord. Despite the animosity expressed in the corre-spondence between the two camps, all of these maneuverings for control remained behind the scenes, and over time, "God Bless America" has largely shed its associations with either Berlin or Smith as its origins have become lost to history. Yet the sense of contestation between Berlin and Smith continued even after Smith's death in 1986. Her obituary described the singer's ongoing affiliation with "God Bless America" by stating that in 1938 she had "introduced a new song written expressly for her by Irving Berlin."[109] A correction ran a few days later, noting that the obituary had "incorrectly described the origin of the song 'God Bless America.' Irving

Berlin wrote it for his 1918 musical, *Yip, Yip, Yaphank*, according to the American Society of Composers, Authors and Publishers (ASCAP). He dropped the song from the show before it opened. Miss Smith introduced it, extensively revised, on 11 November 1938."[110] Here, ASCAP stepped forward to protect the legacy of the then ninety-eight-year-old Berlin, as embattled as ever, defending his right to call the song his own.

But Smith may have won the battle for association with "God Bless America" in the long run. In an online survey that I conducted on attitudes about the song, 43 percent of more than 1,800 respondents reported that they associate the song with Kate Smith, but less than one-quarter correctly identified Irving Berlin as its composer.[111] Smith's voice remains entangled with the song, as her iconic recordings continue to be played in public venues, her captured performance infused with the power of nostalgia long after her own star had faded. Yet over the course of the twentieth century, "God Bless America" became disassociated from Berlin, taking on the "composerless" quality of a folk song or anthem as it has been absorbed into the American subconscious.

CHAPTER 2

⊙ぅ⊙

Grateful That We're Far from There

Irving Berlin, Kate Smith, and the Forging of an Interventionist Anthem

I'd like to write a great peace song, . . . a great marching song that would make people march toward peace.

—Irving Berlin, September 1938[1]

Viewers of the World Series in 2011 may have noticed a trend in the nightly performances of "God Bless America" during the seventh inning stretch: at five of the seven games of the series, the song was performed by a soldier in uniform. (See the companion website for links to these renditions of the song. ◐)

These performances sit in stark contrast to Irving Berlin's initial feeling that the song was not appropriate for soldiers to sing in *Yip, Yip, Yaphank*, but this is just the most recent incarnation of the song's longtime association with American interventionism. It began during World War II, when Kate Smith became the quintessential voice of the home front, mounting elaborate shows at North American military bases and holding several war-bond drives on the radio, thirteen-hour marathon fundraising efforts that broke records for war bond sales.[2] Smith's association with "God Bless America" essentially created and reinforced her patriotic image, and her wartime use of the song in turn solidified the song's role as a signifier for home-front support for war, a connection that would continue into the twenty-first century.

Figure 2.1
Kate Smith with soldiers during World War II. Photograph courtesy of the Kate Smith Collection, Howard Gotlieb Archival Research Center at Boston University.

But why did "God Bless America" take on this strong association with interventionism in the first place? There is no martial imagery in the lyrics of the song's familiar chorus specifically linking the song to war, no "bombs bursting in air" or "land where my fathers died" or "terrible swift swords." How did *this* patriotic song become the anthem of choice for military supporters, rather than another?

In fact, the early history of "God Bless America" reveals a shifting relationship with war. It was originally written in 1918 for soldiers to sing onstage but took on a very different meaning during the period directly before the US entry into World War II, when changes made by both Irving Berlin and Kate Smith first aligned it with isolationism before positioning it to become a song in support of the war. These shifting associations reflect larger changes in public opinion about intervention in the war during the late 1930s and early 1940s. In addition, Berlin and Smith's compositional and interpretive decisions distanced the song from the pop music conventions of its Tin Pan Alley roots, framing it instead as an anthem to be sung by the public.

THE COMPOSER'S MARK: A "PEACE SONG" AND INTERVENTIONISM

When Irving Berlin recovered "God Bless America" from his trunk of rejected songs in September 1938, much had changed since he had first sketched his song in 1918. A wartime marked by the zeal of Cohan's "Over There" had given way to an increasing mood of isolationism in response to a new, escalating conflict in Europe. But by the end of 1938, public opinion had shifted again, this time toward intervention in the looming war abroad. Berlin's compositional and lyrical revisions to "God Bless America" in the fall of 1938 were shaped by the historical landscape within the twenty years separating the song's original composition and its radio premiere.

Non-interventionism was part of the American mainstream during the mid-1930s. In a 1936 poll, 95 percent of Americans were opposed to US participation in another European war.[3] Much of this sentiment arose out of the belief that the Great War had been what the historian David Kennedy characterized as "an unpardonably costly mistake never to be repeated."[4] In her 1938 autobiography, Kate Smith expressed skepticism and remorse about American involvement in the First World War:

> In 1917, there was a great hue and cry about making the world safe for democracy! Yet, right now, with Fascism, Naziism, and Communism, there is less democracy in the world than there was twenty-one years ago. What happened to that promise to our boys who laid down their lives in the World War?[5]

No radical pacifist, Smith wrote that her desire for peace grew out of her work with veterans, and she articulated an unquestionably non-interventionist stance, writing, "I'm frank to say, if I had a son, I wouldn't want to send him off to battle in a strange land, to fight other nation's battles."[6] Smith, who would later prove to be a huge supporter of the war effort, was expressing views that were widely shared by many Americans in early 1938. In fact, Armistice Day itself, the occasion for which Smith and Collins approached Berlin for a new song to sing, was first made a legal holiday in May 1938, when an act of Congress declared it "a day to be dedicated to the cause of world peace."[7]

Returning from London in September 1938, as the Munich Pact precipitated the Nazi takeover of the Sudetenland in Czechoslovakia, Irving Berlin told a reporter, "I'd like to write a great peace song, . . . a great marching song that would make people march toward peace."[8] Kate Smith expressed similar sentiments on her talk show on the day of the song's premiere, saying: "As I stand before the microphone and sing it with all my heart, I'll be thinking of our veterans and I'll be praying with every breath I draw that we shall never have another war."[9] Against this backdrop, "God Bless America" appears to have been positioned as an anthem for non-interventionism in the escalating war in Europe. Yet "God Bless America" was called a "peace song" only in advance press surrounding its debut.[10] In later articles and interviews, such language was not used.

Although the premiere of "God Bless America" took place on the first official observance of Armistice Day, it also happened to coincide with a pivotal event in the history of World War II: *Kristallnacht*, the Nazi's calculated attacks on Jewish communities throughout Germany and its annexed territories, which began on 9 November 1938. As Smith described to listeners of *Kate Smith Speaks* on the day of the song's premiere, "In Germany, the Nazis are taking vengeance for the killing of an official by a Jewish youth. Mobs roamed the cities and towns last night, wrecking Jewish shops and setting fire to synagogues. It was a night of terror for German Jews."[11] According to many scholars of World War II, the brutality of *Kristallnacht* signaled a turning point for a growing American attitude of revulsion and condemnation of Nazi Germany, and a consequent move away from staunch isolationism.[12] In an October 1937 survey, 62 percent of Americans reported feeling neutral toward Germany, whereas a post-*Kristallnacht* poll showed 61 percent in favor of a boycott of German goods.[13] While a "peace song" may have suited the public mood in September 1938, as Kate Smith continued to perform the song in late 1938 and early 1939, a march toward peace seemed less and less appropriate.

Examining the details of the lyrical and musical revisions that Berlin made between October 1938 and March 1939 illustrates how these cultural shifts are expressed in successive versions of "God Bless America," as it transitions from a war song to a peace song and back again. Berlin's revisions also move the song away from its pop music origins, positioning it instead as an anthem and a hymn to be sung by the public.

In the song's original 1918 incarnation, the initial lyrics were appropriate for a country at war, with the words "make her victorious on land and foam" evoking the battlefronts in Europe (ex. 2.1). As originally sketched, the song followed an ABAC form common in Tin Pan Alley tunes, with a repetition of the opening melody on the words, "make her victorious."[14] The rhythm is in a martial 2/4 time, with no syncopation other than the dotted rhythmic figure on the words "America" and "victorious." The melody features bugle-call leaps, such as those in the opening of the A section and on the final "America" in the C section, as well as rhythmic patterns that evoke "Stars and Stripes Forever" on the line "to the right with a light from above."[15]

Example 2.1: "God Bless America," 1918 version

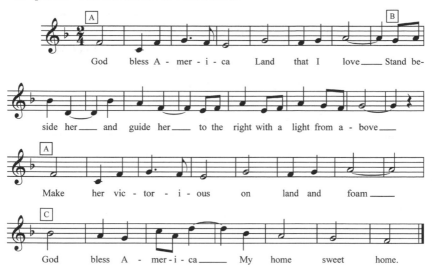

Example 2.2: Chorus (first revision, 25 October 1938)

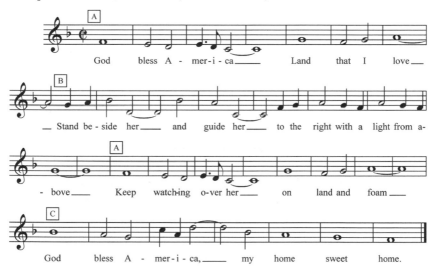

In the first 1938 revision in Berlin's files at the Library of Congress, dated 25 October, the song follows the same form as the original, but Berlin has made several changes that position it away from war (ex. 2.2).[16] Berlin altered the line "make her victorious on land and foam"—obviously not applicable to a country no longer at war—to *keep watching over her* on land and foam," but otherwise the lyrics remained unchanged.[17] While retaining the

dotted quarter–eighth note figure on the word "America," Berlin lengthened
the other note values, creating a new feeling of a ballad rather than a march
for soldiers to sing. He also eliminated the bugle-call leaping melody in the
original, substituting stepwise motion on the line "to the right with a light,"
and created a smoother vocal line by removing a similar leap in the first few
measures of the A section. The only other musical change at this point was
to modify the line "stand beside her and guide her" in the B section to now
include two sequential leaps of a major sixth, strengthening the melodic
coherence.

At this stage, Berlin also added an introductory verse, which includes a
direct reference to anti-interventionism:

> While the storm clouds gather
> Far across the sea
> Let us swear allegiance
> To a land that's free
> Let us all be grateful
> That we're far from there
> As we raise our voices
> In a solemn prayer[18]

The "storm clouds" in the first line are an obvious reference to the growing
strife in Europe, and follow Tin Pan Alley conventions linking bad weather
to troubled times.[19] Berlin's use of the first-person plural ("let us swear allegiance," "let us all be grateful," and "as we raise our voices") positions the
song as an anthem to be sung by a crowd, a subtle distinction from the
singular "land that I love" of the chorus that follows. And the last line that
labels the song "a solemn prayer" specifically frames the song as a hymn.

But most importantly, the line "let us all be grateful *that we're far from
there*" strongly points to a non-interventionist position, one that may have
been sympathetic to the suffering in Europe but that did not urge action to
bring Americans into the fray. Berlin's lyrics here are subtler than the sentiments expressed in a small but significant number of non-interventionist
songs that were released during this prewar period, including a 1939 song
titled "Over Here" by Al Maister and Chick Floyd in which listeners were
told to "be thankful we're living OVER HERE."[20] While this song projects a
more direct isolationist message than Berlin's, both lines riff on George
M. Cohan's World War I–era "Over There" while expressing viewpoints in
pointed opposition to Cohan's rousing war song.

This latest version of "God Bless America" remained unchanged on
proofs of sheet music dated 31 October and 4 November 1938—just one

Example 2.3: Verse (first 1938 revision)

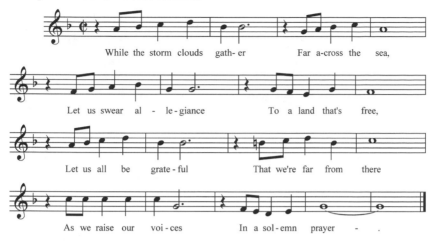

While the storm clouds gath-er   Far a-cross the   sea,

Let us swear al - le-giance   To a land that's   free,

Let us all be   grate-ful   That we're far from   there

As we raise our   voi-ces   In a sol-emn   prayer - .

week before it was to be performed by Smith.[21] These proofs also include music for the verse (ex. 2.3).[22] Charles Hamm has compared the relationship between verse and chorus in Tin Pan Alley songs to that of the recitative-aria setting in opera, with the verse serving as an introduction to a chorus that is considered the heart of the song, and Berlin's verse follows this convention, with short sequential phrases that ultimately move to a dominant harmony, propelling us toward the chorus.[23] The "non-interventionist" line ("grateful that we're far from there") is given melodic, harmonic, and formal emphasis within this short verse. The only chromaticism in the song's melody (verse or chorus) occurs with a B-natural at the beginning of this phrase, and Berlin also increases the tension and emphasis by using the phrase to break up expected repetition. After the first eight measures, Berlin repeats the opening melody on the words "let us all be grateful," but then deviates from a direct restatement of the entire opening phrase, so that instead of a dominant harmony resolving to the tonic F major (as on the line "far across the sea"), there is a surprising shift to E major moving to A minor coinciding with this phrase.

But critical last-minute changes to the song were still to come. A handwritten piano score dated 2 November 1938 indicates that Berlin was continuing to edit the words and music between the two rounds of proofs mentioned above, a little more than a week before the song's premiere. Although the score does not include words, it contains changes to the form and melody that fit the song's final lyrics.[24] The song appears in its final incarnation in an undated handwritten score that may be one of the final versions exchanged between Berlin and Collins before the song's debut (ex. 2.4).[25]

Example 2.4: Chorus (final revision)

This version includes a drastic shift in the song's formal structure—instead of a return to the A melody in the chorus, Berlin has added a new C section, with new lyrics in praise of the country's natural landscape set to a sequential melody that leads to a climactic restatement of the title phrase in the song's last line. In the B section of the chorus, Berlin has replaced the words "stand beside her and guide her *to the right*," with "*through the night*," an acknowledgement of the new, politically charged association of "the right" with Fascism and right-wing politics.[26] In the final phrase, Berlin eliminated the somewhat awkward leaps on the word "America" in favor of a smoother line descending by step from the word "God," a change that alters the climactic center of the song. Whereas in the 1918 and first revised 1938 versions, the highest note fell on the last syllable of "America," in the final version the highest note sounds on "God," effectively highlighting the prayerful aspect of the song and further framing it as a hymn. The song's new form, a more unconventional ABCD, also serves to distance the song from typical pop music compositional styles.

At this point, the verse continued to include the pivotal line, "let us all be grateful that we're far from there," and Kate Smith sang this non-interventionist verse in her earliest performances. However, Berlin and his associates expressed dissatisfaction with this version of the verse early on. Saul Bornstein wrote Berlin that he and a group of broadcasting and music publishing executives had listened to Smith's rendition of the song in her Thanksgiving 1938 broadcast: "all feel that it should have a verse, but without the 'storm-clouds' line and the 'grateful-we-are-over-here' line."[27] Perhaps these executives wanted to purge the verse of any reference to a specific time and place in history, or to distance themselves from any remotely political stance regarding US involvement in the war, or to avoid placing the song on the wrong side of shifting public opinion. Whatever the reason, by 20 February 1939, when the printed sheet music was copyrighted, the storm clouds stayed, but Berlin changed the line to "Let us all be grateful *for a land so fair.*"[28] In a letter to Bornstein in early February 1939, Berlin expressed satisfaction with his new verse, "Regarding 'God Bless America,' I think it is wise to go through with the original verse, although I regret very much that I didn't have the new verse in the beginning."[29] Berlin's regret underscores the importance of removing the "far from there" line from the original verse, since it was the only major change between the two versions.

Berlin's desire to remove the "non-interventionist" line in the verse was likely in response to his own changing views as much as to shifts in public opinion about intervention in the war. As a Jewish immigrant, Berlin showed growing concern about the events in Europe and began to give large donations to Jewish relief work during this period.[30] In her memoir, Berlin's daughter Mary Ellin Barrett wrote that by 1940, "isolationists in our interventionist family became the enemy, or at best, if close friends, the misguided ones."[31] A "peace song" was no longer necessary.

In September 1939, a music teacher in Detroit, Michigan, wrote to Berlin, asking his permission to reprint and distribute a new version of the chorus written by two of her students:

God Bless America
Keep her from war
Stand beside her and guide her
Through the troubles she must endure
Save her government, save her citizens
Save her army and navy too
God bless America and we'll prove true[32]

This chorus may have taken its cue from the song's original "non-interventionist" verse, but in his response Berlin made it clear that he did not want the song linked with such a specifically anti-interventionist message, even if it was only sung by music students in Detroit. In a letter to Bornstein asking him to respond to this request on his behalf, Berlin wrote that he would prefer that these students sing the song's original lyrics, "because the whole point of the song is to keep it away from any feeling of war. And the lyric they have written, definitely is on the propaganda angle, and you don't think children should be taught to sing those lyrics at this time."[33] Here, Berlin reveals not only an awareness of the power of song lyrics to shape public opinion (even that of children) but also a distaste for anything smacking of propaganda, isolationist or otherwise.

Despite his professed desire to keep the song "away from any feeling of war," both Berlin and his song became increasingly associated with interventionism during the prewar years. In May 1941 alone, Berlin sang it at a Madison Square Garden rally for new army inductees, as well as at a large interventionist rally in Philadelphia organized to counter an appeasement speech by Charles Lindbergh sponsored by the isolationist organization America First.[34] In fact, the song was booed when song leaders tried to lead it at two separate America First rallies (one in Chicago in December 1940, and another in New York in May 1941), purportedly because it was "regarded as an interventionist song."[35]

"God Bless America" was thus a fitting anthem for this prewar period, when mainstream public opinion moved away from anti-interventionism to embrace a more sympathetic stance toward American involvement in the war. In October 1939, a Gallup poll revealed that while 84 percent of Americans were pro-Ally, there remained little support for entering the war.[36] But by September 1940, a Princeton Public Opinion Survey reported that 53 percent of Americans thought defeating Hitler was more important than staying out of the war, and in January 1941, 68 percent were in favor of aid to the Allies even at risk of war.[37]

On the other hand, Berlin's revisions to "God Bless America" might also reflect a desire to disentangle the song from any political messages or associations. He even tried to distance the song from an explicitly patriotic message, claiming in a 1940 interview that "it's not a patriotic song, but rather an expression of gratitude for what this country has done for its citizens, of what home really means."[38] Cleansed of any specific political meaning, "God Bless America" emerged as a song with a universal message that could be interpreted as the listener saw fit. Its adaptability made it timeless, no doubt contributing to its ongoing popularity. In his 1938 revisions, Berlin purged the song of any reference—however oblique—to events that would tie the song to a particular time and place. The verse, with its vague references to storm clouds across the sea, retained the only vestige of the song's historical roots, but it soon became an optional introduction that was frequently omitted in later performances and songbook publications, as was the custom with many popular songs from that era.[39] Nonetheless, Kate Smith's nightly performances would leave their own stamp on the song and its shifting meanings.

THE PERFORMER'S MARK: A BALLAD BECOMES AN ANTHEM

American radio listeners heard Kate Smith sing "God Bless America" more than anyone else during this prewar period, giving her a critical role in shaping the song's reception. An analysis of Smith's first radio performance of "God Bless America"—as well as a later live performance recorded in February 1939 and her Victor recording released in March 1939—reveals the extent to which Smith, along with arranger Tony Gale and music director Jack Miller, influenced the song and its staying power. Elements of Smith's performance and Gale's arrangement continued the shift away from pop tune sensibilities that Berlin's revisions had begun. The arrangements also specifically positioned the song as a vehicle for group singing, infusing Berlin's song with the musical conventions of both a hymn and an unofficial anthem. But it is a recording that Smith made two decades later that completely disengages the song from its Tin Pan Alley origins to become a timeless anthem.

Smith's premiere performance on 10 November 1938 begins with a brass fanfare featuring sequential declamations of the song's opening phrase, taken at a stately andante tempo.[40] (See table 2.1 for a schematic of this performance. A recording is available on tracks 1 and 2 of the companion website. ◉) This instrumental introduction leads to a climactic drumroll, after which Smith gives her spoken introduction over strings, a statement that both positions Smith as playing a central role in the song's creation and predicts its popularity:

> And now it's going to be my very great privilege to sing you a song that's never been sung before by anybody, and that was written especially for me by one of the greatest composers in the music field today. It's something more than a song—I feel it's one of the most beautiful compositions ever written, a song that will never die. The author: Mr. Irving Berlin. The title: "God Bless America."

After this introduction, Smith sings Berlin's original verse (including the "grateful-that-we're-far-from-there" line), accompanied by solo piano in a free, improvisatory style characteristic of popular song verses. On the last note of the verse—on the word "prayer"—the strings return and set a faster tempo for the chorus that follows, a sprightly andante with a strong backbeat.

Table 2.1. SCHEMATIC OF KATE SMITH'S 10 NOVEMBER 1938 PERFORMANCE

Timing	Description	
:00	Instrumental introduction	
:20	Spoken introduction (Smith)	
:55	Verse (Smith)	
	While the storm clouds gather far across the sea	
	Let us swear allegiance to a land that's free	
	Let us all be grateful that we're far from there	
	As we raise our voices in a solemn prayer	
1:40	Chorus 1 (Smith)	
	A	*God bless America, land that I love*
	B	*Stand beside her and guide her through the night with a light from above*
	C	*From the mountains to the prairies to the oceans white with foam*
	D	*God bless America, my home sweet home*
2:20	Chorus 2	
	A & B	Smith + choir (all sing lyrics)
	C	Smith on lyrics, choir background
	D	Smith + choir (all sing lyrics)
3:17	Coda	
	C	Smith on new lyrics, choir background
		From the green fields in Virginia to the gold fields out in Nome
	D & D′	Smith + chorus (all sing lyrics)

Through multiple repetitions, the song's chorus undergoes an intriguing combination of stylistic treatments, borrowing conventions from the popular song, march, anthem, and hymn. The chorus is first sung solo by Smith, then repeated by Smith and a chorus, followed by a coda of the song's last two phrases. In the first section, where Smith is accompanied by her full orchestra, the song has a "swing" feel typical of other Tin Pan Alley song performances, with the rhythm section offering punctuation on the backbeat and the piano continuing the improvisational, jazz-influenced style introduced in the verse. Smith adds a subtle "swing" element to her vocal performance by syncopating her entrance on the phrase "land that I love" rather than beginning the phrase on the beat. The brass section plays fanfares between the phrases of the vocal line, echoing the brass opening and reflecting the "martial air" that Smith thought the song needed. Such militaristic musical tropes evoked by the brass throughout the arrangement may have subtly strengthened listener's association of the song with interventionism.

When the chorus is repeated, Smith is joined by a mixed choir singing the lyrics in four-part harmony. The swing in Smith's vocals is absent, but a backbeat in the rhythm section persists. At the C section ("From the mountains . . ."), there is a dramatic shift in the arrangement: the tempo slows; Smith sings the lyrics with plenty of rubato as the chorus backs her up on "ah"; the rhythm section drops out; and the harp becomes the only accompaniment. The final D phrase ("God bless America, my home sweet home") is even slower, and the choir joins Smith in singing the lyrics in an a cappella, chorale-style vocal arrangement. Here, all stylistic references to the pop ballad and the march have vanished, replaced by the anthem and the hymn.

But Smith and her crew aren't done with us. As a final coda, the C and D phrases return for a third time, heralded by the brass fanfares that again punctuate each phrase, and marked by a return to the brisk andante tempo of the beginning. Here, Smith sings the somewhat awkward lyrics "From the green fields in Virginia to the gold fields out in Nome," which were cut in later renditions. At the very end of the song, the D section is performed twice at successively slower speeds; the first iteration—sung by Smith and the chorus accompanied by the full orchestra—cadences on the dominant rather than the tonic on the word "home," propelling the song into a final repetition of "God Bless America, my home sweet home." In this ending phrase, there is a lengthy pause after "America," and the final four words are delivered slowly and climactically, punctuated by brass as Smith ascends to the upper octave until she reaches the last word, "home," which she sings unaccompanied. As Smith holds her final note, the chorus and orchestra join her and bring the song to an end with a triumphant, four-note ascending line in the chorus and brass, followed by a drumroll flourish. The broadcast recording ends to the sound of loud audience applause and shouts, evidence that the premiere was enthusiastically received.

It is quite a performance. After listening to this broadcast, I can't help but feel that there is some truth to the *Look* magazine caption that so incensed Berlin, the one that gave arranger Tony Gale credit for reworking the song so that its performance "was neither the song Berlin had written at Camp Upton nor the one he had sung for Collins."[41] Gale and his musicians have thrown everything they could at this arrangement, with a dizzying array of stylistic references, as well as vocal and instrumental textures: a pop ballad verse and first chorus, martial brass fanfares, hymnlike part-singing, and a show-stopping, ever-repeating finale. The use of the chorus served as a cue to listeners that the song lent itself to be sung en masse, but most other aspects of the arrangement emphasize a performative virtuosity.

Perhaps not surprisingly, Smith and Berlin apparently had different ideas about the way the song should be performed. Collins told the radio critic Ben Gross that Smith thought it "should have more of a martial air" and that Berlin disagreed; Richard Hayes elaborates that Berlin wanted it to be more of a ballad.[42] Smith and Collins seem to have followed Berlin's wishes for its first performance, but her later renditions reflect different sensibilities. Hayes claims that a change in the song's arrangement occurred on Thanksgiving night, 24 November, two weeks after the premiere, and that it was this arrangement that persisted in Smith later performances.[43] Correspondence within the Berlin camp provides evidence that this Thanksgiving rendition had a slower tempo than the two performances that preceded it, but there was no general agreement that the new arrangement was an improvement. After Smith's Thanksgiving broadcast, Bornstein wrote to Berlin that "mostly all here, including Sam Katz, Disney, Winslow and the others liked her original rendition. While her rendition on Thanksgiving night was forceful, effective and full of reverence, it seemed to lose something of that inspired, patriotic 'salute the flag' spirit her first rendition gave and which the song seems to need."[44] Bornstein added that the "few here that liked her Thanksgiving night rendition explained that they liked it because she did not do the song so fast." Berlin expressed the opposite opinion about Smith's approach to the song, writing in February 1939 that he "had a feeling that she is doing 'God Bless America' a little too slow. Maybe its because I am used to the original way she did it."[45]

A recording of a live broadcast on 16 February 1939 sheds some light on these changes to the song's arrangement.[46] (Track 3 on the companion website. ◐) By this time, Smith had performed the song on her show every week for fourteen weeks, and her spoken introduction reflects its popularity (as well as the continued contested nature of its origins):

> Of all the songs I've sung in the years that I've been in radio, none has received the response as the one I sing now. As long as your letters insist that you want to hear it, why I'll sing it. The song was written for me by Mr. Irving Berlin. The title: "God Bless America."

One subtle change from Smith's original performance takes place directly after her spoken introduction, when a harp glissando leads into the first piano chords of the verse, serving perhaps to strengthen the distancing of the song from pop music by using an instrument often associated with liturgical and classical music.

The general form and instrumentation of the arrangement remain unchanged in this 1939 performance. The most significant change is that the tempo has been slowed dramatically, from 100 to 76 bpm. At this stately speed, the swing backbeat is less perceptible, the string and horn interludes more prominent. The song has lost the jaunty undercurrent of Tin Pan Alley, further drawing on the musical conventions of anthem and hymn.[47]

Several minor changes to the lyrics can be heard in this performance. In addition to the removal of the line about Virginia and Nome, there is a slight change to the non-interventionist line in the verse, so that Smith sings "Let us all be *thankful* that we're far from there," instead of *"grateful"* as it appears in Berlin's lyrics. Although it is a small adjustment, this word choice reflects nuanced meaning. According to one online definition, *"Grateful* means that you appreciate what someone has done for you and you want to express your thanks. *Thankful* means that you are relieved/pleased that what you hoped for has actually happened."[48] Here Smith subtly shifts the *gratitude* that the immigrant Berlin had expressed for all that the United States had done for him to *thankfulness*, which can be understood as coming from a more comfortable position within American culture, where one is praising that which is expected rather than being earnestly "grateful."

Just one month after this broadcast performance, Smith released her first recording of "God Bless America" on Victor, in March 1939.[49] (Track 4 on the companion website. ◉) The arrangement is nearly identical to her live performances from this period, but the verse has been omitted completely. Of course, there were practical reasons behind the decision to cut the verse—it was common practice for Tin Pan Alley songs to lose their verses, and it was an easy way to trim the song's length in order to fit within the three-minute limit imposed by the recording technology of the time. But there were likely more strategic reasons as well. For one, the opening line of the verse ("As the storm clouds gather") positions the song within a specific historical moment. Without the verse's symbolic reference to the escalating conflict in Europe, the recording carries a sense of timelessness that allowed it to remain popular beyond this prewar period. In addition, the verse's last phrase ("in a solemn prayer") calls attention to its religiosity, which would become a sensitive subject when anti-Semitic criticism of the song arose in 1940.

Smith's Victor recording became a best seller, and she went on to record "God Bless America" several times for other record labels throughout her career.[50] On an album called *Kate Smith Sings "God Bless America" and Other American Favorites*, which she recorded for Tops in the fall of 1959, Smith's rendition of the song is much shorter than her 1939 recording, omitting both the verse and the full repetition of the chorus, and lasting just over two minutes.[51] (Track 5 on the companion website. ◉) It is this later, streamlined version that has now become a staple at baseball games and on the radio, likely because of its shorter length and more straightforward presentation of the song.

Many aspects of this later recording seem designed to purge the song of any remnants of its Tin Pan Alley past and to strengthen its association as an anthem. Smith sings the melody straight (without swing), and the piano, with its nightclub tinge, is absent. Also gone is the a cappella choral singing in the full second repeat of the chorus, which had been so evocative of a hymn in the broadcast recording. What remains are the brass fanfares, Smith's straightforward but forceful singing style, and chorus accompanied by orchestra, all of which position the song as an anthem.

This streamlined arrangement also solidifies the song's associations with group singing. It retains mixed chorus singing during the coda section, but perhaps most intriguingly, the song is performed in a lower key. Smith sang the broadcast version and earlier recordings in C-sharp, while the Tops recording is in B, a whole step lower. This key change makes it easier for nonprofessionals to sing, but it also has a dramatic effect on the timbre of Smith's voice. Since it doesn't require her to move into her head voice, she could be mistaken for a male tenor, and the key change thus increases the song's universality by removing any gendered assumptions about the singer and giving all listeners the feeling that they could sing it. Such vocal androgyny also negates the power and sensuality associated with the high female voice, which feminist theorists have argued is "a source of sexual power, an object at once of desire and fear."[52] Thus neutered of any threat signified by a high singing voice, Smith's "God Bless America" evoked a universality that helped this later recording to become the iconic version of the song for decades to come.

"God Bless America" began its life as a rousing soldier's march during World War I, then was briefly reincarnated as a "peace song" before becoming an interventionist anthem during the years leading up to the US entry into World War II and beyond. The song's associations with interventionism, once established, have remained constant into the present, as its repeated use as a home-front war anthem has continued to strengthen its symbolic power. The verse is now performed only rarely, and its "grateful-we-are-far-from-there" line has been erased from memory, but the song's early history reflects shifts in attitudes about American war that are often forgotten.

The song is a product of the creative efforts of Berlin, Smith, Tony Gale, Jack Miller, and Ted Collins, informed by the shifting mood of the times. Through Berlin's tinkering with a classic Tin Pan Alley song form and Smith and Gale's use of musical tropes from a wide array of styles, the song transcended its pop song status and came to inhabit a liminal space between ballad, hymn, march, and anthem. Over time, Smith's performances shifted from an emphasis on performative virtuosity to a simpler arrangement in a lower key, finally positioning the song as an anthem suitable for a crowd. And as a result of Berlin's removal of lyrics that linked the song to a particular time, place, or point of view, and Smith's gender-transcending performance in her low vocal range, the song became universal on multiple levels, allowing it to take on an array of meanings that could be adapted to a shifting historical landscape.

CHAPTER 3

ᏬᎶ

Land That I Love

Early Embrace, Critique, and Backlash

The mob is always right. It seems to be able to sense instinctively what is good, and I believe that there are darned few good songs which have not been whistled or sung by the crowd.

—Irving Berlin, July 1940[1]

No song has ever flamed into our country's consciousness more spectacularly than "God Bless America."

—*Chicago Radio Guide*, August 1940[2]

Beginning in July 1940, an explosion of press articles about "God Bless America" began to appear in newspapers across the country.[3] Berlin believed that this phenomenon was truly a grassroots response by the people, writing in 1940, "One of the finest things that can be said about the song is that this is *one* song that the public picked rather than a songwriter or a publisher. I never labeled it an anthem, not did I realize when I first set the phrase 'God Bless America, Land That I Love' to music that I was really writing a hymn. However, there it is. Millions of people sing it seriously."[4] Others have commented on Berlin's unique ability to channel the public mood through his songs. In his biography of Berlin, Philip Furia calls him "the man who gave voice to the masses"; to Jody Rosen, he was a "*public* songwriter, who pledged his allegiance not to his muse but to 'the mob.'"[5]

By 1940 "God Bless America" had transcended its Tin Pan Alley roots to become a popular vehicle for group singing, which served to strengthen community ties during a prewar period marked by uncertainty and fear.

At the same time, strong dissent against the song emerged from across the political spectrum. Some disdained what they saw as the song's simplistic jingoism, but other criticism contained a dark subtext of anti-Semitism and xenophobia aimed at Irving Berlin, showing that "God Bless America" touched a nerve in a prewar United States where some ideas about Jews and cultural outsiders veered perilously close to those of the Nazis.

PUBLIC EMBRACE: "GOD BLESS AMERICA" AS AN UNOFFICIAL ANTHEM

A handwritten note, dated "July 20, 1940, midnight," reads:

> Dear Mr. Berlin:
>
> Thought you might be interested in this. I'm on my way to Cleveland for a vacation—and everyone in this lounge car is singing "God Bless America"—singing it at the top of their voices, letter-perfect in word and melody. Someone started singing it spontaneously—over his Tom Collins—and the whole car took it up.[6]

A letter to the editor in November 1940 describes a similar scene in Louisville, Kentucky: "This morning while sitting in our office in the Starks Building reading about the war-torn Europe, the men in one of the insurance offices sang 'God Bless America.' The voices echoed and re-echoed in the court of the building."[7]

The popularity of "God Bless America" during this period is not only reflected in its robust sheet music and recordings sales, but also in the extent to which it was embraced by ordinary Americans and sung in public. One small-town reporter wrote in late 1940 that the radio broadcaster's impending ban on all ASCAP songs was "unfortunate, but not a calamity," since "we can still sing it wherever we choose, and it is the singing rather than the hearing of those words that give them meaning for each of us."[8] A cross-section of clippings saved by Berlin from newspapers across the country reveal that by September 1940, the song was sung at the meetings of an extraordinary array of civic organizations and clubs, ranging from such bastions of middle-class respectability as Kiwanis, Odd Fellows, American Legion, United War Veterans, and the Daughters of the American Revolution, to events sponsored by the WPA Recreation Division, the American Labor Party, and the Union Hispano-Americana.[9] It became a part of the core repertory in school music programs across the country.[10] Churches and synagogues included the song in their services—possibly a first for a tune with origins in Tin Pan Alley. Its popularity seems to have transcended the racial divide, being sung at meetings of African American civic groups such as the Negro Welfare League and the Sigma Gamma Rho sorority, and was included along with the anthem "Lift Every Voice and Sing" at a meeting to unionize African American railroad workers.[11]

The song also became a part of larger public events, like the New York World's Fair, the Portland Rose Festival, the "Cavalcade of Music" concert in San Francisco, and the *Chicago Defender*'s Bud Billiken picnic.[12] It was played and sung at every Brooklyn Dodgers home game in 1940, as well as during halftime at college football games.[13] Audiences were encouraged to sing along to renditions of "God Bless America" at countless community concerts, after shows at Radio City Music Hall, at Broadway plays, and on film trailers in movie theaters across the country.[14]

The reasons for this public embrace of "God Bless America" are multilayered. On a basic level, the song's simple melody and lyrics made it easy to sing. As one reporter put it, "If you can't sing 'God Bless America' you can't sing anything."[15] Leopold Stokowski, whose All-American Youth Orchestra

Figure 3.1
Irving Berlin leads the band as it plays "God Bless America" at "I Am An American Day" ceremonies at New York City Hall in May 1942. Photograph by *The New York Times*/Redux, courtesy of Rodgers & Hammerstein: an Imagem Company, on behalf of the Estate of Irving Berlin.

played the song on many concerts, called it "very singable—that is, [it] can be carried along handsomely by a great number of people, and it has dignity, simplicity and a wonderful sincerity; and it's not surprising that people all over the nation love to sing it."[16]

The song's straightforward patriotism gave it added power during this period before the United States entered the war, when patriotic displays became an important part of public life. Democrats chose it as the theme song of their 1940 convention despite the fact that the Republicans were already using it in Wendell Willkie's presidential campaign.[17] And the embrace of the song by progressive groups such as the American Labor Party may have allowed them to demonstrate their loyalty to the United States even as they criticized aspects that they found unjust. In the face of mounting anti-German and anti-Japanese sentiment, a German translation of the song was sung by a large gathering of German Americans in Rochester, New York, and young Japanese Americans in El Centro, California, sang it as they presented their county supervisors with a formal resolution of loyalty to the United States.[18] In a more menacing use of the song as a signifier for patriotism, the Nazi anthem "Horst Wessel" was briefly replaced by "God Bless America" at Camp Nordlund, a New Jersey retreat run by the pro-Nazi German American Bund, as part of an attempt to "make the camp 100 percent American"—that is, until they called for a boycott of the song upon discovering that it was written by a Jew.[19]

The singing of patriotic songs became a powerful tool for instilling patriotism and loyalty during this period, as one Los Angeles newspaper declared in July 1940:

> An effective way to combat "fifth column" activities here is to rouse the patriotic emotions of Americans by anthems and songs. There should be community "sings" in every town and village of the country from now on. They should sing "The Star-Spangled Banner," Sousa's "Stars and Stripes Forever," and Berlin's "God Bless America." These songs should be played and sung in all public places.[20]

This editorial calls attention to the power of group singing to forge national identity and quiet dissent. But this kind of communal singing did more than promote patriotism and nationalist loyalty—for many, the act of singing itself allowed these public events to strengthen a sense of shared community as a response to increasing anxiety during this period. Newspaper clippings reveal that many community sings were added to outdoor concerts of local bands and orchestras across the country during the summer of 1940, often as a result of public demand.[21] One article explained that a community sing was planned after "an outburst of singing by the audience as the orchestra played 'God Bless America' at a concert," as well as in response to requests for community singing from those attending concerts.[22] Such enthusiasm for group singing could be a manifestation of what Warren Susman, in his study of the culture of the Depression era, characterized as a general interest in "participation in some group, community, or movement," of a "need to feel one's self a part of some larger body, some larger sense of purpose."[23]

"God Bless America" seemed to ease anxiety fed by increasing conflict abroad and ongoing economic Depression at home. Laurence Bergreen contrasts the song with Orson Welles's *War of the Worlds*, which was broadcast the week before the premiere of "God Bless America" in 1938, noting that while Welles exploited the public unease of this period, Berlin's song served as a calming force.[24] The idea that the song had a soothing effect in the face of escalating violence is supported by reports that record sales swelled during Nazi invasions of Poland, the Low Countries, and France.[25]

Given the unease of the period—and more specifically, the turbulent events of the fall of 1938—the song's timing has to be considered an important factor in its success. As one reporter wrote in 1940, "Two years ago, Irving Berlin dusted off a composition written twenty years previously for a soldier show, a composition which he believes might not have been accepted by the public of only five years ago and would have been rejected as maudlin by the America of little over a decade ago."[26] Berlin seems to have felt that the song was particularly resonant for pre–World War II Americans. In 1940, Berlin explained the song's popularity as he saw it:

> I believe its great appeal is the fact that it comes at a time when people feel very keenly about their patriotism and want to express it. This song seems to say what we all feel. Personally, I make no great claims for the merit of the song itself. But, because of the circumstances and of its timeliness, I sincerely believe that those thirty-two bars of words and music are the most important I have ever written. Certainly they are closest to my heart.[27]

He reflected decades later, "It was a very ordinary patriotic song that any child could have written . . . 'Land that I love'—what child couldn't write that? It was the timing that counted."[28] The song's dual sentiments of patriotism and faith were thus seen as particularly appropriate for a cultural moment marked by prospects of continued economic Depression and the threat of war.

The perception that "God Bless America" was already "old" likely contributed to its strength as an unofficial anthem. By 1940, the song's World War

I origins were well publicized, and at least one newspaper story referred to it as "Irving Berlin's old song" just two years after its first performance.[29] This sense of age distanced the song from its roots in popular music and lent it a sense of history that allowed it to be embraced as a hymn or an anthem, rather than a pop tune. It also may have imbued the song with a sense of nostalgia for an idealized shared past, which would have appealed to an American public worried about the future.

Strategic decisions about the song's initial performances also contributed to the public perception of the song as an anthem or a hymn to be sung in groups. Performance restrictions were purposefully imposed to distinguish it from other pop tunes and avoid their typically short lifespans. In addition to giving Kate Smith exclusive radio performance rights, Berlin prohibited any dance arrangements and stipulated that it could be played only in connection with patriotic, religious, civic, or educational events.[30] At the same time, schools, civic groups, and religious organizations interested in using the song in collective performance were encouraged to do so, free of charge.[31] These measures enabled "God Bless America" to achieve a different kind of popularity—as a timeless anthem meant not only to be listened to, but to be sung.

DISSENTING VOICES, PART I: "THAT SONG AGAIN"

Of course, not everyone was singing along. Criticism of "God Bless America" came from everywhere—right, left, and center. Some commentators simply didn't like the song, its message, or its principal performer. One journalist acknowledged that although he did not share this opinion, "there are a great many citizens in this nation who become nauseated the moment Kate Smith swings into the strains of 'God Bless America.'"[32] In her book about her father, Mary Ellin Barrett recounts how her mother, Ellin Berlin, walked out on a radio appearance for the Roosevelt campaign when the host asked if she "didn't find 'God Bless America' a little corny and sentimental."[33]

Part of this may have stemmed from listener fatigue; despite restrictions on its use, "God Bless America" seemed to be everywhere by 1940. In addition to its omnipresence at public events, Kate Smith sang it on the radio nearly every week from November 1938 to January 1941.[34] By December 1940, her 1939 Victor recording had sold more than half a million copies, and once her record was released other labels followed suit, issuing new versions by their own recording stars in an attempt to capitalize on the song's popularity.[35]

Such fatigue was likely made worse by a proliferation of other patriotic Tin Pan Alley songs released after 1939, spurred in part by the success of "God Bless America."[36] In a satirical poem appearing in *Variety* in December 1940, the lyricist Al Stillman complained of this phenomenon:

> This is my country and I love it
> And I don't have to be reminded of it
> On the red, white and blue networks, night and day,
> By Gray Gordon and Sammy Kaye.
> Mine ears have heard and have been badly bent
> By patriotic compositions of indubitably meritorious intent.[37]

Even those who liked "God Bless America" acknowledged the negative effect of this glut of patriotic songs and sentiments: "Kate Smith may be corny and you may be tired of some of the current vehement patriotism, but there's no denying it that when Kate sings this Irving Berlin tune, you've heard something fine."[38] Berlin himself expressed cynicism about the use of patriotism in entertainment, pointing out that "a patriotic song has got to be good, or it's unworthy of publication. It can be simply a trick—an applause trap, like waving a flag at the end of the third act, which just about forces an audience to clap."[39]

Others objected to the song on aesthetic grounds. The singer W. Wallace Ashley caused something of an uproar when he called the song a "trashy ballad," asserting that "it is not great music regardless of any publicity tie-up with Boy Scouts, Kate Smith, or press agent stories about Irving Berlin. It is smartly done, no doubt of that, and has enough religious inference to mask its type. But it is a ballad. Its accompaniment is jazz, and the melody will never stand without accompaniment, which is the test of a good melody."[40] Berlin himself said that he made "no great claims for the merit of the song itself" and wrote to one of his critics, "I have no quarrel with those who find fault with the quality of the song."[41]

Some commentators resented the notion that singing "God Bless America" could substitute for genuine patriotic action, arguing, "there is more to be done than the singing of 'God Bless America.'"[42] Several college newspapers took aim at the song for promoting a simplistic patriotism; the *Dartmouth* proclaimed, "It seems as though we could do a little more than place America's well-being musically in God's hands and call it patriotism," and Santa Barbara State College's *El Gaucho* agreed: "One's ability to bellow forth chauvinistic babble is hardly an indication of one's feelings toward the United States."[43]

Such negative sentiments represent the darker, coercive side of group singing; while building a sense of community among participants, it can alienate and exclude outsiders who find themselves unmoved or at odds with the song and its message. "God Bless America" not only provoked spontaneous affirmations of community but also became a vehicle for defining the "outsiderness" of those who may not have been completely in step with the majority. Suspicion swirled around people who chose not to sing it or not to stand when it was played in public. In October 1940, the singer Harry Richman described how during his show at Ben Marden's Riviera in Fort Lee, New Jersey, audience members came to his dressing room demanding the song, asking "How dare you not sing it?"[44] Once he added it to his show, he commented: "Now almost everybody in the place stands up when it's sung and you know, there's something strange about those who don't." A short newspaper item from San Francisco in July 1941 reiterates this theme of outsiderness: "At the Top of the Mark the other twilight a crowd of nice people were so annoyed at one crabbed individualist who wouldn't stand up when 'God Bless America' was played."[45] In these instances, the song became an imperative, an important marker of patriotism and loyalty, and those who did not participate were seen as dangerously out of sync with the group.

Perhaps the most famous dissenter against the song during this period was Woody Guthrie. "God Bless America" had plenty in it to rankle Guthrie, a self-proclaimed atheist and "the ultimate proletarian."[46] According to Guthrie biographer Joe Klein, the singer's hatred of the song took hold in early 1940, while he was hitchhiking his way from Texas to New York City during a cold, snowy winter:

> Worse than the weather, though, was the fact that "God Bless America," Irving Berlin's patriotic pop tune, seemed to be everywhere that winter. . . . [I]t seemed that every time he stopped in a roadhouse for a shot of warm-up whiskey some maudlin joker would plunk a nickel in a jukebox and play it just for spite. . . . "God Bless America," indeed—it was just another of those songs that told people not to worry, that God was in the driver's seat.[47]

Soon after arriving in New York, from his perch in a rundown hotel near Times Square, Guthrie wrote his own song in angry response to it. Originally called "God Blessed America," its title was later changed to "This Land Is Your Land," and it went on to become an unofficial anthem, just like the song it satirized.[48] In his song's well-known verses, Guthrie evoked the beauty of the land to praise the United States, following Berlin's lead (and that of "America the Beautiful" before him). However, Guthrie's original song also included two "protest" verses, which were cut when the song was later recorded and published:

Verse 4:
Was a big high wall that tried to stop me
A sign was painted said: Private Property,
But on the back side it didn't say nothing—
God blessed America for me

Verse 6 (final):
One bright sunny morning in the shadow of the steeple
By the relief office I saw my people—
As they stood hungry, I stood there wondering if
God blessed America for me[49]

The refrain "God blessed America for me" (which was of course later changed to "this land was made for you and me") brings the emphasis back to the people. Instead of extolling America's virtues and asking God to bless the country as it is, Guthrie's song is an open critique of the way America does not share its blessings with all of its citizens. The last verse addresses the suffering of ordinary Americans, which Guthrie felt was ignored in the simplistic praise offered in "God Bless America."

While Guthrie may not necessarily have had the song's copyright restrictions in mind when he wrote the fourth verse, it does resonate with one of the main sources of criticism of "God Bless America": its status as Berlin's "private property."[50] In an article in the *Daily Worker* in early 1941, leftist critic Mike Gold echoed this same objection, writing that although "God Bless America" may have been embraced by the masses, the song "really belongs to Irving Berlin. If you want to express your patriotism through the song you must pay anything from two-bits up to a hundred dollars for the right to warble or whang it. 'God Bless America' is private property."[51]

In fact, the copyright and performance restrictions on the song were a source of resentment and misunderstanding from all sides. Berlin's office would grant permission for a performance providing it "preserves the spirit in which it is written, and further providing it is for a religious, educational, patriotic and charitable function or program."[52] The song was free for any group to sing in noncommercial contexts, but these policies created confusion among those who wanted to sing it. For example, a short article in a Prescott, Arizona, newspaper tells of a Sunday School teacher who contacted ASCAP, concerned that her class's weekly rendition of the song was illegal after reading that the song was restricted (ASCAP informed her that she was free to use the song without payment).[53]

Such misunderstanding was likely fueled by the rancor between ASCAP, which protected the rights of composers, and radio broadcasters, who had long believed that the royalty fees paid to composers were too high.[54] This clash reached its peak in 1941, when broadcasters banned all ASCAP-affiliated songs (including "God Bless America") from the airwaves, a boycott that lasted from January to October of that year.[55] During the boycott, broadcasters successfully blocked "God Bless America" from being performed at Roosevelt's inauguration in January 1941, despite the fact that ASCAP waived its licensing fees for the event.[56]

Six months before the ASCAP ban and just after Berlin announced the formation of the God Bless America Fund in June 1940, one radio station program director wrote an open letter to Berlin criticizing the song's high royalty fee, acknowledging that donating the royalties was patriotic, but "it was not enough."[57] He continued, "I respectfully submit that you are in the position of having written a song that no longer belongs to you, to Miss Kate Smith, or even to ASCAP; it rightfully belongs to the American people as a whole." He suggested that Berlin present the song to the US government "so that it may be played and sung everywhere, at any time, without the possibility that ASCAP could assess punitive measures against a musician, a singer, a hotel, a barroom, a church, or a radio station, whose patriotism led to an infringement of your, and ASCAP's, doubtful rights in the performance of the song." The letter here feeds the misperception that performance of the song always required a royalty fee—even when sung in church.

Berlin was a founder of ASCAP and fierce protector of his copyrighted material, and thus was predictably incensed at this attack on his song.[58] He fired back, stating that this suggestion

> would I think be in much better taste if advanced by an executive of a radio station which had not been a party to defrauding composers and authors of their royalties for a period of years. . . . Your letter so obviously has for its true purpose an attack upon the American Society of Composers, Authors and Publishers, which represents the songwriters of the world against stations such as yours which seem willing and anxious to confiscate for their free use all music, that it does not merit any reply in respect of the suggestion made and intended as a peg upon which to hang your attack.[59]

The broadcasters' depiction of ASCAP as overly greedy in its protection of composer royalties seems to have tapped into a shift in the public perception of popular music, toward a focus on performers rather than composers. The rise of radio had dealt a huge financial blow to composers, who reigned when sheet music sales defined the music industry; recording and broadcast industries also moved the composer farther from the public eye, while increasing the exposure of performers.[60] Although the broadcasters' anti-ASCAP position stemmed from their own economic self-interest, it touched a populist nerve with the idea that a song like "God Bless America," which had been embraced as a patriotic hymn, should no longer be guided by the dictates of the popular music industry. In his history of the rise of the music business, David Suisman argues that the concept of "popular music" institutionalized within Tin Pan Alley was "deeply misleading, for however many people sang these airs, Tin Pan Alley's songs did not come *from* the people at all. Rather, the songs were crafted specifically, deliberately, and essentially as commercial products."[61]

Detractors of "God Bless America" were critical of both Smith and Berlin in their perceived exploitation of the patriotic mood to make a profit. One 1939 newspaper profile of Smith emphasized that "sincere flag-waving, in her case at least, pays big dividends," noting that she had just signed a three-year, noncancelable contract for $7,000 per week.[62] In today's dollars, this is the equivalent of just over $110,000 per week, or about $5.7 million per year—a high salary by any era's standards and a truly staggering amount in a country still reeling from the Depression.[63] Criticism aimed at Berlin tended to focus on the song's restricted use and its high royalty fee of eight cents per performance (two cents was standard, and most Berlin songs were four cents).[64]

The existence of the God Bless America fund and its unassailably American beneficiaries was often cited to counter criticism regarding Berlin's commercial intentions. And it worked—to some extent. As one critic of the song complained, "when Tin Pan Alley puts out a purely patriotic number, not an ounce of patriotism went into the manufacture of it. The song was written for profit and nothing else, although, of course, this would not apply to 'God Bless America,' the proceeds from which go to a worthy cause."[65] But the song was infected with a popular music taint despite the fact that Berlin earned no money from it, as this critic continued: "Even so, 'God Bless America' has the sound and the metallic ring and the false swagger of Tin Pan Alley, regardless of its talent-origin."

Another source of criticism was the perception that Berlin and Smith intended "God Bless America" to replace "The Star-Spangled Banner" as the national anthem, an idea that emerged from a spontaneous popular reaction to the song but which both Berlin and Smith vehemently opposed.[66] In September 1940, one newspaper reported that the sheet music sales of "God Bless America" had surpassed those of the anthem by a wide margin, and several accounts of the song's performances at public events refer to the audience treating the song as an anthem by standing and removing their hats.[67] Smith was emphatic in her response to fan mail regarding the inappropriateness of this behavior, saying that the song "is not our national anthem and must not be accorded the same tribute . . . there is no song in the world that can take the place of 'The Star-Spangled Banner.'"[68] In a letter expressing his dismay at the perception that he meant the song to replace the national anthem, Berlin wrote "No patriotic American wants to replace The 'Star-Spangled Banner'; no one can. . . . As an American I feel The 'Star-Spangled Banner' is the most inspiring National song we have."[69] Any attempt to replace the national anthem was seen as a threat to an established American identity, and Berlin and Smith were eager to prove their "Americanness" in the face of such criticism.

DISSENTING VOICES, PART II: ANTI-SEMITIC BACKLASH AND "A (JEW) NEW NATIONAL ANTHEM"

In response to yet another article hinting at a campaign by Berlin to supplant "The Star-Spangled Banner" as the national anthem, the chairman of the God Bless America Fund, Herbert Bayard Swope, wrote to Berlin in August 1940, "One would almost believe there was an organized propaganda against this beautiful song."[70] Berlin replied that he didn't know if there was "planned propaganda against 'God Bless America,' but from the many clippings I get every day there is certainly a definite minority taking cracks at the song."[71] It turned out that Swope's fears were not far from the truth. In December 1940 the head of the New York Council of the Girl Scouts wrote to Swope: "You will understand, I am sure, that ever since the announcement was made of the generous award to the Girl Scouts from the 'God Bless America' fund we have received many letters of inquiry from many sources. . . . Today a letter has appeared of such a scurrilous nature that I felt perhaps the Trustees ought to be aware of it."[72] That letter, which the Girl Scout director called "perfectly appalling evidence of bigotry and hatred" and which Swope turned over to the FBI, was from the head of the pro-Nazi Protestant War Veterans of the United States.[73] It articulates a chilling paranoia about a Jewish conspiracy involving "God Bless America." After questioning the Girl Scouts about the form of Berlin's donation ("Was this given to you outright as a lump sum, or do you receive so much per month?"), the letter went on to declare:

The reason of these questions is the fact that millions of Christian Americans resent certain forces using a great Patriotic organization such as yours to further their own selfish interests, and further the lid is about to be blown right off this slimy trick.

Are you aware that Irving Berlin owns this song? that he is not only the publisher but likewise the selling organization? and that his press agents stated to the American people through the newspapers of the Country that the proceeds are being donated to your organization to further Americanism? what a story this will make when it becomes known (which it already is) that he paid your organization $15,000 dollars to put over a (Jew) New National Anthem.

It will serve your interests to tell the truth in this matter, for it is about to break loose in the press through the National, the South and the West leading where the newspapers is yet *FREE from JEW control*. We want the facts, let us have them.[74]

From our perspective today, such a vitriolic response to a song like "God Bless America" may be incomprehensible, but in fact criticism of "God Bless America" during its early years was tinged with anti-Semitic and xenophobic rhetoric aimed at Berlin. This dissent—against a song written by a Jew who dared to ask God to bless America, who dared to call the country his "home sweet home"—is a stark reminder of the anti-Semitism that permeated American culture during this prewar period, not just from the minority on the far Right but within mainstream society as well.

Predictably, the most venomous anti-Semitism against the song often came from groups aligned with the Nazis, such as the Protestant War Veterans or the German American Bund. Before the United States entered the war, such an affiliation may have been condemned by a majority of Americans but was not yet treasonous. At a joint rally of the German American Bund and the Ku Klux Klan in August 1940 (where the head of the Protestant War Veterans also spoke), group leaders called for a boycott of "God Bless America."[75] A week later, an article mockingly titled "G-A-W-D Bless A-M-E-R-I-K-E-R!" appeared in the newspaper of the German American Bund and was quite explicit in its anti-Semitic and anti-immigrant stance. After warning of a Jewish conspiracy to replace the national anthem, the author of the article writes that he

does not consider G-B-A a "patriotic" song, in the sense of expressing the real American attitude toward his country, but considers that it smacks of the "How glad I am" attitude of the refugee horde of which Theodore Roosevelt said, "We wish no further additions to the persons whose affection for this country is merely a species of pawnbroker patriotism—whose coming here represents nothing but the purpose to change one feeding trough for another feeding trough."[76]

This snide reference to the "refugee horde" is a personal attack aimed at Berlin, since there is nothing in the song that would feed into such an interpretation other than its composer's identity as a Jewish immigrant. These attacks from pro-Nazi groups make even more poignant Berlin's change to his original lyrics—from "guide her to the right" to "through the night"— underscoring a sense of urgency for Berlin to eradicate any reference to "the Right," not only because of its ties to Fascism but also to anti-Semitism.

Though it may be easy to dismiss such hate speech as the predictably extreme views of the outer fringe of society, one should not underestimate the strength of the Right and the persuasiveness of their anti-Semitic and anti-immigrant rhetoric during this period. Anti-Semitism in the United States during the 1930s has been described as "more virulent and more vicious than at any time before or since."[77] Despite growing sympathy toward the plight of European Jews in the aftermath of *Kristallnacht*, anti-immigration attitudes in the United States paradoxically persisted, with no popular support for raising the immigration quotas imposed in 1924.[78] And with the deepening economic depression, Hitler's scapegoating of the Jews as the main source of all economic and social ills gained traction. Describing the increasing violence and prejudice against Jews in Europe, a commentator in the *Chicago Defender* wrote, "American Jews do well to sing 'God Bless America' while eying the changing scene."[79]

Perhaps the most notorious figure associated with this phenomenon in the United States was Father Charles Coughlin, who disseminated vitriolic anti-Semitism and isolationism through national radio broadcasts, his newspaper *Social Justice*, and the activities of the Christian Front, an organization he founded in May 1938.[80] Vilified by many, Coughlin nonetheless had a wide listenership, with a regular radio audience of 3.5 million and 15 million who reported that they had heard him at least once.[81] Just ten days after *Kristallnacht*—and, coincidentally, after the premiere of "God Bless America"—Father Coughlin gave "the most incredible radio address of his career," launching an "expansive anti-Semitic diatribe" that tied Jews to the evils of Communism.[82] In his history of anti-Semitism in the United States, Leonard Dinnerstein characterizes the activities of the Christian Front between 1939 and 1941 as "roving gangs" who "picketed, and placarded obscene stickers on Jewish-owned retail establishments, desecrated synagogues, and indiscriminately attacked Jewish children and adults on the streets of cities like New York and Boston[.]"[83]

Dinnerstein's description of violence in urban Jewish neighborhoods evokes chilling echoes of the Nazis' campaign against European Jews, though such anti-Semitic activities in the United States were not, of course, sponsored by the state. A 1939 memo from the American Jewish Committee emphasized the high stakes of their mission to combat anti-Semitism, which they saw as directly tied to Nazism: "It is not yet too late to turn the tide. . . . [W]hat we are concerned with is, not merely the saving of the Jews, but the saving of civilization."[84] A 1940 article in the American Jewish Congress *Bulletin* described mounting fear among American Jews who "did not know what calamity might next occur in the United States."[85]

Philip Roth captures this feeling of the country on a precipice in his novel *The Plot Against America*, which imagines the United States tilting toward increasing anti-Semitism and Nazism when the isolationist war hero Charles Lindbergh defeats President Roosevelt in the 1940 election. It is a disturbing portrait that attempts to show how close the United States was to succumbing to its own prejudices during this period. And it also depicts a genuine fear among Jews who weren't sure about which direction the war would go, anxiety that was present in the Irving Berlin household of 1940. Berlin's daughter Mary Ellin Barrett writes that for her parents, "the war in Europe remained frighteningly close."[86] She continued that her mother, Ellin Berlin, who was raised Catholic, would later say that "they genuinely believed, in the summer and fall of 1940 and well into the next year, that the Germans would win" and "make an arrangement" with the United States. "And if that happened, how would they protect their half-Jewish children?"

Since anti-Semitism was part of the mainstream during this period, it should not come as a surprise that mainstream criticism of "God Bless America" was often tinged with anti-Semitism and xenophobia. For example, many of the complaints about the song's supposed profit drew on stereotypes about Jews and economic exploitation, as a September 1940 article from *Time* described, "Chief headache that *God Bless America* has brought on is a wave of snide anti-Semitism directed at Composer Berlin. Frequent are the letters to [Smith's manager Ted] Collins berating him as an Irishman for swelling Jewish coffers."[87]

In addition, the fear of a Tin Pan Alley song replacing "The Star-Spangled Banner"—an anthem with roots in nineteenth-century America—reflects anxieties about outsiders making irrevocable changes to American culture. These critics often questioned the right of a Jewish immigrant to compose a song staking his claim on America. In a sermon delivered at New York's West End Collegiate Reformed Church in July 1940, Rev. Edgar Romig spoke out against the song's popularity, proclaiming, "The great national

anthems that have survived, and that will outlive most contemporary doggerel, came out of the hearts of men who knew what it was to sacrifice for
America."[88] In a letter to the editor defending the song, Herbert Bayard
Swope subtly questions the sermon's anti-Semitic subtext: "I wonder why
the Rev. Dr. Romig, with so much to engage his clerical attention, chose to
pick on 'God Bless America.'"[89]

Although "God Bless America" was embraced by many Christian organizations and incorporated into hymnals and church services, the song's popularity appears to have rankled many prominent clergymen during this
prewar period. Bishop Ashton Oldham of Albany, New York decried singing
the song "in an utterly superficial and un-Christian spirit," and complained
of "complacency and unctuousness" in its assumption "that God should
and must bless America."[90] In a sermon called "Why Should God Bless
America," the Presbyterian minister Peter Marshall of Washington, DC, admonished, "But singing 'God Bless America' is not enough. Waving our flag
is not enough. A maudlin, sticky, sentimental, pseudo-patriotism is not
enough. God is not going to bless America just because a nation sings the
song."[91] If anti-Semitism had remained a subtle undertone within some of
this criticism from the pulpit, Rev. Marshall made his position more explicit as he continued his sermon:

> Considering the treatment meted out to the Jews of other lands, we might well
> ask if the Jews in America are any better than their unfortunate brethren across
> the seas? Is it merely a coincidence that so many Jews own liquor stores and
> make their fortunes from the sale of alcoholic beverages? Is it merely a coinci-
> dence that the Jews practically control the amusement world, moulding the Hol-
> lywood morals that infect our national life and lower our national morality?"

Marshall evokes the fear of a Jewish influence on American popular culture, fear that seems to have stoked criticism of "God Bless America."

Within this context of an anti-Semitism that permeated American culture, "God Bless America" can be viewed as a radical move on Berlin's part,
an answer to those who questioned the character and loyalty of Jews in the
United States. By evoking tropes of prayerful patriotism, Berlin staked his
claim on a discourse of home and country that had not only excluded Jews
but that anti-Semites held up to represent everything that Jews and other
immigrants wanted to take away from Christian Americans. The Protestant
War Veterans signed off the letter to the Girl Scouts, "For God, Home &
Country"—an ironic summary of the themes of Berlin's song and a neat
synopsis of what they must have felt was at stake in their tirades against
"God Bless America."

Despite criticism of the song from all sides, for Berlin, "God Bless America" remained a sincere expression of thanks to his adopted country. Acknowledging that the words were "a little too tender" for soldiers to sing in *Yip Yip Yaphank*, he said, "I couldn't help it. That's the way I felt. I always write the way I feel."[92] This sincerity comes across clearly in a recording of Berlin performing the song on a radio broadcast in 1939—a performance that transforms the song into a love ballad.[93] (Track 6 on the companion website. ◉) Berlin accompanies himself on the piano with simple but elegant embellishments and sings in a crackly baritone. He omits the verse, which he appears to have found irrelevant, as he told one reporter in 1940, "I had said everything I wanted to say in the chorus."[94] The march tempo from Smith's rendition is absent; Berlin's performance is a slow rubato, a ballad to be crooned. He elongates words like "prairies" and "oceans" with a vocal glissando in an almost playful way. In the last repetition of the title phrase, there is a plaintive quality to Berlin's delivery of the word "God," which falls at the uppermost reaches of his register. He pauses before uttering the word "America," emphasizing the country's name in a way that evokes the name of a beloved in a ballad. Berlin's voice cracks when he first sings the word "home" in the last rendition of the phrase "home sweet home," giving a sense of poignancy and urgency to this idea of homeland. He doesn't quite recover on "sweet" but finds a warm, rich tone on the final word, "home," a compact symbol for an immigrant's search for a sense of belonging.

Berlin's performance lasts only a minute and twenty-five seconds. Without the ornate orchestration, the brass fanfares, the rhythm section, the choir, and the elaborate repetitions of Smith's rendition, it is less an anthem or hymn than a heartfelt love song. His daughter writes of her own mixed feelings about the song:

> After a while I became aware of negative talk. Not just the crazies who asked what right an immigrant Jew had to call on God to bless America or a protest artist like Woody Guthrie, who would write, "This Land is Your Land" as an ironic comment, but middle-of-the-road columnists and broadcasters who called the song flag-waving, sentimental, jingoistic, simplistic. I didn't understand what they were saying. The song was what it was. But I was troubled. Then, one day at a Boy Scouts rally in the Catskills, I heard my father sing "God Bless America." No other singer, not Crosby, not Judy Garland, not Kate Smith herself, or a long procession of opera stars performing it on state occasions, could give it quite that conviction. He meant every word. . . . It *was* the land he loved. It *was* his home sweet home. He, the immigrant who had made good, was saying thank you. And even if in later years he and I disagreed sometimes about the way that land did things, when he sang that song, I could not fail to be profoundly moved.[95]

Berlin's sincerity resonated with many Americans during this period, as evidenced by the embrace of his song as a vehicle for group singing in a wide range of social contexts. During and directly after this prewar period—and perhaps in response to the anti-Semitic backlash against the song—"God Bless America" became associated with cultural tolerance, signaling a growing acceptance within mainstream America that a Jewish immigrant like Irving Berlin had every right to call the United States his "home sweet home." But the song's meaning and associations would shift radically over the course of the century, as it was increasingly used as a conservative anthem charged with protecting the status quo.

CHAPTER 4

༄

Through the Night (to the Right)

The Evolution of a Conservative Anthem

I suppose that everyone who hears or sings the song has a distinct and individual interpretation of the petition: "God Bless America." Some hope that God will keep America just as it is, others hope that God will help this nation solve its vast social and economic problems, still others desire God to preserve us from the threat of aggression, and yet others hope that in the inscrutable providence of God, Mr. Willkie will win the election in November. In a word, a thousand hopes, longings, and desires are voiced in the phrase, "God Bless America."

—"Through the Eyes of the Church Mouse," *Hopkinsville (KY) Era,*
24 August 1940

I rving Berlin was the master of writing songs with lyrics vague enough to become universal, and "God Bless America" may represent the pinnacle of this art.[1] The lack of specificity in its lyrics has allowed the song to embody multiple, sometimes contrary, points of view, with shifting meanings that depend upon who is singing and listening as well as upon the social and historical context of any given performance. Who is the "I" in "land that I love"? Who claims America as "my home sweet home?" What hardship is signified by "the night," and in what direction does the country need to be guided? Whose God is being invoked?

In 1938, Berlin changed his original World War I–era lyrics from "guide her to the right" to "through the night," because by 1938 "the right" had acquired associations with Fascism. But the idea of a move "to the right" is quite relevant in looking at the changing meaning of "God Bless America" over time, as it began to be used in and associated with increasingly conservative contexts. During the 1940s, the song acquired associations with religious, ethnic, and racial tolerance, largely a result of its strong connections with Irving Berlin, a Jewish immigrant. But beginning with the cultural upheaval of the Vietnam War and its aftermath, the meaning of "God Bless America" became more and more aligned with the Right, embodying a worldview focused on maintaining a white, Christian, status quo. The song and phrase also became a potent political symbol, emerging as a bipartisan political imperative by the beginning of the twenty-first century.

In explaining how music can accumulate a variety of meanings over time, Thomas Turino coined the term "semantic snowball" to describe the phenomenon when songs are sung again and again in different contexts, each time adding new meanings while retaining older associations.[2] But in tracking the meaning of "God Bless America," a more apt metaphor might be that of sedimentary rock, which reveals traces of its history over time, rather than the accumulation within a snowball, where each successive layer obliterates that which it covers.

PRELUDE: A BRIEF HISTORY OF THE PHRASE "GOD BLESS AMERICA"

While the focus of this book is on the uses and meanings of the *song* "God Bless America," relevant uses of the phrase also need to be part of the discussion, since the increased use of the phrase in American public life was a direct outgrowth of the song's popularity and absorption into American culture. Before the song's debut in 1938, the phrase "God Bless America" was not in regular use within American public life. The phrase had appeared in the *New York Times* only fourteen times since 1885, and all but two of these references involved offering of thanks within an international context or as a benediction spoken by a religious leader. (See fig. I.1 in the introduction for a visual representation of these references. A longer discussion of the earliest references to the phrase "God Bless America" can be found on the companion website ●). In contrast, there were thirty-two references to the phrase in the *New York Times* just within the two-year period between the song's November 1938 radio premiere and the end of 1940—more than twice as many appearances as within the eighty years before the song's debut. And most of these references occurred in domestic, secular American life, as opposed to the international and sacred contexts in which they appeared before the song's premiere.

The first few instances of the phrase appearing after November 1938 reflected its instant popularity on the domestic front in the wake of the song's debut: two fashion articles described the phrase newly emblazoned on women's belts and hats.[3] Many of these new references to the phrase were within classified advertisements aimed at banner salesmen, with a flurry of ads that trumpeted the slogan's new popularity during the summer of 1940: "'God Bless America' banners sweeping the country," with "timely sales appeal" and "good profits."[4] As a profile about the song in *Variety* noted in 1940, "The success of the song also has resulted in a large novelty business, catering to the millions who like to wear buttons or wave Pennants inscribed with 'God Bless America.'"[5] This spike in the usage of the phrase after the song's premiere—and especially its new function outside of international or religious settings—shows that the phrase's role within the domestic and secular realms of twentieth-century American culture was a direct result of the song and its popularity, and is thus a relevant part of its story.

WHOSE "HOME SWEET HOME"?
"GOD BLESS AMERICA" AND TOLERANCE

America is an ideal which permits a man to stand up in 1940 and sing 'God Bless America' and include in that blessing 12,000,000 Negroes, 20,000,000 Catholics, 4,000,000 Jews and 40,000,000 citizens of foreign stock. That, whether you like it or not, is America. And that, if you are an American, is the way you will want it.
    —"Who Do We Include in 'God Bless America,'" *Googhland (VA) Times*,
                        4 October 1940

Although not explicitly referenced in its lyrics, "God Bless America" was weighted with a subtext of religious, ethnic, and racial tolerance during its early years, as Berlin's immigrant success story connected the song to a burgeoning public appeal for tolerance in response to the rise of Nazism in Europe. The song's association with a Jewish immigrant also challenged the assumption of the centrality of a Christian God within American religious discourse, and the song's rise to prominence coincided with growing mainstream acceptance of the acceptance of a Judeo-Christian religious pluralism after World War II.

This connection to religious tolerance began within weeks of its radio premiere. In fact, the very first reference to the song in the *New York Times*, which appeared less than three weeks after its radio debut, makes no mention of Kate Smith's weekly performances. Instead, the article describes the song's performance at a dinner sponsored by the National Conference of

Christians and Jews (NCCJ), where Catholic, Jewish, and Protestant speakers repudiated the "doctrine of race and hate" in totalitarian Europe and urged Americans not to let it happen within their own communities.[6] The article erroneously states that the song "had been written by Irving Berlin especially for the conference," a telling misperception that demonstrated—and perhaps perpetuated—the song's initial connections with religious tolerance.

At the NCCJ event, "God Bless America" was sung first by opera singer Dorothea Flexer and then by the audience, illustrating the song's immediate appeal as a vehicle for group singing, since people sang along despite the fact that many of them had likely never heard it before. Irving Berlin himself was in attendance at this event, providing evidence of the composer's own interest in the issue of cultural tolerance and willingness to link his song to this cause. And Berlin's presence also may have strengthened the song's tolerance message. Sung from his perspective as a Jewish immigrant, the song's first and last lines—"God bless America, land that I love" and "God bless America, my home sweet home"—could be interpreted as both an invocation of an ecumenical God and a validation of an immigrant's claim to Americanness.

Correspondence between Berlin and NCCJ's director Everett Clinchy reveal a direct, behind-the-scenes connection between "God Bless America" and religious tolerance during the song's early history. In two separate letters written in 1939 and 1940, Clinchy recalled Berlin playing the song for him before it was published, writing that partly because of this private concert, "I am coming to feel that . . . at least in a spiritual sense your song belongs to the National Conference."[7] Berlin responded, "I am particularly touched by your expression of how much the song means spiritually to the National Conference and I hope that it will always continue to have this significance."[8] Berlin began what would become his lifelong financial support of the NCCJ in December 1938, shortly after the song's debut and its performance at the NCCJ dinner.[9] The Nazis' increasing violence against Jews likely fed Berlin's interest in the NCCJ during this period, and the song's implicit appeal for religious tolerance became all the more powerful in the wake of the anti-Semitic backlash against it (see chap. 3).

This link to religious tolerance seems related to Berlin's own biography; his wife, Ellin, was a Roman Catholic who, according to their daughter Mary Ellin Barrett, taught their children "her own informal version of the Judeo-Christian tradition, acceptable to my father, interesting to her."[10] Barrett writes that such religious duality pervaded her household: "Everything made sense—Jewish and Christian holidays, Jewish and Christian relatives, Jewish and Christian friends."[11]

Berlin's support for religious pluralism and tolerance was also made explicit in his establishment of the God Bless America Fund, through which all of the royalties from the song were donated to the Boy Scouts and Girl Scouts of America. The official statement articulating the choice of the beneficiaries of this fund explained: "It was felt that the completely nonsectarian work of the Boy and Girl Scouts was calculated to best promote unity of mind and patriotism, two sentiments that are inherent in the song itself."[12] This emphasis on the Scouts' nonsectarianism points to an interest in promoting religious tolerance, and in fact, the internal structure of the fund itself seems designed to send an important message. Berlin appointed three public figures to serve as the fund's trustees: a Jew (the journalist Herbert Bayard Swope), a Roman Catholic (the boxer Gene Tunney), and a Protestant (Theodore Roosevelt Jr.), a deliberate ecumenical distribution that persists to this day.[13] Berlin may have modeled this triumvirate on the structure of the NCCJ itself, which was also governed by three trustees, one from each faith.[14] The symbolism here is too strong to ignore. Berlin could have named anyone he wanted to serve as a trustee; why would he have decided on this structure if not to promote religious pluralism, and perhaps to refute any suggestion of a Jewish conspiracy behind the song?

Coincidentally, the period when "God Bless America" debuted and became famous marked the beginning of a burgeoning recognition of a shared Judeo-Christian worldview in the United States, as well as an increased acceptance of religion in public life.[15] In the late 1930s a nascent use of the term "Judeo-Christian" became a signifier for anti-Fascist views, since the term "Christian" had been appropriated by pro-Fascist, anti-Semitic groups like the Christian Front.[16] Most scholars date a solid acceptance of the American Judeo-Christian tradition to the period during and directly after World War II, forged in response to Nazi atrocities in the name of Christianity and the specter of a faithless Fascism (and later, Communism).[17] Another turning point in the acceptance of a Judeo-Christian ideal occurred in 1952, when president-elect Dwight Eisenhower spoke of the intertwining of pluralistic religion and politics, "Our form of government has no sense unless it is founded in a deeply felt religious faith, and I don't care what it is. With us of course it is the Judeo-Christian concept, but it must be a religion that all men are created equal."[18]

This postwar period was marked by increased interest in religion and acceptance of religion in public life, when the words "under God" were inserted into the Pledge of Allegiance and "In God We Trust" became the official national motto.[19] The song's popularity during the period before the US entry into World War II may serve as an early indication of these shifts, or perhaps the song's ubiquity on the radio and public gatherings actually served to guide and reinforce both an acceptance of religiosity and the Judeo-Christian concept. In two earlier American patriotic songs, God is either absent ("My Country 'Tis of Thee") or hidden away in the fourth stanza ("The Star Spangled Banner"). "America, the Beautiful" includes the refrain, "God shed his grace on thee," but when it was composed in the nineteenth century, this religious reference was likely interpreted as a straightforward invocation of a Christian God, without the complicated pluralism of the ecumenical higher power in "God Bless America."

In many ways, the reception and uses of "God Bless America" parallel that of the Judeo-Christian concept. Both were used in the fight against anti-Fascism, and both were marked by a vagueness that gave them power, as Harvard's Douglas Bush wrote in 1945, "One could wish for fuller hints of what the Hebraic-Christian tradition, to which all pay at least vague lip service, actually does or can mean in modern terms for modern men of good will."[20] Just as the lack of specificity in the lyrics to "God Bless America" allowed the song to carry multiple meanings, the vague definition of Judeo-Christianity facilitated an avoidance of conflict, as the religious historian Mark Silk notes that "greater precision might have provoked unwanted disagreement when the idea was to invoke a common faith for a united democratic front."[21]

During the years leading up to America's entry into World War II, this subtext for religious and ethnic tolerance appears to have been widely understood. Three months after its first use by the NCCJ, Berlin led a crowd in singing "God Bless America" after a speech against bigotry by Eleanor Roosevelt, in which she warned, "Fear arising from intolerance and injustice constitutes the chief danger to our country."[22] The song continued to be used by immigrants as an expression of thanks to their new country, as one family of German Jewish refugees recounted to their small-town newspaper, "We sang it on the train as we gazed upon the beautiful countryside, we sang it when we arrived in Danville . . . and we find ourselves all day long humming the tune and echoing the words—God Bless America."[23] These simple words resonated with the lucky few who had escaped persecution in Europe. The neuroscientist Daniel Levitin later wrote that his grandmother, who escaped Germany after her parents had been shot, sang "God Bless America" every morning, "her voice trembling through her thick accent, her body shaking and overflowing with joy and thankfulness that she had been saved, that she had lived long enough to see her freedom and the freedom of six grandchildren."[24] In fact, the song itself has roots in Berlin's own immigrant experience; Berlin reportedly first heard the phrase "God Bless America" from his mother, who frequently spoke the words with emotion that "was almost exaltation," despite the poverty of their immigrant household.[25]

The song's debut also coincided with a new government interest in promoting cultural tolerance. In her history of radio and race in the World War II era, Barbara Savage notes that war and economic depression fed an increased need on the part of the government "to foster a broader notion of acceptance and inclusiveness for the sake of national unity."[26] Interestingly, "God Bless America" debuted the same week as the premiere of *Americans All, Immigrants All*, a radio show produced by the Department of Interior's Office of Education, aired by CBS and written by the cultural critic Gilbert Seldes.[27] The goal of the program was to "create a state-sanctioned narrative of American history that made immigrants, African Americans, and Jews visible."[28] The show, which later included Irving Berlin in its program on Jews in America, would have been heard by radio audiences during the same period as Smith's performances of "God Bless America," and the message of *Americans All* dovetailed nicely with the song's status as a signifier for racial and ethnic tolerance.[29] In his book about the gradual categorization of European immigrants as "white," Matthew Frye Jacobson notes that such a message of acceptance gained momentum after World War II, when a "sober, war-chastened 'tolerance'" replaced racialized categorizations of ethnic immigrants after the horrors of Nazi Germany were revealed.[30]

Many scholars point to the late 1930s and early 1940s as the beginning of "the long civil rights movement" that began as an alliance between New Deal intellectuals, leftist radicals, and labor and civil rights activists.[31] One dramatic and strange performance from this period reveals a vivid connection between "God Bless America" and a move toward racial tolerance. The occasion was the opening of the 1940 American Negro Exposition, a large-scale event that highlighted the African American contributions to American history. A reporter for the *Pittsburgh Courier* described the exposition's opening ceremonies held in the Chicago Coliseum:

> Four thousand people were standing in the partially lighted exposition hall. The official family of the nation, State and city, was standing in the balcony. All eyes were pointed toward the heavens because the multitude was engaged in song. At the climax of 'God Bless America,' the giant batteries of flood lights emblazoned the entire place. President Roosevelt in his Hyde Park (N.Y.) home, had touched a diamond-studded button, which caused the illumination."[32]

The symbolism here is powerful: the president of the United States literally illuminated the role of African Americans in American history as a racially mixed audience sang, "God bless America, *my* home sweet home." The song, in this context, served to validate the Americanness of all of those present.

In fact, some of the activities of the God Bless America Fund appear specifically designed to promote racial and ethnic tolerance. At the suggestion of Herbert Bayard Swope, the fund's chairman, all monies given to both the Boy and Girl Scouts from the God Bless America Fund were earmarked for low-income communities, what was referred to as "Special-Area scouting" or "less chance areas."[33] One newspaper article ascribes this choice to Berlin's own background on the rough streets of the Lower East Side, quoting Berlin as saying, "In my day it would have been worth a boy's life to appear in my neighborhood in a Boy Scout uniform," but this initiative also seems related to an interest in racial and ethnic inclusion.[34] As the first progress report from the Boy Scouts notes, "An effort will be made in Detroit to work especially among Negro boys and, if possible, a Negro Executive will be employed; in Cleveland, work was to be focused in the Polish district."[35] Subsequent reports show that donations from the God Bless America Fund allowed the Boy Scouts to form new troops in African American communities in Detroit and Jacksonville, Florida.[36]

Fund correspondence reveals a particular interest in racial equality, In 1941 Berlin ascertained that the Camp Fire Girls admitted African Americans before including the organization as a one-time Fund beneficiary in 1941, and in 1949 Swope's letter to the Boy Scouts underlined the fund's priorities: "Because we believe that the Boy Scouts is conducted on a policy freed from racial or religious prejudice, we are happy to make this contribution."[37] Swope later called the Girl Scouts "a leading factor in the fight to end race, color, and religious discrimination in the United States."[38]

At the same time, Kate Smith was becoming known for her use of radio as a medium for the promotion of tolerance. In a 1945 radio commentary, she explicitly linked tolerance with the war effort: "I know that our statesmen—our armies of occupation—our military strategists—may all fail if the peoples of the world don't learn to *understand* and *tolerate* each other. Race hatreds—social prejudices—religious bigotry—they are all the diseases that eat away the fibers of peace."[39] Smith was also recognized for her role in promoting tolerance by the NCCJ, who presented her with a citation of Distinguished Merit in 1945 because "her radio programs throughout the year embodied the message of understanding and good will among all Americans," and because "she has consistently dedicated herself to the advancement of these ideals."[40] She received a similar citation in 1947 from the Hebrew Institute of Long Island, for "outstanding patriotism and unselfish and inspiring work in helping to combat racial hatred, bigotry, and inequality."[41] The twin associations of the song with both Berlin and Smith likely contributed to its connections with tolerance during this period.

Of course, "tolerance" does not equal "justice" or "equality," as a 1939 memo within the American Jewish Committee noted in stating the organization's principles in combating anti-Semitism: "We don't believe in approaching the whole thing merely from the standpoint of promoting 'tolerance,' [which,] we think, is an undignified thing—nobody wants to be tolerated."[42] Although Berlin and the God Bless America Fund showed an interest in promoting racial inclusion, in the early years they did not challenge the segregation policies of the Boy Scouts, admittedly an accepted reality during this period but indicative of the limits of "tolerance."[43] And of course there were some who agreed with Woody Guthrie that the song was an attempt to mask the country's social ills, including bigotry and violence. In a letter to the *Chicago Defender*, one anonymous soldier described the violence inflicted upon African American servicemen by American military police and noted that "God Bless America" and other patriotic songs "all sound to me like a lot of propaganda behind which this country has hidden for years."[44] The song was not a revolutionary battle cry by any means, but its use appears to be influenced by an interest in cultural and racial tolerance and inclusion that grew out of the long civil rights movement and entered into elements of mainstream American culture during the late 1930s and 1940s.

By the 1950s, the song's associations with ethnic and religious tolerance had begun to fade. Perhaps it was a result of a general acceptance of the idea of a Judeo-Christian religious pluralism, or because Irving Berlin's prominence as a famous Jewish songwriter waned. Or perhaps the song's pluralistic associations were an imperative connected to the need for unity during the war effort, and were not as necessary after victory over the Nazis and the rise of new, divisive threats of the Cold War. Whatever the reason, connections with tolerance and inclusion largely disappeared over the course of the latter half of the twentieth century, as the song became increasingly linked to a conservative agenda fearful of the infringement of outsiders.

In a disturbing counterpoint to the song's original pro-tolerance, anti-Fascist message, in 1998 "God Bless America" served as the soundtrack to a propaganda video by the neo-Nazi group Aryan Nation.[45] This song—which sixty years earlier had been boycotted by the anti-Semitic Right and used to uphold the ideals of tolerance in the face of Nazi atrocities—was now viewed as the appropriate sonic background for neo-Nazi propaganda. This dramatic shift serves as a stark illustration of the changing meaning of "God Bless America" over the course of the twentieth century.

STAND BESIDE HER AND GUIDE HER: THE EVOLUTION OF A CONSERVATIVE PROTEST ANTHEM

In February 1991, during the final weeks of the first Iraq war, a man stood up to speak at the First Congregational Church in Kennebunkport, Maine, where President George H. W. Bush was in attendance:

> About 10 minutes into the service, the Rev. Patricia Adam invited members of the congregation to speak or share a prayer. John Schuchardt, a longtime antiwar demonstrator, took the opportunity to denounce the war. "We must think of what it means to be bombed by more than 2,000 planes every day," Mr. Schuchardt said. As Mr. Bush looked on with a stoicism that seemed to give way to a mixture of embarrassment and distress, members of the congregation tried to drown out the protest with a chorus of "God Bless America."[46]

This church confrontation is an example of what I call a *"Casablanca* moment," when group singing is used to demarcate the sonic space of protest, named after the iconic scene from the film in which expatriates at Rick's bar loudly sing the "Marseillaise" in order to drown out the sound of Nazi officers singing the anthem "Die Wacht am Rhein." (A link to this scene is available on the companion website. ◑) Of course, the focus of the protest in these two contexts is quite different—In *Casablanca* it is the oppressed French who overwhelm the occupying Nazi's anthem with their own, while the church protestors sang "God Bless America" to uphold the status quo in response to dissent. Most studies of music and protest focus on progressive social movements, especially the integral role of music within the civil rights and labor movements.[47] But by the end of the century, "God Bless America" was increasingly used as a means to silence dissent, becoming an anthem for those who wanted things to stay exactly as they were.

The chameleon-like lyrics of "God Bless America" made it a powerful vehicle for a wide range of protest contexts during the twenty-five years after its debut. In a protest setting, the vague "stand beside her and guide her" allowed the song to be imbued with different meaning depending on which direction the singers wanted the country to be "guided through the night." Between 1940 and the early 1960s, it was sung by a diverse range of political constituencies, including anti-Communist protestors, striking laborers, and civil rights activists. But this multiplicity of meanings became largely unified during the cultural rifts of the mid- and late-1960s, as the song was embraced by those who felt threatened by the upheaval of the period. It became an anthem for those who supported the Vietnam War, opposed school integration, and railed against the socially progressive agendas of the feminist, abortion rights, and gay rights movements. Previously malleable lyrics became fixed, and the song's pluralist subtext vanished. Instead, there emerged a tacit understanding that the song represented a warning to those challenging the status quo and upheld the ideals of the newly powerful Christian Right.

In its early years, the most common use of "God Bless America" as a protest song served an anti-Communist message, likely drawing on its invocation of religion and patriotism as a symbolic weapon against "Godless Communism."[48] The first *New York Times* citation of such a use described a St. Louis United Auto Workers meeting in August 1940, during which the workers passed a resolution condemning the totalitarian regimes of Germany, Italy, Russia, and Japan. The article notes that there was a vigorous debate over the inclusion of Russia in this statement, and that the resolution's passage represented the first defeat of the left wing and Communist-supported factions within the union. During the heated discussion, supporters of the proposal sang "God Bless America" to suppress verbal attacks by the minority opposition.[49] The song's earlier associations with interventionism and against totalitarianism may have added to its power in this anti-Communist context, and the song would continue to be used as a vehicle to suppress Communist expression before, during, and after World War II. A group of teenagers sang it to disrupt a Communist meeting in a downtown Milwaukee park in 1941, and in 1947 war veterans broke up a Communist party rally in Bridgeport by singing "God Bless America" and the national anthem.[50] In 1949, protestors sang "God Bless America" outside the Soviet-sponsored Cultural and Scientific Conference for World Peace at the Waldorf-Astoria in New York, and anti-Communist counterdemonstrators sang it in response to leftists' "We Are Fighting for Freedom" at a New York rally supporting American Communist leaders convicted of advocating the overthrow of the US government.[51] These instances offer an interesting reflection of the trajectory of the anti-Communist movement, from anti-totalitarianism abroad during World War II to the Cold War–era fight against domestic Communism.[52]

"God Bless America" was also used as a protest song on the left during this period. Within the labor movement, the song was sung by striking garment workers (joined by Eleanor Roosevelt) in Brooklyn in 1941, and by subway workers protesting a lockout in 1956.[53] And in 1961, left-wing protestors sang it at a demonstration against the House Un-American Activities Commission in San Francisco.[54]

Civil rights activists also used the song frequently in the early 1960s. It was sung in 1960 by jailed protestors in South Carolina and lunch-counter protestors in Texas.[55] Demonstrators in favor of Maryland's state civil rights legislation sang it on the steps of the statehouse in 1962.[56] In 1963, protestors sang it while picketing a housing development in Torrance, California, which refused to sell homes to African Americans.[57] And within a two-day period in early summer 1963, young African American students sang "God Bless America" at school segregation protests in Jackson, Mississippi, and Baton Rouge, Louisiana, hinting, perhaps, at a strategic, unified use of the song by the movement.[58] After all, what could be threatening about schoolchildren, some as young as nine, peacefully singing that staple of elementary school music programs, declaring their love for God and country in support of their right to an equal education? The tactical use of music within the civil rights movement has been well-documented, and the proximity of the dates of these two protests indicates that "God Bless America" may have been used with a specific purpose in mind: to uphold the patriotism—and perhaps project the harmlessness—of the nonviolent protestors, pointing out that they, too, had a land that they loved, a country they hoped would be guided toward justice.

Within a movement led by a preacher and steeped in the black church, the religiosity of "God Bless America" fit in among the African American spirituals and hymns that often evoked a higher power. One description of Martin Luther King Jr.'s 1963 march on Detroit noted, "occasionally a group sang 'God Bless America' or chanted 'we want freedom.'"[59] The protestor's use of "God Bless America" challenges the assumption—put forward by Woody Guthrie and others—that the sentiments of "God Bless America" ran counter to the spirit of dissent. Of course, it also connects to the song's earlier associations with tolerance, where the lyrics "land that I love" and "home sweet home" could be imbued with a message of inclusion, depending on who is singing. The song was later used in a South Carolina demonstration marking the twenty-fifth anniversary of the school desegregation law, where a black children's choir led in the singing of "God Bless America."[60] But such pluralistic uses of the song would become rare as the song's meaning shifted to the Right during the tumultuous period of the late 1960s.

Through the early 1960s, the song appeared able to retain multiple layers of meaning, but beginning in the mid-1960s its meaning and uses became increasingly connected to conservatism. Beginning in 1965, the song's protest-related use (as reported in the *New York Times* and other newspapers) was almost exclusively in the service of conservative positions, primarily support for the Vietnam War, and opposition to progressive social movements like school integration, feminism, and abortion.[61]

"God Bless America" seems to have come into its own as a protest song in response to the antiwar movement of the late 1960s and early 1970s. First composed during World War I and embraced as an interventionist anthem before World War II, it is no surprise that the song continued its long associations with war. Reporters took note of prowar activists using the phrase on signs and banners beginning in 1965,[62] but the big story related to "God Bless America" involved a lone counterprotestor at a peace event. It was during the "Read-in for Peace in Vietnam" at New York's Town Hall in February 1966, when a police detective walked onto the stage, seized the microphone, and began to sing "God Bless America," urging the silent audience to sing along. Joel Oppenheimer, a poet participating in the read-in, challenged the officer to leave, saying, "What do you think we are here for? We've been hearing that song too long." When the detective asked the crowd if they would let him be heard, members of the crowd shouted, "No, No!" and he left the stage.[63] Thus by 1966, the song had already become a symbol of support for the Vietnam War, one that elicited an almost visceral response from antiwar protestors.

This episode serves as a bizarre counterpoint to a similar occurrence during the period before the United States entered World War II, when isolationists booed a performer who sang "God Bless America" at rallies sponsored by America First in 1940. At this pre–World War II occasion, though, the song was not intended as protest but rather introduced by a song leader who wasn't aware of its meaning as an interventionist anthem. In 1940, some interpreted America First's disdain for "God Bless America" as an expression of anti-Semitism, an association that had completely evaporated by the mid-1960s. During the Vietnam War, the song's earlier association with military intervention could have heightened the song's power for those who supported American involvement in the conflict (at least for those old enough to remember World War II). By 1966 the song's meaning had become clear to all sides, and it was continually used as a symbol for pro–Vietnam War views. It was sung by veterans, construction workers, and others at prowar rallies in 1967, 1969, and 1970.[64]

"God Bless America" was often used as a sonic weapon in conflicts with antiwar protestors, such as a confrontation in 1973 between prowar construction workers and peace rally participants in which a "pro-Administration crowd sang 'God Bless America' at an antiwar group who confronted them with peace signs."[65] This image of a group of protestors "singing at" an opposing group demonstrates the power of songs like "God Bless America" to communicate hidden layers of meaning, as well as simply to allow masses of people to demonstrate their strength in sonic terms.

The uses of "God Bless America" by prowar activists paint a stark portrait of the cultural divide that roiled American society during this period: rallies for and against the war occurred month after month, and people on both sides clashed angrily, with "God Bless America" used by those supporting the Vietnam War, and, perhaps more important, opposed to those who protested it. For the vehemence with which conservatives expressed their views at antiwar rallies highlights that it was not just that they were in favor of the country's involvement in Vietnam, but that they felt threatened by the very nature of the peace movement, the dissolution of the culture of "consensus" that had marked the preceding years, the foreign nature of the youth culture that challenged many of their basic assumptions of American life. In their history of the cultural rifts of the 1960s, Maurice Isserman and Michael Kazin write, "In the course of the 1960s, many Americans came to regard groups of fellow countrymen as enemies with whom they were engaged in a struggle for the nation's very soul."[66]

Changes in the uses of "God Bless America" also point to larger shifts in the discourse of patriotism. During World War II, the song was used on the home front to represent American domestic values of tolerance and inclusion in the face of Nazi totalitarianism. But within the context of the Vietnam War, the song's use was linked with a claim to the virtue of the conduct of the United States on the world stage, a claim that progressives could not support. Those opposed to the war could not "bless" America's violence in Vietnam, and this shame over the country's conduct meant that the language of patriotism was increasingly ceded to a conservative point of view.

The generational rifts that became so apparent in the 1960s, with the rise of a youth culture increasingly disenchanted with the mores of its elders, also influenced the shifting meanings of "God Bless America." For older Americans, this song was likely tinged with nostalgia, invoking memories of Kate Smith and the cozy shared community of radio, for the united sacrifice of the World War II home front, and perhaps for a musical world dominated by Tin Pan Alley, rather than the alien sounds of rock 'n' roll.[67] For those born after World War II, "God Bless America" was likely a song they were forced to sing in elementary school, or one they heard on one of their parents' corny TV shows, devoid of any cultural meaning other than its simple patriotic religiosity and the bland mainstream that the youth of the 1960s rebelled against.

With the culture clashes of the Vietnam War as a kind of catalyst, "God Bless America" quickly became a symbol for a white, conservative worldview in the late 1960s and 1970s. In 1967, the song was played on a Memorial Day parade float in Norwalk, Connecticut, by the John Birch Society, an extreme Right organization whose links to anti-Semitism and intolerance prompted the NAACP and Jewish and disabled veteran's groups to withdraw from the parade in protest.[68] During this same period, the segregationist politician Lester Maddox used the song as a political anthem, playing it no less than three times at one public event and often proclaiming that he sang it "with all of my heart."[69]

The historian Lisa McGirr points to the early and mid-1960s as the beginning of a "conservative revival," dubbing religious conservatives to be the "other radicals of the 1960s" and framing the Right as a grassroots social movement during this period.[70] By the late 1960s, "God Bless America" had become an anthem for this conservative "counter-counterculture."

In the late 1960s and '70s, "God Bless America" was increasingly used by conservative activists opposed to school integration and public housing, imbuing the song with a new connection to embattled whiteness. In a dramatic reversal of the song's earlier use in civil rights protests, by the late 1960s "God Bless America" was the song of choice for white demonstrators opposed to school integration: at a 1969 "mother's march" in Cairo, Illinois; by angry protestors blocking school buses in Pontiac, Michigan, in 1971; by a group of busing opponents in Boston on more than one occasion during the 1970s.[71] It was also sung by white demonstrators at the building site of the Kawaida Towers, a proposed public housing project in a predominantly Italian Newark, New Jersey, neighborhood, which was sponsored by the Congress of African People, a project of the black power movement.[72]

The song's meaning had thus undergone a dramatic shift from the tolerance and inclusion of the 1940s. In these anti-integration and anti–public housing contexts, it became clear that the "I" in "land that I love" was white, and that the request for guidance "through the night" had become a kind of coded language for protection from encroachments on "Americanness" by the nonwhite other. This shift parallels the changes in racialized thinking that began in the 1940s, when, as Matthew Frye Jacobson argues, the burgeoning civil rights movement and struggle against Jim Crow brought the black-white binary to the center of American thinking about race, allowing ethnic European immigrants (like Irving Berlin) to become "white" in opposition to African Americans and other people of color.[73] By the 1970s, this binary had broadened into what Jacobson calls a "persistent, naturalized whiteness of the white republic" in response to the perceived encroachments of African Americans, Asians, and Latinos.[74]

Throughout the 1970s and beyond, the song continued to be sung in support of a myriad of conservative social issues, embraced by the Christian Right that rose to power with Ronald Reagan in 1980. In 1977, a group of conservative women sang "God Bless America" while angrily marching out of the National Women's Conference to protest the passage of a progressive agenda endorsing legalized abortion, lesbian rights, and the passage of the Equal Rights Amendment.[75] Anti-abortion marchers sang it at Buffalo's "Right to Life Day" in 1982.[76] With the ascendency of Christian conservatives, "God Bless America" tilted away from its prewar Judeo-Christian roots, becoming reappropriated to represent the Christian God of the evangelical Right.

If conservatives can be understood as revolutionaries reacting against the progressive social change movements of the 1960s, then "God Bless America" was their "We Shall Overcome." In a vivid example of a *Casablanca* moment involving these two songs, protestors at a 1982 nuclear disarmament rally outside the UN sang "We Shall Overcome," and a squad of policemen countered with "God Bless America."[77] This instance is an intriguing illustration of two warring songs whose power derived partly from the meanings that each had accumulated over time. In his study of the role of music in social life, Thomas Turino points out that the use of a hymn such as "We Shall Overcome" in the civil rights movement drew upon its earlier associations with "religious righteousness and progressive politics," deepening the historical and emotional power of these songs and the messages the activists hoped to convey.[78] By the 1980s, "We Shall Overcome" had an even stronger association with righteous protest because of its earlier use within the civil rights movement. "God Bless America" was its obvious counteranthem, as it had acquired equally strong connections with upholding the status quo after years of use in conservative contexts.

After maintaining an initial association with religious and racial tolerance, "God Bless America" emerged from the cultural upheaval of the 1960s as an anthem for the Christian Right. For the most part, there was no longer a question of whose land was "home sweet home," and from what forces the country needed protection. The uses of both the song and the phrase in politics provide further evidence of this rightward trend, but also show that by the turn of the twenty-first century, the phrase "God Bless America" became less a partisan symbol than a political imperative.

"THANK YOU, AND GOD BLESS AMERICA": THE SONG AND PHRASE IN AMERICAN POLITICS

During the 1940 presidential campaign, both FDR and his Republican challenger Wendell Willkie adopted "God Bless America"—then at the height of its prewar popularity—as campaign theme songs. This bipartisan use followed the wishes of Irving Berlin and the God Bless America Fund, as Berlin wrote in July 1940, "no political party has the exclusive rights to the song 'God Bless America.' In our grant to the Republican Party Campaign Committee for Wendell L. Wilkie, we specifically mentioned the fact that we could not give the exclusive rights to any political party to a song that is obviously for all Americans."[79]

After the bipartisan "God Bless America" blitz of the 1940 presidential campaign, the song and the phrase continued to be used by politicians throughout the twentieth century. But it was the phrase that became a ubiquitous part of American political discourse, as the conservative columnist William Safire joked in a 1992 essay:

> Let us bow our heads in thanksgiving: Never has the name of God been so frequently invoked, and never has this or any nation been so thoroughly and systematically blessed, as in the 1992 campaign. . . . Thank you. God bless each and every reader of this column, even you lefties. And God bless America (which is not to say that God should not also bless the rest of the world).[80]

Figure 4.1 shows *New York Times* references to the song and phrase associated with the twelve presidents in office between 1940 and 2008.[81] This chart illustrates two important trends: (1) over time, the *song* increasingly became associated more with Republicans, while the *phrase* came to be a bipartisan imperative; and (2) as the political use of the *song* waned, the popularity of the *phrase* among politicians grew. The first point is yet more evidence of the song's shift to the Right, while the second links to larger issues about the changing role of group singing in American public life.

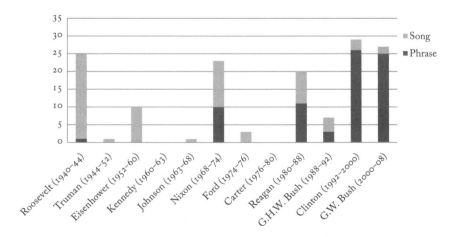

Figure 4.1
New York Times references to "God Bless America" associated with US presidents from FDR to George W. Bush.

There are several interesting features of this graph that are worth noting. The high number of references to the song during FDR's last term serves as testament to its enormous popularity during that period. This spike may also be related to the fact that the song was a new facet of American politics in 1940 and thus was deemed noteworthy by journalists. The increase in usage during Eisenhower's two terms might be linked to the song's burgeoning associations with Republicans, but its popularity was just as likely influenced by Irving Berlin's personal support for the president—he wrote "I Like Ike" for the 1952 campaign and led crowds in singing "God Bless America" at campaign events.[82] On the other hand, the absence of the phrase and song in association with John Kennedy's campaign and short administration is striking but not particularly surprising, given the trepidation surrounding his status as the first Roman Catholic president. Along similar lines, it is interesting that Jimmy Carter, a self-proclaimed evangelical Christian, largely avoided the song and phrase that had come to be associated with conservatism by the time of his term of office.

In *The God Strategy*, an account of the incorporation of religion into contemporary American politics, David Domke and Kevin Coe argue that it was Ronald Reagan who first made the intertwining of politics and religion a political imperative, that Clinton's combination of faith and politics won him the White House, and that faith-based governing was at the center of George W. Bush's presidency.[83] They begin their book with Reagan's first, rather self-conscious use of the phrase "God Bless America" to conclude his 1980 speech accepting the Republican presidential nomination:

> I have thought of something that's not a part of my speech and worried over whether I should do it. [pause] Can we doubt that only a Divine Providence placed this land, this island of freedom, here as a refuge for all those people in the world who yearn to breathe free? Jews and Christians enduring persecution behind the Iron Curtain; the boat people of Southeast Asia, Cuba and of Haiti; the victims of drought and famine in Africa, the freedom fighters in Afghanistan, and our own countrymen held in savage captivity. I'll confess that I've been a little afraid to suggest what I'm going to suggest. I'm more afraid not to. Can we begin our crusade joined together in a moment of silent prayer? [pause; audience silent with heads bowed] God bless America.[84]

Coe and Domke point to this moment as the beginning of the infusion of religion into present-day politics, and Reagan's presidency is often framed as the crowning moment of the Christian Right's rise to power.[85] The authors also identify Reagan as the first president to make political use of the phrase "God Bless America." Analyzing the inclusion of that phrase and related benedictions in major presidential addresses, they argue that such statements uniting God and country "were *almost entirely absent* from the modern presidency," having been spoken only once before Reagan took office, by Richard Nixon in his 1973 address about the Watergate scandal."[86]

It is a satisfying and intriguing coincidence that Reagan, who would become so strongly associated with the phrase "God Bless America," was the star of the 1943 film *This is the Army*, in which the song made its movie debut—in fact, Reagan first appears on screen while the song is playing, during a reenactment of Kate Smith's premiere of the song on her radio show. (See the companion website for a link to this scene. ◗) But as fig. 4.1 indicates, the information gathered from the *New York Times* paints a different picture than that drawn by Domke and Coe. Here, the first political use of the phrase "God Bless America" dates back to a 1940 FDR campaign rally in Manhattan.[87] But this data also shows that it was indeed Nixon, swept into office by conservatives reacting against the 1960s counterculture, who first made regular political use of both the song and the phrase. When including more informal speeches and campaign events (rather than only major speeches, as Domke and Coe do), there were ten references in the *New York Times* to Nixon's use of the phrase, just one fewer than Reagan. In addition to his use of the phrase to conclude his April 1973 Watergate speech, Nixon ended two earlier speeches that February with the words "God Bless America."[88]

But it is Nixon's use of the *song* "God Bless America" that is most interesting here. While ending speeches with the phrase became a bipartisan political necessity in the later part of the twentieth century, Nixon used the song to an extent not seen since its heyday in 1940. It was played by the US Marine Corps band at his inauguration, and sung by celebrities campaigning for him in New Hampshire in 1972.[89] In addition to these routine instances of the song's use at campaign and presidential events, Nixon added an important twist: he sang the song himself, sometimes playing along on the piano.

The first instance of such a performance occurred in May 1973, where Nixon and Irving Berlin led the crowd in singing "God Bless America" at a state dinner for POWs recently returned from Vietnam. The evening was full of high-profile entertainers (including Vic Damone, Sammy Davis Jr., and Roy Acuff), but as one newspaper account described:

> the man who squeezed tears from all the eyes was 88-year-old Irving Berlin. He sang a wheezy, broken version of his World War II classic, "God Bless America." The President himself bounded on the stage with Mrs. Nixon to line up with the show-biz folks, including Bob Hope, Jimmy Stewart, John Wayne, and Phyllis Diller, to join a final chorus. 'We've never had a night like this one at the White House,' the President told his guests.[90]

To Irving Berlin
God Bless America, God Bless You,

Richard Nixon

Figure 4.2
President Nixon and Irving Berlin singing "God Bless America" at a state dinner for former prisoners of war in May 1973. Photograph by the Associated Press, courtesy of Rodgers & Hammerstein: an Imagem Company, on behalf of the Estate of Irving Berlin.

This scene serves as a dramatic indicator of the generational divide of this period: all of the stars singing "God Bless America" with Nixon came from a generation that remembered World War II and the great mobilization of the home front in support of the troops. Perhaps they even remembered Irving Berlin singing "God Bless America" at Allied Relief events, or Kate Smith singing it during her marathon war bond drives.[91] The image of Nixon singing "God Bless America" at an event for Vietnam POWs, with his arm around an aged Irving Berlin, provides a vivid illustration of the song's generational associations, in addition to its ideological ones. For these aging celebrities, the song was imbued with nostalgia for an earlier era, one marked by consensus and a common purpose. But here, toward the end of Nixon's embattled presidency and just months after the United States withdrew from its calamitous involvement in the Vietnam War, "God Bless America" was once again used as a symbol of support for the war and the president.[92]

Berlin and Nixon appear to have shared a warm personal regard. A few months before the POW state dinner in 1973 where the singing took place, Nixon wrote to Berlin: "[N]ever have I received a more cherished gift than your original manuscript of the chorus of 'God Bless America.' This song expressed the sentiments which most of us feel but cannot convey."[93] The sing-along at the White House appears to have carried poignant meaning for both President Nixon and Berlin. The president wrote to Berlin that singing "God Bless America" was "one of the most memorable moments" at the POW event, and Berlin responded that it was "one of the most moving experiences I ever had."[94] Berlin's personal involvement shows how his own political alliances map the same rightward shift as the song's associations—from FDR to Eisenhower to Nixon.

But this sing-along with Berlin was not the last of Nixon's performances. At a White House dinner in March 1974, "God Bless America" was among the songs sung by Pearl Bailey, accompanied by the president on the piano.[95] That same month, Nixon played the piano and sang at the opening of the new Grand Ole Opry House in Nashville. After playing "Happy Birthday" and "My Wild Irish Rose" in honor of his wife's birthday, Nixon announced that "country music is America" and began to play and sing "God Bless America," to which the crowd sang along.[96] (See the link to archival video of this performance on the companion website. ⊚)

Nixon's forays into musical performance just four months before his resignation were likely meant to distract the country from the escalating Watergate scandal, but for some they had the opposite effect. Russell Baker derided the "clownishness of this public straining to play the nice guy," and there is certainly something contrived about the president's public piano recitals and their accompanying media coverage during that fraught political climate.[97] But Nixon's performances effectively cemented the relationship between the song "God Bless America" and conservative politics, which continued with Reagan's presidency.

President Reagan's copious use of "God Bless America" served two purposes: as a signal to conservatives and a symbol of nostalgia for an older generation of voters. His use of the phrase sent a message to his evangelical base that he would not shrink from infusing his politics with religion. This was a critical part of what Domke and Coe have dubbed the "God strategy," which entails maintaining a primarily secular agenda to avoid alienating moderate Americans, while "deliberately finding opportunities to 'signal' sympathy for religious conservatives' views."[98] "God Bless America" was the perfect conduit for such a message. It was a patriotic song that children learned in school, but it had acquired new meanings beginning in the

Figure 4.3
Presidential candidate Ronald Reagan and his wife, Nancy, sing "God Bless America" at the conclusion of the campaign's final rally in San Diego, 3 November 1980. Photograph by Teresa Zabala/The New York Times/Redux.

mid-1960s, as it was wielded by Christian conservatives in battles against secular liberalism. When FDR adopted the song in his 1940 campaign, it represented an embrace of cultural and religious tolerance and an inclusive, ecumenical God; by 1980, the Christian Right used the song to signify an incorporation of Christian faith and values into politics. At a 1984 meeting of religious broadcasters at which Reagan appeared, attendees "virtually serenaded" the president with "God Bless America," and the singer and conservative icon Pat Boone boomed through the microphone, "How wonderful to have a President who believes these words."[99]

In addition to this function as a symbol for the Christian Right, the song was, again, a nostalgic reminder of the World War II era, when Reagan was a Hollywood star and "God Bless America" was at the height of its popularity. As one journalist described Reagan's relationship with the song near the end of the 1980 presidential campaign, "Mr. Reagan has taken that song and the American flag out of the sports arena and made them a prominent feature at his political rallies. Old-fashioned flag-waving patriotism is no longer unsophisticated and passé, at least at the G.O.P. gatherings."[100] Such flag-waving echoes the patriotic fever that swept the nation in the 1940s. It evokes the song's past, which would have resonated with most Americans who were over the age of forty in the 1980s: memories of pre-TV radio, and of Kate Smith, the quintessential patriot of that era. In fact, Reagan awarded Smith the Presidential Medal of Freedom in 1982, specifically citing her association with the song:

> The voice of Kate Smith is known and loved by millions of Americans, young and old. In war and peace, it has been an inspiration. Those simple but deeply moving words, "God bless America," have taken on added meaning for all of us because of the way Kate Smith sang them. Thanks to her they have become a cherished part of all our lives, an undying reminder of the beauty, the courage and the heart of this great land of ours. In giving us a magnificent, selfless talent like Kate Smith, God has truly blessed America.[101]

Here, Reagan evokes the heyday of Smith's brand of populist patriotism and links it to a song (and phrase) that he helped bring into the center of political rhetoric. Although he attributes the song's "added meaning" to Smith, its use by Reagan and his conservative supporters did as much to shape the song's symbolic meaning in the 1980s as Smith's orchestrated performances had in the late 1930s and 1940s.

George H. W. Bush departed from his predecessor's dependence on the phrase "God Bless America," preferring the more expansive "God bless the United States of America" or "may God continue to bless America."[102] The first President Bush also seems to have used the *song* much less than Reagan, perhaps as a way to distance himself from his predecessor's formidable shadow. For his campaign, Bush in fact chose "This Land Is Your Land," a song written in the same year and in direct opposition to "God Bless America." Although by 1988 Woody Guthrie's song had been neutered of its rebellious spirit, its history as a protest against the more conservative values espoused by "God Bless America" gives Bush's use of the song an ironic historical twist.

The phrase "God Bless America" came roaring back with Bill Clinton, who borrowed a page from the Republican playbook by invoking religion to bring his party to the White House in 1992.[103] According to references in the *New York Times*, Clinton's association with the phrase even edged out that of his successor, whom Domke and Coe view as the apotheosis of the intertwining of politics, conservatism, and religion. Like his father, George W. Bush often used variants such as "May God continue to bless America," but his presidency certainly solidified the political imperative of uttering the phrase "God Bless America."

In addition to telling a story about a growing acceptance of religion in American politics, this presidential data also shows that by the 1990s, the phrase essentially became a substitute for the song, which could be an indication of a decline of public singing in American life more generally. As shown in fig. 4.1, during FDR's 1940 campaign and last term of office, there were twenty-five references to the song and only one use of the phrase. But in the sixteen combined years of the Clinton and G. W. Bush presidencies, there were only five references to the song's use and fifty-one of the phrase, indicating a dramatic decrease in the use of group singing in politics. In fact, as shown in the chart of all *New York Times* references in fig. I.1 in the introduction, in 2000 references to the phrase far outnumber references to the song overall.[104]

Clinton's 1992 campaign signaled the end of the campaign song as a vehicle for group singing. Before that year, new songs were commissioned (such as "I Like Ike" in 1952) or old songs appropriated (Truman's "I'm Just Wild About Harry" in 1948 or George H. W. Bush's "This Land is Your Land" in 1988 and 1992), usually designed to be learned and sung by supporters at campaign events.[105] But Clinton's campaign song—Fleetwood Mac's "Don't Stop"—was a 1970s rock song positioned to appeal to the baby boomers of Clinton's own generation.[106] A campaign song like "Don't Stop" is not as powerful without its instrumental accompaniment and the iconic voices of its original performers, and thus is designed to be listened to rather than sung. In the past twenty years, presidential campaign songs have been chosen from the vast repertory of American popular music since the 1960s, calculated to evoke already-established associations with a specific pop song or genre, rather than forge an image with a newly composed campaign song meant to be sung by a crowd.[107] Similarly, the political role of "God Bless America" shifted from a vehicle for singing at campaign events to a phrase that became a mandatory political trope by the beginning of the twenty-first century.

This chapter has traced the shifting meanings associated with "God Bless America," from the tolerance movements of the early 1940s to the

Christian Right of the 1980s through the end of the twentieth century. Until the late 1960s, the song's diverse uses reflected its ability to convey multiple, sometimes contradictory, messages. But as a result of continued use to uphold the status quo beginning in the Vietnam War era, the song's meaning became largely entrenched within conservatism, losing past associations with cultural and religious pluralism as it became an anthem for the Christian Right, ushered into the political arena by Nixon and Reagan.

These changes represent more than a simple rightward trajectory. They also underscore larger themes within twentieth-century American history: the "whitening" of European immigrants in the wake of World War II, the shift from a Judeo-Christian ideal to an expanded intertwining of Christian religion and politics, and the rise of modern popular music as embodied in presidential campaign songs. Examining the song and the phrase together shows a decline of the use of the song in favor of the phrase, perhaps an indicator of a general wane in group singing in public life. However, all of this changed again with the 9/11 attacks, as the song temporarily fulfilled a new, nonpartisan function as a vehicle for public mourning and a poignant symbol for post-9/11 unity.

CHAPTER 5

⌒⌒⌒

My Home Sweet Home

Commemoration, Coercion, and
Commerce after 9/11

I think I told you once that when conditions for America are not so hot, people are very
glad to God bless America.
                        —Irving Berlin, 1952[1]

In a national poll conducted a few weeks after 9/11, 70 percent of Americans reported that they had sung "God Bless America" as a direct result of the attacks. This was slightly fewer than those who said that they had told someone they loved them (79 percent), but more than those who had prayed or attended a religious ceremony (67 percent), cried (64 percent), sang the "Star Spangled Banner" (63 percent), or kept in closer contact with relatives (61 percent) in response to 9/11.[2]

These astonishing figures reveal the central role that "God Bless America" played in the public response to the attacks. It began on the evening of September 11, when members of Congress burst into a spontaneous rendition of the song after a press conference on the steps of the Capitol. This event, viewed by millions of Americans glued to their television sets in the aftermath of the attacks, appears to have anointed the singing of "God Bless America" as the appropriate vehicle for group mourning and commemoration.[3] Workers at the crash sites in New York and the Pentagon sang it on more than one occasion.[4] It became the song of choice at 9/11 memorials—both official and ad hoc—sung at spontaneous memorial sites in Manhattan and beyond, at a service in Chicago's Daley Plaza, at candlelight vigils on a suburban lawn in New Jersey, and along a highway on the Maryland shore.[5]

The song came to symbolize remembrance and commemoration as people returned to their normal lives, marking the resumption of everyday activities. Singing "God Bless America" allowed people to acknowledge the horrors of 9/11 while trying to move beyond them, and assuaged the guilt of the living for indulging in life's pleasures in the midst of heartrending loss and destruction. When Broadway shows reopened on September 13, audiences joined in singing "God Bless America" after the final curtain.[6] Stock traders sang along as it was sung at the opening bell of the New York Stock Exchange on September 17.[7] That same day, baseball fans sang it at stadiums across the country as professional baseball games resumed.[8] In the jittery weeks following the attacks, a flight attendant "rallied passengers with an impromptu chorus of 'God Bless America' as a plane landed," and diners "enjoying a respite from the sadness of recent days" sang it after a rendition of "Happy Birthday" at Smith & Wollensky's in Manhattan.[9]

Perhaps as striking as the instant popularity of "God Bless America" was the fact that people were singing at all. As a rule, people don't sing together in secular public life in the United States, but a momentary interest in group singing was one of many things that changed, at least momentarily, after 9/11. During times of crisis, communal singing often fulfills a critical function in American public life, facilitating an instant, temporary sense of community that suddenly becomes overwhelmingly necessary. This period of public mourning directly after 9/11 is significant not just because of the sudden popularity of "God Bless America" but also because of the dramatic ascension of group singing to the forefront of public life.

And yet there was a flip side to this spontaneous embrace of "God Bless America." For those who felt unmoved by or opposed to the intertwining of religion and patriotism within its lyrics, the song took on an oppressive power, and this sense of coercion intensified in the years following the attacks, when "God Bless America" became a symbol of support for the wars in Afghanistan and Iraq. In addition, the song's spike in popularity revealed its otherwise hidden economic underpinnings: still under copyright, the song's new role as a vehicle for mourning was earning hundreds of thousands of dollars behind the scenes, a financial boon that some perceived as being at odds with the newfound sense of unity that briefly emerged in the wake of tragedy.

CONGRESS, "GOD BLESS AMERICA," AND
COLLECTIVE MEMORY AFTER 9/11

"God Bless America" was anointed as a post-9/11 anthem on the evening of the attacks, when many members of Congress assembled for a press conference on the steps of the Capitol. Yet according to two former congressmen whom I interviewed, this gathering almost didn't take place, as Capitol security officials were so concerned about additional attacks that they warned everyone to disperse. But congressional leaders eventually decided that a press conference could send an important message about unity and bravery to a shaken American public.[10]

The press conference itself featured short speeches by Speaker of the House Dennis Hastert and Senate majority leader Tom Daschle, surrounded by members of Congress from both parties. Both speakers touched on the same themes, emphasizing that America's leaders stood united, would bring the perpetrators of the attacks to justice, and were sending their thoughts and prayers to the injured and families of those who were lost.[11] (Links to video of this press conference can be found on the companion website. ◑) On the television broadcast, these speeches were shown in split-screen, in tandem with images of the falling twin towers and burning Pentagon. After a moment of silence, the conference ended; on the TV broadcast, Tom Brokaw spoke over footage of Senate leaders beginning to leave, noting, "A remarkable tableau of political unity, there on the steps of the Capitol building. Party leaders from both houses, and a number of members . . ." He stopped his commentary mid-sentence when strains of "God Bless America" were heard emerging from the crowd, becoming perceptible by the song's second line, "land that I love." At this point, the camera panned—for the first time—to the full group of congressmen and women still standing on the steps. The camera lingered on two congresswomen standing toward the front of the group—Carrie Meek, an African American Democrat from Florida, and Kay Granger, a white Republican from Texas. The two women held hands and, like most participants in this impromptu sing-along, looked stricken, resolute, moved. By the last refrain, "God bless America, my home sweet home," viewers saw a wide camera shot encompassing the entire group, mostly made up of men in dark suits and ties, accented by a smaller number of congresswomen in brighter colors.

These demographics are also expressed in sonic terms, as the singing on the broadcast *sounds* male, dominated by baritone voices. It remains tentative and not entirely settled on a unified key until the line "to the oceans,

Figure 5.1
Members of Congress singing "God Bless America" on 11 September 2001. Photograph by
Kevin Clark/The Washington Post/Getty Images.

white with foam," leading into the climactic refrain, "God bless America,
my home sweet home." A few participants and commentators took note of
the song's lack of tonal unity, which lent the rendition a poignant sincerity
that may have contributed to its emotional power. One former congressman wrote, "The singing was pretty bad but the song never sounded
sweeter to my ears," and the music critic Terry Teachout proclaimed,
"though I've heard it sung better, I've never heard it sound better."[12] When
the song ended, everyone broke into applause. Many of the participants
embraced. As Brokaw reflected:

> If somebody told me two days ago—in the midst of the political struggle on
> Capitol Hill and down at the other end of Pennsylvania Avenue, over the budget
> and taxes and Social Security, with a congressional election coming up in the
> year ahead—that the leaders of the House and Senate joined by many members
> from both parties would stand on the steps of the Capitol to declare their unity
> and sing "God Bless America" spontaneously, I would have not said that that was
> a likely event. Um, [pause] it was something to see. An unusual spectacle indeed,
> brought about by events that no one could have foretold and, of course, that no
> one would ever have wanted.

The moment was a perfect encapsulation of the public mood directly
after the attacks: sincere patriotism, bewilderment, mourning, a desire for

unity, and for commemoration. As Martin Daughtry noted in his introduction to *Music in the Post-9/11 World*, "This strange and spontaneous performance, drawing simultaneously on the iconicity of the united chorus, the indexical associations of patriotic music, and the symbolic attributes of political authority, delivered its message to its disparate audiences more emphatically than the words that preceded it ever could."[13]

There are some precedents of staged versions of "God Bless America" being sung publicly by members of Congress. The first reference in the *New York Times* described a playful moment in 1955, at a traditional vaudeville songfest held as the House of Representatives adjourned. One representative began the singing with the barbershop standard, "Let the Rest of the World Go By," and others joined in until "at one point the entire House joined the singing, and from that point on, the dam burst."[14] In a performance that featured sing-alongs of old standards, a harmonica solo, a joke bird impression, and a solemn rendition of the Lord's Prayer, the legislators, "in a burst of patriotic fervor, stood en masse and sang 'God Bless America.' The galleries, caught up by it, stood and joined the singing." A more politically pointed performance occurred on the steps of the Capitol in September 1980, when the presidential nominee Ronald Reagan led Republican congressmen in singing "God Bless America" at a pre-election rally in which participants pledged to take a unified approach if they controlled the White House and Congress.[15] In 1988, a nonpartisan performance took place on the Capitol steps, when lawmakers were asked to join together to sing "Happy Birthday" and "God Bless America" in honor of Irving Berlin's one hundredth birthday.[16] But what is striking about the 9/11 performance is the utter sincerity and bewilderment of the participants, which so captures the public mood directly after the attacks.

Viewing the television broadcast, it is impossible to detect where the singing originated, but it does seem as if the performance was a purely spontaneous response to tragedy, one without a calculated purpose as one might imagine in that political milieu. In order to find out more about how this singing came about, in 2009 I sent out a short survey targeted to retired members of Congress who had served during the fall of 2001. From the 104 former members of Congress I was able to track down on the Internet, I received thirty completed surveys—a respectable 29 percent return rate.[17] In addition to these survey responses, two former congressmen contacted me on their own to talk about their 9/11 experiences in phone interviews.

Identifying the person who first began to sing "God Bless America" on the steps of the Capitol proved more difficult than I had imagined. Through the survey, I learned that the performance was helped by at least one enthusiastic singer within the group: former representative David Phelps, who wrote, "I'm not sure who started it but I came in quickly!"[18] Phelps, a professional singer who regularly led the hymn singing at House prayer breakfasts on Thursday mornings, apparently helped turn the song from a murmur into a full-fledged performance: "So when someone started murmuring God Bless America, I believe I helped us get in tune and find a reasonable key. . . . I do remember Senator Jay Rockefeller behind me and saying, 'Good job!'"

But what about the mysterious instigator of the singing? I was excited to read Rep. Ken Bentsen's confident assertion that "Nebraska Rep. Tom Osborne, former Univ. of Nebraska football coach, just began singing 'God Bless America' and everyone just joined in."[19] Yet in the same batch of mailed surveys, Tom Osborne himself wrote that he didn't remember who started the song. The former House majority leader Dick Armey responded that the singing was started by Rep. Dana Rohrabocher, a fellow conservative Republican standing directly behind Armey at the press conference, but Rohrabocher declined to participate in my survey to confirm this assertion.[20] None of the other former members of Congress who responded to my survey identified a specific person as the singing's point of origin.

This difficulty in identifying the person who started the singing is a result, in part, of logistical limitations and a relatively small pool of respondents. Of the 540 members of the 107th Congress (in session from January 2001 to January 2003), I heard from thirty-two—only nineteen of whom reported being present at the 9/11 press conference.[21] So it is possible that I simply didn't find the right person to ask. Then there is the obvious practical difficulty of identifying where, precisely, the song originated in a crowd, in which people are most aware of those directly surrounding them. How can one know if the first person he or she heard was truly the original source of the singing?

In addition to these logistical issues, the elusive nature of the singing's origins demonstrates the complexity of untangling spontaneous collective action through the fog of memory. Eight years later, who could remember who actually began singing? Is it possible that whoever started the singing might not necessarily remember his or her own actions, once they were taken up by the collective? In other words, could the individual spark of the song's first few words become lost in the crowd? This is an especially intriguing question since this particular rendition of the song would go on to attain iconic status as a symbol of the American response to the 9/11 attacks. The spontaneity of this performance becomes critical to the song's authenticity as a response to tragedy, yet the origins of the singing have become nearly impossible to reconstruct in hindsight.

My attempt to reconstruct the events behind this congressional performance is further complicated by the fact that the performance has now
become an annual ritual, reenacted on the Capitol steps each year on the
anniversary of 9/11, creating additional layers of memory to compete
with the original.[22] Almost all survey respondents who attended the press
conference agreed that the singing of "God Bless America" was spontaneous, but the two responses that reflect uncertainty about the event's
spontaneity seem related to issues of memory. As one former congress-
woman described her own confusion about the 2001 event, "I am not sure
but I think the word circulated—time, place, song. I know our all being on
the steps was planned. Not sure if we knew about singing together or if it
erupted. I think it was spontaneous."[23] Another survey respondent
thought that the song had been a planned performance at the beginning
of the press conference: "I recall the idea was to gather at the Capitol to
show bipartisan unity and someone suggested we start with the song."[24]
The original, spontaneous moment faded from memory, replaced with a
planned exercise, likely influenced by subsequent reenactments of the
singing on anniversaries of 9/11.

Such confusion is related to the fluid nature of individual and collective
memory. In his landmark study of collective memory published in 1952,
Maurice Halbwachs wrote that "the past is not preserved but is reconstructed on the basis of the present," taking note of how layers of experience impact our memory of past events.[25] More recently, the historian Jay
Winter has argued that "the act of recalling the past is a dynamic, shifting
process, dependent on notions of the future as much as on images of the
past."[26] Winter draws on the cognitive psychologist Daniel Schacter's description of how memory works: "Sometimes in the process of reconstructing [memories] we add feelings, beliefs, or even knowledge we obtained
after the experience. In other words, we bias our memories of the past by
attributing to them emotions or knowledge we acquired after the event."[27]
Karim Nader, a behavioral neuroscientist, has conducted experiments that
suggest that the act of remembering itself can allow memories to become
distorted, influenced by whatever is present in the environment when the
memory is recalled and retold.[28] The repeated post-9/11 performances of
"God Bless America" have now melded into a composite of experiences and
memories that resist disentanglement.

It is also possible that the singing had been planned by at least some
who were on the Capitol steps on 9/11. In 2011, at the commemorations
of the tenth anniversary of the attacks, the Senate majority leader
Harry Reid noted that it was Sen. Barbara Mikulski's idea to sing "God
Bless America" at the 9/11 press conference.[29] Perhaps the singing had

been planned among a few of those in attendance who began the song together. Unfortunately, Senator Mikulski's office did not respond to my inquiries regarding her role in the singing, so this story will need to join the chorus of competing narratives regarding the song's appearance on 9/11.

One former representative, James Greenwood, contacted me to tell the story of that day as he remembered it. According to Greenwood, when the plane hit the Pentagon, everyone in the Capitol was ordered to disperse. He, like many others, described how difficult communication was, with cell phones not working and phone lines jammed. But for those who stayed close to the Capitol, the order came through various channels to return to the headquarters of the Capitol police for a conference call with the congressional leadership, who had been taken to a secure location. According to Greenwood, it was after this conference call that "God Bless America" was first sung:

> And then what happened is, a member of Congress—and I don't remember which one it was, but it was an African American Democrat female—stood up and spontaneously began to sing "God Bless America." . . . Most people don't know this, but the [singing on the] Capitol steps was really a repeat performance. So the first time it happened was in the Capitol police headquarters, and she just stood up and started to sing that, and we all—all of us who were there—stood up and we sang along. It was a very, very emotional moment.[30]

While the conference call was mentioned in a few other survey responses, no one else described this earlier moment of group singing. Perhaps it occurred after most people had left the room, or there were multiple rooms in which smaller groups of people participated in the conference call—or it was simply forgotten. It was obviously a poignant memory for Greenwood, who contacted me independently after receiving my survey to talk in more detail about this experience.

Viewed this way, the performance on the Capitol steps can be understood as the public expression of a private, spontaneous experience, of an attempt to recapture a moment of intimate communion for a larger audience. In this context, the singing was a performance both calculated and spontaneous, which served two distinct purposes. It provided a commemorative moment for those participating in the singing, and it conveyed meaning to the television audience—to show unity in the face of crisis, to show that Americans would not hide in the face of terror, and as it turns out, to begin a ritualized response to the tragedy that would reverberate for years.

WHY "GOD BLESS AMERICA"?

In the weeks after the attacks, newspapers took note of the sudden ubiquity of "God Bless America." This proliferation of articles—with headlines like, "No. 1 Anthem: 'God Bless America,'" "'God Bless America,' The Song in A Nation's Heart," and "'God Bless America' a Balm for Nation's Grief"—serves as further evidence of the song's central role during this post-9/11 period.[31] The articles themselves provide insight into the reasons behind the song's sudden popularity, as journalists retraced its history and interviewed various experts about why it so resonated with a grieving public. Many of the reasons given in the press echo those from the song's initial popularity in 1940: the simplicity of the melody and a patriotic message suited the public mood. But other aspects of this post-9/11 embrace of "God Bless America" reflect that specific time and place in history, when a national tragedy sparked a desire for unity that was satisfied by singing together in public.

Why did "God Bless America" become the anthem of choice at this moment? If a song of patriotism and unity was called for, why not the national anthem? One simple answer given by former members of Congress is that "God Bless America" is easier to sing than "The Star-Spangled Banner."[32] As Celeste Bohlen wrote in her analysis of the relative absence of the national anthem post-9/11: "[A]s everyone knows, the anthem is not an easy song to sing, and in times like these, people tend to want to sing their hearts out, without having to stretch to reach the high notes."[33]

Some commentators pointed to the appeal of the song's modern lyrics in response to a modern tragedy. As the musician Ian Whitcomb told the *San Francisco Chronicle*, "I don't think 'The Star-Spangled Banner' has the same kind of resonance, because it's not written in the American vernacular."[34] Susan Elliott, editor of MusicalAmerica.com, put it a different way, noting that the song's lyrics represented precisely the right sentiment, without ornamented language: "The lyrics do not beat around the bush. It's 'God bless America, land that I love . . .' That's exactly the way we all feel right now. We don't have to weave our way through 'O! say, can you see by the dawn's early light' or 'My country, 'tis of thee.'"[35] Another obvious reason for avoiding the national anthem was the martial imagery of its lyrics, as the music critic and author Robert Kimball told the *Washington Post*, "The idea of bombs bursting in air has suddenly taken on a strange connotation."[36]

A few former members of Congress also noted that the anthem already had ceremonial meaning attached to it, which did not feel appropriate for the commemorative moment on 9/11. Former congressman David Phelps noted that "at different public gatherings (ballgames, festivals, patriotic events, etc.) the National Anthem is appropriate and follows traditional protocol." Former Rep. Henry Bonilla wrote, "I think it is viewed as more of a song of national pride and unity versus the national anthem which is more ceremonial." As an alternate anthem, "God Bless America" had no previous ceremonial associations on a national scale, and thus represented a clean slate on to which new ritual meanings could be projected.[37]

Another reason that "God Bless America" served well in this regard is that it was simply a song that everyone knew well enough to sing. Alex Ross described the crowd at a vigil in the East Village: "When one part of the crowd is devoted to Jay-Z and another part to John Zorn, the common ground becomes 'God Bless America.'"[38] Another former congressman noted that "both parties had sung it repeatedly at their national conventions," implying that the song was a natural choice for politicians needing a vehicle for group singing, simply because it was so familiar.[39] "God Bless America" does seem to be among a small handful of songs that most Americans know, though the subject of a shared American song repertory needs further study.[40]

David Sedaris described his own experience with the power of "God Bless America" in a story that aired on the radio show *This American Life* the week after 9/11. He talked with a mixture of humor and pathos about living as an expatriate in Paris and attending a memorial service two days after the attack. He noted that although the service was held in an American church, the sermon was delivered in French to accommodate a national television broadcast, which left the Americans in attendance wanting more: "It's different for visiting tourists, but the Americans who actually live here go to great lengths to avoid one another. Now we wanted to hang out and share our emptiness, but it wasn't on the program."[41] In an echo of the singing on the Capitol steps, a spontaneous sing-along of "God Bless America" erupted after the official service was over:

> The service ended, and just as the last politician filed out of the room, a man in the balcony started singing "God Bless America." It's a song I'd always associated with homeroom and high school sporting events, but under the circumstances, and on foreign soil, the lyrics became significant. The man started singing, and little by little, the rest of us joined in. The couples with bilingual children, the college students, the nannies, and across the aisle, soprano Jessye Norman, who placed her hand over her heart and sang as if she were just a normal, shattered woman and not an opera star.

The vague, universal aspects of Berlin's lyrics allowed "God Bless America" to adapt and resonate with new meaning in the bewildering context of

9/11, despite previous associations with the banality of high school. As a humorist, though, Sedaris was able to step back from this poignant moment to reflect on the more ridiculous aspects of the song's lyrics:

> The thing about "God Bless America" is that after a certain point, nobody seems to know the words. "Stand beside her and guide her" is almost always followed by a prolonged mumbling that lasts until we reach the mountains and prairies. Then there's that strange bit about "the oceans, white with foam," which is odd, in that it's not in any way a national phenomenon. Lots of countries have foam. They just don't talk about it.

But for Sedaris and his fellow expatriates, the song's last line was the most powerful, resonating with the question of what "home" truly means for those living abroad:

> What killed me, what killed us all, was the very end: "my home sweet home." Because regardless of what we tell ourselves, Paris is not our home. It's just a place where we have our apartments and furniture. If it were our home, we'd have wanted to stay put, rather than catch the next flight back to New York or Kansas or wherever our families sat helpless in front of their televisions.

In addition to the song's specific reference to a sense of "home," the main significance of the singing, for Sedaris, was its ability to connect the community of expatriates in a way that the service itself could not. In a sociological study of the aftermath of 9/11, Edward Tiryakian argues that the attacks produced "a massive national solidarity" in which "all segments of the population, all regions of the country felt the attack on the World Trade Center and on the Pentagon was an attack against the American people, a crime of violence which made all segments realize what they shared as Americans."[42] In her book *A Paradise Built in Hell*, Rebecca Solnit argues that in the aftermath of disasters, a newfound "purposefulness and connectedness bring joy even amid death, chaos, fear, and loss."[43] She writes that a "somber version of that strange pleasure in disaster emerged after September 11, 2001, when many Americans seemed stirred, moved, and motivated by the newfound sense of urgency, purpose, solidarity, and danger they had encountered. They abhorred what had happened, but they clearly relished who they briefly became."[44]

While Solnit focuses her study on the bravery and kindness of strangers spurred to action by disaster, her notion of a sense of joy in tragic events also applies to those involved in the spontaneous communal singing that arose in response to 9/11. Many former members of Congress describe singing on the steps of the Capitol in positive terms, as one effused, "It was one of the greatest events of my six years in Congress."[45] And Alex Ross wrote. "Everyone who was in New York on September 11th will remember not only the sun-drenched terror of the day but also the fullness of human contact in the weeks that followed. Often, the connection was made through music."[46]

Many descriptions of singing "God Bless America" after 9/11 indicate that the music was particularly charged with emotion. One former congressman called the performance on the Capitol steps "an emotional catharsis" and another said, "It was an emotional relief to join in the singing."[47] Senator Trent Lott wrote that he "felt chills" as the group sang, and an article describing the scene on the Capitol steps noted that Sen. Hillary Rodham Clinton was in tears.[48] Later renditions continued to wield emotional power for those participating in the singing: a performance of "God Bless America" after The Producers on Broadway "brought the entire audience to its feet and many to tears"; business and real estate executives "wiped away tears" as the song was sung at the opening of the New York Stock Exchange; and as Oscar de la Renta described a high-fashion gala, "When at the close we all sang 'God Bless America,' I could see tears in the eyes of a lot of people. For one time, it really didn't matter what people were wearing."[49]

Above all, former members of Congress emphasized in surveys and interviews that the song—and the act of singing itself—allowed those present to transcend divisions and foster a rare sense of unity, as Dick Armey wrote, "It was the most non-partisan, patriotic moment of my 18 years in Congress."[50] This sentiment was echoed by many former members of Congress, with comments such as: "There was no partisan divide"; "No partisanship, just citizenship"; "No one cared who was Democrat or Republican. We were united!"; "It produced a sense of togetherness that hasn't been felt since."[51] One spiritual leader later noted, "It's amazing—the capacity of that simple melody to unite the country in a way that was both comforting and brought strength—it crossed all divides."[52] The singing fed a need for connection, and the song invoked an intertwining of God and country that was, for many, not merely tolerated but in demand during the period directly after the attacks. As former Rep. Connie Morella wrote emphatically, "What better song to exemplify our love for our country, our solidarity, and our quest for guidance beyond the material as we faced such a shocking tragedy?!"[53]

The embrace of the song and its direct evocation of God coincided with a general turn to religion and spirituality during this period. One former senator put it plainly: "The country turns to God when the world gets dangerous."[54] Another congressperson described "God Bless America" as a "national hymn," fulfilling a different function from the national anthem.[55] In fact, after the attacks a bill was put forward to make "God Bless America" the official "national hymn," a congressional designation that had never before been proposed.[56] Polls in September and October 2001 showed increases in church and synagogue attendance and other indicators of religious sentiment, although this religious upsurge proved to be short-lived, a temporary bereavement process rather than a revival or awakening.[57] And of course, there were some who objected to the interweaving of religion and patriotism embodied by "God Bless America" from the outset, who felt in the singing a not-so-subtle coercion to utter words they did not believe.

"A PLAGUE OF AFTERMATH THEISM": GOD, COUNTRY, AND COERCION

Despite its newfound poignancy, "God Bless America" was not without its critics. For some on the political Left, the song's previous associations with conservative politics and ideologies could not be overlooked. Writing in the *Nation* one month after the attack, Eric Alterman protested, "My patriotism is . . . not Kate Smith singing 'God Bless America'; it's Bruce Springsteen singing 'This Land Is Your Land,'" echoing the ideological battle between those two songs that began in 1940.[58] Three weeks after the attacks, one music journalist saw the need for songs like "God Bless America" as coming to an end, writing, "as we return to a semblance of normalcy, I suggest radio stations move beyond playing understandably knee-jerk, ego/ethno-centric fare."[59] But even here, the criticism was aimed at Kate Smith's recording and other performances of the song, not at the kind of group singing that had become such a ubiquitous part of the public response to the attacks. In fact, the emotional power of group singing did appear to quiet many of those who might otherwise recoil from "God Bless America." One self-proclaimed agnostic wrote that the song was "soothing simply for its tune," demonstrating her ability to ignore the message of the words in favor of participating in public mourning.[60]

There were some who felt assaulted by the new infusion of religion into public life—dubbed "a plague of aftermath theism" by the New York City Atheists—in which "God Bless America" played a starring role.[61] Tom Flynn, editor of the Secular Humanist journal *Free Inquiry*, lamented that the post-9/11 intertwining of religion and patriotism effectively excluded the nonreligious from participating in public mourning.[62] Greg Epstein,

Harvard's Humanist chaplain and author of the book *Good Without God*, told me about his experience with the song a few months after the attacks. Epstein was then a graduate student in Judaic Studies at the University of Michigan in his first year of studying to be a Humanist rabbi, and he recounted his memory of "God Bless America" being sung at the General Assembly of the United Jewish Communities, an annual meeting of thousands of global Jewish leaders, which took place in November 2001:

> And I remember very distinctly standing in a very close huddle with all of these Jewish students from U of M, with thousands and thousands of other people, many of them young people, surrounding me. And everybody's singing along. And I knew at that point that I was a Humanist, which meant that I did not believe in the existence of a God or gods or the supernatural or anything like that. . . . And so there I am in this room, thousands of people are singing this song and commemorating 9/11, and I felt that I could not sing along. And so I had to stand there, very, very, very uncomfortably—silent, at attention. And I remember standing very stiffly, in other words, I remember making a real effort to stand erect and at attention, and with dignity and respect for the sentiment of people who were singing. But I could not assent to the words, and I could not misrepresent myself by singing along as if I believed the message of the song.[63]

Epstein was sympathetic to those able to suspend any of their own beliefs in the song's lyrics, acknowledging that "everyone wants to have a common—you know—melody and a common aesthetically pleasing way of expressing their American-ness, or something that holds them in common. And I can understand that view, and it doesn't upset me tremendously, but it's something that I can't agree with or assent to." There were others, however, for whom the post-9/11 use of "God Bless America" represented an unacceptable breach of the separation of church and state.

In one well-publicized case, Donna Cayot, an atheist and mother living in Somers, New York, took legal action against the singing of "God Bless America" at an assembly that took place the week of the attacks at her son's school, arguing that it forced her son to pray. At the assembly, each student was given a copy of the lyrics, including the rarely sung introductory verse, and it was the last line of the verse, "As we raise our voices in a solemn prayer," which Cayot found particularly objectionable. In an appearance on the Fox News show *Hannity & Colmes*, Cayot pointed out that by requiring students to sing a song "which repeatedly beseeches God to bestow a blessing, which talks about God guiding the nation through the light and through the night with the light from above, and basically says as we raise our voices in a solemn prayer," the school was sending a message that "you cannot be a real American unless you believe in God. . . . He's a fourth grader. They're telling him, 'If you don't believe in God, you're not a real American.'"[64] After the principal, superintendent, and school board president refused to apologize for including "God Bless America" at the assembly and would not agree to discontinue the use of the song, Cayot appealed to the state education commissioner to prohibit the song from being played at school assemblies, arguing that it violated the separation of church and state.[65] Her appeal was dismissed, with the commissioner concluding that "the students were led in singing the song 'God Bless America' for the secular purpose of expressing patriotism and mutual concern," and that the school assembly did not have the effect of endorsing religion.[66]

What is most striking about the Cayot case is the extent to which she appears as a marginalized dissenting voice during this period directly after 9/11, as the imperative of unity in the wake of the attacks overrode any accommodation of a minority point of view. In letters to Westchester's *Journal News* about her case, public opinion was overwhelmingly against her, with only the head of a New York atheist organization writing in her defense.[67] The ACLU declined to take her case, in contrast with their involvement in an effort three years later to remove the words "under God" from the pledge of allegiance.[68] Before Cayot's appearance on Hannity & Colmes, the liberal Colmes confessed that he could not support her position so soon after 9/11.[69] Such stifling of dissent from all sides reveals the coercive elements beneath the sense of unity that emerged in the aftermath of the attacks.

Predictably, Sean Hannity pounced on Cayot during her appearance on his Fox News show, co-opting the language of "tolerance" to criticize her stance: "The Left in America has been lecturing us about how we need to be tolerant and accepting. . . . Most people disagree with you, the overwhelming majority, and it's an opportunity for your son to be tolerant and accepting of how a lot of other people feel because—you know what?— that song's not going to hurt your son in any way."[70] This theme of tolerance and inclusion was also cited by neighbors writing letters to the editor about her case: "How unfortunate that Ms. Cayot did not see this as an opportunity to further her son's education, namely, respect for others. We need more unity and understanding, rather than further separation and selfishness."[71] This connection to the idea of tolerance is an interesting echo of the song's original associations with cultural and religious pluralism in the 1940s—though in this instance, it is the will of the majority that is said to need tolerance, rather than ethnic, racial, or religious minorities.

Of course, it is true that many people found solace within the singing of "God Bless America" after the attacks, and thus Cayot could be considered out of step with—perhaps even "intolerant" of—the majority. But this conservative appropriation of the language of tolerance seems calculated to undermine dissent, since a sense of intolerance for the will of the majority is at the very root of protest. By speaking out, a dissenter is expressing her desire to no longer tolerate the policies of those in power. After 9/11, such a call for accommodation went against the sense of unity that many craved in the aftermath of the attacks. As one letter to the editor admonished, "This woman ought to be completely ashamed of herself. For the first time in such a long time our children are coming together united and proud to be Americans."[72]

Another theme that emerged from the response to Cayot's case is the extent to which many people experience "God Bless America" as a secular song, despite its repeated calls to a higher power. Cayot took pains to mention that it was not the familiar refrain that she objected most to, but the rarely sung verse that defined the song as a prayer. Writing in response to a story about Cayot in the *Journal News*, one local man enthused, "As an atheist, I wouldn't mind 'God Bless America' being our national anthem. It is a great song that I never thought of as religious."[73] And Alan Colmes pointed out to Cayot, "I'm all for, you know, the impenetrable wall they talk about between church and state, but 'God Bless America' has taken on a secular meaning in our society, much like 'In God We Trust' on the coin."[74]

In legal circles, this acceptable level of an interweaving of state and religion is known as "ceremonial deism," a phrase first used in 1962 by Walter Rostow, dean of the Yale Law School, to encompass religious activity that has come to be "accepted as so conventional and uncontroversial as to be constitutional."[75] "God Bless America" easily falls into this category of a generally accepted melding of religion and patriotism. In an article on American popular music, politics, and religion, Katherine Meizel has linked the post-9/11 popularity of songs like "God Bless America" and "God Bless the U.S.A." to the related idea of civil religion, a term coined by Robert Bellah in 1967 to describe a shared set of sacred "beliefs, symbols, and rituals" that permeate American public life.[76]

I should admit that I have this same experience of the song—learned in schools and sung on national holidays, I rarely think of it as a religious song or prayer. And yet, its lyrics do explicitly ask God for blessing, as Cayot herself stated, "if you don't believe in God, you're very aware of the prayerful nature of this song, and that when you mouth these words, you're saying something that is not true in your belief system."[77] This feeling of uttering words the singer does not believe is at the root of the coercive power of communal singing, where the person next to you may wonder why you are not singing along. However, a different kind of dissent emerged in response to the hidden economics of "God Bless America," a confluence of patriotism and profit that sparked controversy about the economic consequences of the song's new function as a vehicle for public mourning.

GOD BLE$$ AMERI©A: ECONOMICS

In the months following 9/11, newspapers began to take note of the economic underpinnings of "God Bless America," with articles pointing out that the song, published in 1939 by Irving Berlin, was under copyright and gathering an increasing sum of royalties as a result of its newfound popularity. Most newspapers were quick to note that Berlin's estate did not make any money on the song, with all royalties given to the God Bless America Fund and it's beneficiaries: the Boy Scouts and Girl Scouts of America.

Headlines in the fall of 2001 conveyed a mixture of enthusiasm and ambivalence to this financial boon, from the *New York Times*'s approving "Irving Berlin Gave the Scouts A Gift of Song" to the *New York Post*'s more provocative "Patriotic Tune's Revival a 'Ble$$ing' for Scouts" to a riff on the song's lyrics from the *Chicago Tribune*: "Through the Night with a Light from a Buck."[78] In that piece, the author provides a summary of all of the channels through which "God Bless America" was making money: synchronization licenses for TV performances ($3,000–4,000 per appearance); publishing fees for music sales (7–8¢ per unit sold), merchandizing fees for anyone wanting to license the phrase "God Bless America" (up to 10 percent of sales); advertising fees (ranging from $5,000 to $500,000, depending on the length and scope of the campaign); and ASCAP "blanket license" fees for private businesses, such as restaurants or baseball stadiums that play recordings of the song. In fact, the dramatic surge in the use of the song and phrase after 9/11 did result in a huge increase in revenue for the God Bless America Fund, from an average of $200,000 per year to more than $900,000 in the period from 1 July 2001 to 30 June 2002.[79]

Within the climate of post-9/11 unity, there was something distasteful about the enormous profits that were being made from the song's use as a mode of public mourning. It was assumed that in that time of crisis, fees would be waived for the public good, but this was not the case for "God Bless America," which Irving Berlin had long ago earmarked for another philanthropic purpose. For example, the God Bless America Fund declined to waive royalty fees from sales of the benefit recording "America: A Tribute to Heroes," an album whose profits otherwise went to the United Way's 9/11 Emergency Fund.[80] When the Oprah Winfrey show called to request a mechanical license so that the song could be played during an appearance by First Lady Laura Bush, they had assumed that royalty fees would be waived, but again, the fund said no.[81]

Bert Fink, the senior VP of communications for the Rodgers & Hammerstein Organization (which oversees the Irving Berlin Music Company and represents the God Bless America Fund), explained their delicate situation as the demand for "God Bless America" skyrocketed after 9/11:

> Our communication response evolved rapidly over the first couple of days as we had to establish, and then expand on, a few key points: number one, there is a song called "God Bless America," which the country was suddenly embracing after 9/11; number two, it was written by somebody, and his name was Irving Berlin; number three, it's under copyright, which means something; number four, the copyright benefits something called the God Bless America Fund; and number five, what is the God Bless America Fund.[82]

As Fink notes, he had a new responsibility to provide the public with a rudimentary education in the functions of music copyright and the place of "God Bless America" within it. There was surprise that a song like "God Bless America," which had entered the American consciousness as an anthem, had actually been composed by someone, and further shock that money was made from its performance—enough surprise that these facts became newsworthy. The end of the Napster era during this same period in the fall of 2001 was also bringing issues of music copyright, which usually linger behind the scenes, to the forefront. Although the recording industry prevailed in their suit against the free music file-sharing company, which adopted a paid subscription model in September 2001, Napster's overriding popularity fostered a sense, especially among young people, that music should be free.[83]

Much of the unease with the economic aspects of "God Bless America" was tempered by the existence of the God Bless America Fund, but this was complicated by the fact that the fund's beneficiaries had themselves become a source of controversy. Since 2000, when the Supreme Court upheld the Boy Scouts' right to exclude gays, the Boy Scouts of America had lost financial support from many of its past funders, the result of a discriminatory policy that went against many corporate sponsors' public commitment to diversity.[84] As the link between royalties from "God Bless America" and the Boy Scouts became more widely known, criticism began to intensify. As Bert Fink wrote in a November 2001 internal memo, "Inevitably, heightened awareness of 'God Bless America' has also drawn attention to the Fund, its support of the Girl Scouts and Boy Scouts, and what executives at the [Boy Scouts of America] refer to as 'the issue'—namely, the Scouts' national gay-discrimination policy."[85] He went on to say that "Since the broadcast of the *Inside Edition* and *NBC Nightly News* features [about "God Bless America"], both of which state that the song's royalties support the Scouts without going into further explanation, I have received inquiring calls from several gay newspaper and radio programs." For example, the *San Francisco Examiner*'s columnist Warren Hinckle lamented, "The insufferable irony is that when 'God Bless America' is being played to honor [Mark] Bingham, the gay hero [of United Flight 93], and the many gays who died in the terrorist kamikaze attack on the twin towers, the royalties are going to an organization which excludes gays. . . . Should gay bars continue to play 'God Bless America' or trade it in for 'America the Beautiful'?"[86]

This controversy posed the next communications challenge for the God Bless America Fund: to distance itself from the national Boy Scouts of America by emphasizing that funds from the God Bless America Fund went to the Greater New York Councils of the Boy Scouts, which broke ranks with the national organization by drafting a nondiscrimination policy that encompassed sexual orientation.[87] In fact, the fund emphasized that continued financial support was contingent upon the New York Boy Scout's ability to demonstrate nondiscrimination. In addition, royalty funds were specifically set aside for children in New York City who were affected by the attacks.[88] These measures stemmed the tide of criticism against the song, but they also reveal the song's economic power, which usually remains comfortably behind the scenes.

CONTINUITIES AND NEW MEANINGS FROM THE BUSH YEARS TO THE AGE OF OBAMA

In the period directly after 9/11, "God Bless America" was embraced to an extent that transcended its earlier associations with conservatism, becoming a sonic emblem of a sense of unity and collective mourning. But by 2003, newly imbued with powerful post-9/11 associations, the song and phrase became instrumental in the Bush administration's campaign to symbolically connect the war in Iraq with the emotive power of the 9/11 attacks.

The phrase even made its way into the military rituals of the president's official declaration of war in March 2003. After President Bush announced, "For the peace of the world and benefit and freedom of the Iraqi people, I hereby give the order to execute Operation Iraqi Freedom. May God Bless the troops," General Tommy Franks responded, "May God bless America," after which the two men exchanged salutes.[89] Soon after becoming a symbol for post-9/11 patriotism and commemoration, the phrase was recruited to serve an official rhetorical purpose, symbolically linking the declaration of war with September 11.[90] And in yet another echo of their spontaneous 9/11 performance just a year and a half before, Congress sang "God Bless America" on the steps of the Capitol while waving flags in an "apparent show of patriotic unity on the war" after Baghdad fell to coalition forces in April 2003.[91] This singing, which had already been reenacted on the first anniversary of the attacks, now served symbolically to link the escalating war in Iraq with the poignancy of public mourning.

The rhetorical power of repeating the congressional performance of "God Bless America" on the steps of the Capitol was also used by those who support the mainstream infusion of religion in public life. In June 2002, when a US Circuit Court of Appeals determined that the inclusion of the words "under God" in the Pledge of Allegiance represented an unconstitutional breach of the separation of church and state, a group of lawmakers gathered on the Capitol steps to recite the pledge in angry protest, after which they erupted into "a spontaneous rendition of 'God Bless America.'"[92] Here, the song's status as a symbol of post-9/11 commemoration served as both evidence of and justification for an accepted intertwining of church and state.

Even as it was embraced as a conservative anthem, the song has continued to be used as a signifier for the inclusion of immigrants in American culture. Citizenship and naturalization ceremonies are a common context in which "God Bless America" appears, echoing Berlin's original understanding of the phrase from his mother, a new immigrant thankful for the life she had found in the United States.[93] In 2006, activists sang "God Bless America" at immigrants' rights rallies across the country, perhaps a reappropriation of the song's use by anti-immigrant conservatives and an unwitting echo of its earlier connection with the inclusion of immigrants in American society.[94]

By the time of the 2008 presidential campaign, the phrase and song "God Bless America" had long been a political imperative. But the song became weighted with new meaning when news outlets reported on the contents of a 2003 sermon given by Barack Obama's pastor Jeremiah Wright, using the song as a symbol within a scathing criticism of US social policies:

The government gives them the drugs, builds bigger prisons, passes a three-strike law and then wants us to sing "God Bless America." No, no, no, God damn America, that's in the Bible for killing innocent people. God damn America for treating our citizens as less than human. God damn America for as long as she acts like she is God and she is supreme.[95]

After the media frenzy surrounding this sermon reached its peak during the 2008 campaign, "God Bless America" became what David Domke and Kevin Coe dubbed the "God and country test," noting that CNN's Anderson Cooper asked Obama, "Just for the record, you have no problem singing 'God Bless America'?"[96] A few days after Wright's sermon became known, Obama ended a speech in Pennsylvania with the phrase "God Bless America," a political trope that some news outlets noted was "rare" and "uncharacteristic" for the candidate.[97]

Given the song's associations with embattled whiteness beginning in the late 1960s, Wright's attack on "God Bless America" had particularly potent symbolism for white voters fearful of Obama's "outsiderness." Ultimately, of course, Obama passed the "'God Bless America' test," but the song's use as a measure of patriotism is an indication of its power as a cultural symbol, imbued with renewed poignancy because of its associations with the memory of post-9/11 solidarity. The recent political uses of "God Bless America" show continuity with the song's previous associations with the triumph of cultural outsiders, as well as with the protest movements of the ideological Right.

During the 2008 campaign, the song "God Bless America" was more prevalent within the McCain/Palin campaign than among Democrats,[98] but it took on new significance after President Obama was elected. With the election of the country's first black president, the song recovered its original meaning of gratitude for a country that allowed an outsider to achieve success—but on a much grander scale. A new subtext was created, expressing gratitude for the country's ability to move beyond a racist past and elect a black president. For example, as the TV critic Alessandra Stanley noted, "Oprah Winfrey walked onto the stage of her postelection special on Wednesday to the tune of 'God Bless America' and just screamed 'Whooooooo!' over and over."[99] At the inauguration, one reporter observed as "uniformed black schoolchildren sang 'God Bless America' en route to the parade, or as close to the parade as they could get."[100] This use of the song as a celebration of racial equality echoes an earlier moment in American history, when Carl Stokes was elected the first black mayor of a major US city in 1967 and told a cheering crowd in Cleveland that he had never before that moment understood "the full meaning of the words 'God Bless America.'"[101]

Yet the song was not the overriding anthem of choice for celebrating Obama's victory. Alex Ross noted the widespread singing of "The Star-Spangled Banner" by gatherings of joyous young people across the country.[102] And "God Bless America" remained absent from official inauguration ceremonies and events—other than a low-profile performance at a pre-inaugural ball.[103] The huge inauguration concert at the Lincoln Memorial featured Pete Seeger leading the crowd in "This Land Is Your Land," followed by Beyoncé performing "America the Beautiful." At the inauguration ceremony itself, Aretha Franklin sang "My Country 'Tis of Thee." In the midst of so many other unofficial anthems, the song's absence—and the president's ongoing preference for the variant "God Bless the United States of America" as his speech-closing phrase—could indicate that the new administration did not want to associate itself with a song so strongly linked to its conservative predecessors in the White House.[104]

Perhaps not surprisingly, the conservative Tea Party revolution that emerged in response to Obama's ascendancy quickly adopted "God Bless America" as a protest anthem. They sang it at an anti-Obama rally in Washington, DC, in September 2009; in Nashville at the first National Tea Party Convention in February 2010; and at Tea Party protests on tax day across the United States.[105] These examples echo the song's use by right-wing activists during the 1970s and 80s, while also drawing on the song's associations with a post-9/11 sense of unity against a common enemy.[106] In the years since the attacks, the song has again become a wedge rather than a unifying symbol, resuming its place as an emblem for the Right in a polarized twenty-first-century America.

Immediately after 9/11, "God Bless America" took on a new, powerful role as a vehicle for public commemoration and a catalyst for unity. On the flip side of this sense of unity lies the song's coercive power, perceived by some as a tool of indoctrination. But just after the attacks, dissent against "God Bless America" was often silenced or ignored, seen as a betrayal of a national solidarity forged in the wake of the attacks. At the same time, the public ambivalence surrounding the song's economic underpinnings—and the enormous spike in royalty fees as a result of its post-9/11 popularity—reveal the complex relationship between the business of music and a song's absorption into American culture.

The song's newfound popularity can be traced to its spontaneous performance on the steps of the Capitol on 9/11, but my attempt to chronicle the events that led to that congressional performance reveals the inherent difficulty of untangling collective action, as well as the murky territory between memory and history. As Jay Winter has noted in his study of war and memory in the twentieth century, "In virtually all acts of remembrance, history and memory are braided together in the public domain, jointly informing our shifting and contested understandings of the past."[107] The Egyptologist Jan Assman's idea of "mnemohistory"—the study of the remembered past—is as relevant to the recent history of 9/11 as it is to ancient Egypt: "The present is 'haunted' by the past and the past is modeled, invented, reinvented, and reconstructed by the present."[108] This sense of a constructed past has been with "God Bless America" from its beginnings, as its origin story was carefully crafted and contested when the song first became popular in the late 1930s.

Looking back to the song's early history reveals striking similarities between its public reception in the early 1940s and after the 9/11 attacks: the spontaneous eruptions of communal singing; the profusion of articles about the song; an outcry related to the song's copyright; the negative response by those who disagreed with the song's message, followed by a coercion that silenced dissenters. After the United States entered World War II, the song continued to be embraced as part of a public desire for national unity, as this description of the first World War II–era blackout in New York City illustrates:

> On the West Side in tenements around Ninth Avenue and Forty-fourth Street a peculiar patriotic fervor swept the neighborhood. Someone hidden in darkness burst into the opening strains of "God Bless America." Other voices in other windows and in the street caught up the tune. It swelled in volume and in fervency of pitch into thrilling chorus. Men's, women's and children's voices blended in the music. It could be heard two streets east in the blackout quiet.[109]

Composed during World War I and first performed in the period just before the US entered World War II, the song possesses a distinct emotional power in times of national crisis.

But what does "God Bless America" mean in a post–post-9/11 world? The next chapter examines the song's continued use in professional baseball, where it was added to the game's ritualized pageantry just after 9/11 and has remained a persistent part of our national pastime.

CHAPTER 6

✧

My Home Sweet Home (Plate)

Baseball and "God Bless America"

It is the only form of field sport known where spectators have an important part and actually participate in the game. . . . [A]ll America has come to regard Base Ball as its very own, to be known throughout the civilized world as the great American National Game.
—Albert G. Spaulding, *America's National Game* (1911)[1]

When professional baseball resumed play after a six-day hiatus following the 9/11 attacks, teams across the country added "God Bless America" to the seventh-inning stretch, infusing what had been a lighthearted break in the game with a sober patriotism that captured the public mood.[2] In fact, baseball stadiums are among the few public venues in which the singing of "God Bless America" persisted after 9/11; most Broadway shows stopped the practice after a few months, and the song was not included in the patriotic display at the Super Bowl's pre-game ceremony in February 2002.[3] Singing "God Bless America" has now become a sustained tradition within the pageantry of professional baseball, offering a unique opportunity to examine the song's public functions in the years following the attacks.

On 14 September 2001, the commissioner of Major League Baseball (MLB) sent a memo to the teams with instructions about appropriate patriotic ceremonies and commemorations to accompany their first games:

In memory of the victims of the horrific tragedy that occurred last Tuesday in New York and Washington, I am asking all clubs to make sure they include the following components in their plans:

- Observe a moment of silence prior to each game until further notice.
- Fly flags at half mast until further notice.
- In addition to the playing of the national anthem, each club should ask its fans to sing "God Bless America" either prior to the game or during the seventh-inning stretch.
- All players and field personnel should be standing on the top steps of the dugout (or at the baseline) with their hats over their hearts during the playing of the national anthem.[4]

These recommendations stayed in place for the remaining months of the 2001 season. In 2002, a memo from MLB scaled back the suggested frequency of "God Bless America," stating that it "should be sung at the seventh-inning stretch on national holidays (Memorial Day, Fourth of July, and Labor Day) during the season, on September 11, and as part of Sunday games."[5] A slightly revised policy laid out in a 2004 memo has remained in place ever since:

> For all home openers, and games played on Sundays, Holidays and Saturday, September 11th, the break between the top and the bottom of the seventh inning should be used for the playing of "God Bless America." Visiting Club players should assume their fielding positions and all other field personnel should be on the field with caps removed.[6]

These memos underscore the alliance between commercial and community interests within the realm of professional baseball. Major League Baseball occupies a strange in-between space between the public and private spheres. It is a for-profit enterprise deemed exempt from antitrust laws by a 1922 Supreme Court decision that stressed its status as a game rather than a business.[7] In addition, some privately owned team franchises play in stadiums financed by taxpayers, creating public facilities that sportswriter Dave Zirin calls "monuments to extortion and corporate welfare."[8] The sociologist Michael Ian Borer takes a kinder view of the tensions between the corporate and community interests within baseball, as he writes: "Of course, claims of civic pride and community-building can be used to mask the business interests of elite firms and groups, but that does not address the motivations behind the business that fans and spectators bring to the ballpark. Are consumption and fan loyalty that far apart? Not at all."[9] For Borer, baseball *is* different from other corporate ventures, with fans and team franchises joining in partnership to support their team. The new tradition of "God Bless America" foregrounds this tension between the commercial and the communal within baseball, created by a corporate directive that served the needs of a grieving public directly after 9/11.[10]

On 29 March 2003—ten days after the United States invaded Iraq—a small item in the sports section of the *New York Times* illustrated a repositioning of "God Bless America" from 9/11 tribute to pro-war anthem: "Major League Baseball teams will pay tribute to the United States armed forces and the nation by having 'God Bless America' sung during the seventh-inning stretch of all home openers."[11] This shift is a surprisingly direct example of the ways in which a genuine post-9/11 desire for patriotic unity was later appropriated to serve as a symbol of support for the Iraq war. Tributes to first responders became tributes to the troops fighting first in Afghanistan and then Iraq, as commemoration of the tragedy elided with support for the military response.

Two sports columns addressing the addition of "God Bless America" to the rituals of baseball highlight the contrast in the public response to the song between the fall of 2001 and the beginning of the Iraq war in 2003. Writing in the *New York Times* on the one-month anniversary of the attacks, Ira Berkow described the poignancy of "God Bless America" in the weeks following 9/11:

> I want to miss "Take Me Out to the Ball Game." I want to miss the inanity of it, of the peanuts and the Cracker Jack and not caring if I never get back. And I indeed miss the time, a lifetime ago, a hundred thousand years ago, it seems, in a world now so utterly unrecognizable, so relatively benign, that we could indeed forget our problems for three hours at a ballpark.
>
> Now, at the seventh-inning stretch in baseball games, instead of the traditional "Take Me Out to the Ball Game," they are playing "God Bless America."
>
> I like "God Bless America," too. And I've been in ballparks in the last few weeks in which they've played it. I've stood, with the rest of the fans, and the ballplayers, who come out and stand in front of the dugouts and appear to be singing their hearts out like the others while facing the fluttering American flag.
>
> It is moving. The game stops dead in its tracks and we remember the atrocities committed at the World Trade Center and at the Pentagon, and the battle in the plane that crashed in Pennsylvania, as well as the bravery and goodness of so many in response.
>
> But I miss that sweet song, "Take Me Out to the Ball Game," that ode to triviality.
>
> "God Bless America" halts the dream world to recall the nightmare. . . . So we go to the pleasure domes that are our playgrounds, and, unable yet to suspend disbelief, we sing with often moist eyes not "Take Me Out to the Ball Game" but "God Bless America."

It's what we need for now. After all, it's still letting us, with raised voices, "root, root, root for the home team."[12]

But by 2003, the sheen had worn off the song's continued inclusion within baseball for some fans. Gersh Kuntzman, then a columnist with the *New York Post* and *Newsweek* Online, wrote his own piece dedicated to "God Bless America" in July 2003, with a decidedly post–post-9/11 tone:

> If you call yourself a baseball fan, you'll no doubt agree. Since 18 September 2001—when Major League baseball returned after the terror attacks—the song "God Bless America" has pushed aside "Take Me Out to the Ballgame" as the new seventh-inning tradition. For the first few months, who could object? It provided catharsis and comfort—a way for Americans to grieve together.
>
> Most teams have continued the "tradition" to this day. . . . And this song is not merely *played* between the top and bottoms of the seventh inning. It is ponderously intoned with all the subtlety of a Mussolini speech. A stadium announcer—typically the same guy who was screaming, "Let's Get Ready to Rummmmblllllle!" only minutes earlier—solemnly tells the crowd to rise in "tribute" to the soldiers who are defending our "way of life." The players stop wherever they are, doff their caps, place them over their hearts and stand at attention. . . . A somber, maudlin feeling fills the air. And the song begins.[13]

Kuntzman goes on to critique the song itself, which he hates, and laments that these renditions of "God Bless America" during the seventh-inning stretch "embody some great things about America—the community, the notion of shared sacrifice—and *all* of the worst things: the self-righteous pride, the forced piety, the earnest self-reverence, the smugness."

Over time, the song would lose its post-9/11 poignancy even for Ira Berkow, who in 2008 wrote an addendum of sorts to his October 2001 column, calling for the regular practice of singing "God Bless America" to come to an end: "No one, in our lifetime certainly, will ever forget the horror of 11 September 2001. I see no need, except perhaps for holidays, to be reminded of it on a regular basis at a ball game."[14]

Examining the changing meanings and functions of "God Bless America" within professional baseball reveals tensions between sincere commemoration and patriotism on one hand, and a sense of coercion and usurpation of older baseball traditions on the other. The research presented here draws on interviews of executives and staff at MLB headquarters and at five professional baseball stadiums: the New York Mets, Boston Red Sox, and San Francisco Giants in the major leagues; and the Staten Island Yankees and Pawtucket Red Sox (Paw Sox) at the minor-league level. In addition to these interviews and observations, current attitudes about the song were gathered in an online survey, in order to capture the viewpoints of as wide a swath of baseball fans as possible. The survey was completed by 1,849 respondents during the summer of 2009.

Those aware that the New York Yankees play "God Bless America" at every game may wonder why the team is excluded from this list of primary research sites. Unfortunately, Yankees staff declined to participate in my research, although I did observe the song in action at Yankee Stadium. And because a link to my survey was posted on a popular Yankees blog, more than half of all survey participants self-identified as Yankees fans, ensuring that their perspectives are well represented.

PRELUDE: A BRIEF HISTORY OF MUSIC AT THE BALLPARK

Music has become a constant presence at contemporary baseball games, beginning with the national anthem before the game ("The Star Spangled Banner," and "O Canada" when appropriate) and "Take Me Out to the Ball Game" during the seventh-inning stretch. In addition to these ritualized performances, a soundtrack of recorded pop music is ever present, accompanying the action on the field and entertaining the crowd between innings. Many teams play a specific "at-bat" song for each home team player as they walk to the plate, often serving as a projection of a player's identity through the use of coded musical genres such as country, hard rock, hip-hop, and salsa.[15]

This infusion of music within professional baseball is a product of modern technological advances. Before the mid-twentieth century, most baseball games were conducted without any musical accompaniment whatsoever. Bands were present in nineteenth-century games, but as professional baseball expanded and stadiums increased in size, it became too expensive for teams to hire bands to play at every game, so music was usually played only on special occasions, such as opening day, national holidays, and the World Series.[16] The first permanent public-address system was installed by the New York Giants in 1929, and it wasn't until 1941 that the Chicago Cubs became the first team to add an organ in their stadium.[17] The sound of the organ remained at the heart of music at baseball stadiums until the 1970s and '80s, when teams began to play recorded pop music to appeal to younger fans.[18] (The Cubs are the only major league team to continue to rely exclusively on the organ, though many teams still use an organ in addition to recorded sound.) The inclusion of "God Bless America" fits within both the traditions of live performance and the newer introduction of prerecorded music, since some teams choose to recruit a singer to perform it live and others opt to play a recording.

And how did the national anthem come to be played before every game? Famously penned by Francis Scott Key in 1814 and set to the drinking song "To Anacreon in Heaven," "The Star-Spangled Banner" quickly became popular and was often played at public ceremonies during the nineteenth and early-twentieth centuries, long before it attained its state-mandated role as the official national anthem.[19] Within baseball, a *Brooklyn Eagle* article from May 1862 noted that a band played "The Star-Spangled Banner" at the opening game of the new Union Base Ball and Cricket Grounds, one of the country's first enclosed baseball parks.[20] In the twentieth century, it was first played at a professional baseball game at Chicago's Wrigley Field, during the 1918 World Series between the Cubs and the Red Sox. Amid the patriotic fervor of this wartime period, the seventh-inning stretch (which did not yet include "Take Me Out to the Ball Game") was given over to a salute to the flag, during which the band "spontaneously" began to play "The Star-Spangled Banner."[21] When the 1918 series moved to Boston, the song was performed at a ceremony before each game. This new tradition of playing the song before special games continued after the war ended, but the expense of hiring a band large enough to be heard without amplification prohibited "The Star-Spangled Banner" from becoming a regular part of all games, even after it became the official national anthem by an act of Congress in 1931.

The playing of the national anthem became a permanent part of professional baseball during the years leading up to the US entry into World War II—the same period in which "God Bless America" became overwhelmingly popular. Inspired by Canadian hockey teams that played their anthem when Canada entered the war in 1939, the practice became nearly universal by 1941.[22] The anthem provided a public venue for the demonstration of patriotism by players and fans, both, perhaps, plagued by concerns that playing and attending a baseball game was not appropriate during wartime. Richard Crepeau, the sports historian, describes how this wartime convention became permanent: "Four years of war, followed by the Cold War and the emergence of the American Empire solidified the practice and made it into a national ritual."[23] The playing of the national anthem at sporting events has certainly been contested over the years, especially in the wake of the black power protest during the playing of the anthem at the 1968 Olympics, as well as subsequent racially charged incidents in which African

American athletes refused to stand for the anthem.[24] But despite such protests, the tradition persists to this day in baseball, as well as in almost every other American sport.[25]

When "God Bless America" was added to professional baseball games in 2001, the song already had a long history of connection with sports. There are frequent references to the song being played at Brooklyn Dodgers games in the 1940s; in 1966 the Chicago White Sox briefly replaced the national anthem with "God Bless America," a song the team felt was easier for fans to sing, though Irving Berlin himself urged the team to return to the national anthem.[26] In the 1970s, replacing the anthem with "God Bless America" became a good-luck charm for the Philadelphia Flyers hockey team, and by 1978 the team's cumulative record when the song was played stood at fifty-two wins, seven losses, and two ties since the song was first played in December 1969.[27] The song and Kate Smith's performance of it have taken on near-mythic status within the culture of the Flyers, who often invited the singer to perform it live and later erected a statue in Smith's honor outside the stadium.[28] Some even argue that the phrase "It ain't over 'til the fat lady sings" originates with Smith's live performances of "God Bless America" at Flyers games.[29]

While "God Bless America" effectively replaced "Take Me Out to the Ball Game" after 9/11, today the two songs are often juxtaposed, sharing the sonic space of the seventh-inning stretch. Like "God Bless America," "Take Me Out to the Ball Game" has roots in Tin Pan Alley, written in 1908 by Albert von Tilzer and Jack Norworth, two songwriters who claimed they had never attended a baseball game when they wrote their hit tune.[30] The song attained extraordinary popularity in its day, but singing it during the seventh-inning stretch became standard practice only when the broadcaster Harry Caray's iconic off-key performances became famous among Chicago White Sox fans in the 1970s. The song didn't become a universal ritual of professional baseball until the early 1980s, when Caray moved across town to the Cubs, where the games were broadcast nationally.[31]

The practical aspects of adding "God Bless America" to the seventh-inning stretch are worth noting. While the singing of "Take Me Out to the Ball Game" takes place while the players are warming up between innings, "God Bless America" represents a complete break in the game, in which players stand outside their dugouts, facing the flag in the outfield, just as when the national anthem is played. Because of this, "God Bless America" adds time to the break between innings, a unique infringement onto the field by ballpark music, which usually accompanies rather than intrudes upon the game itself. In fact, some have argued that this break can impact the game's outcome. This was especially true of live performances at Yankee

Figure 6.1
Kate Smith Statue outside the Wachovia Spectrum arena, home of the Philadelphia Flyers.
Photograph by Wally Gobetz.

Stadium by Irish tenor Ronan Tynan, who performed a slow rendition of the song (further extended by his inclusion of the rarely heard verse) during post-season games. Critics have said that this kind of elaborate performance can allow the opposing pitchers' arms to cool off and tighten, as the managers of both the Minnesota Twins and the Boston Red Sox publicly complained during the 2003 playoffs.[32] During the regular season, time constraints for performances of "God Bless America" are often strictly enforced, which effectively limits the song's live performances to solo singers or instrumentalists, who can move on and off the field quickly.[33] The Yankees appear to have responded to these time limits by truncating Kate Smith's recorded performance, cutting the musical introduction and the repeat of the song's last phrase to keep their regular inclusion of the song within the time allotted for the seventh-inning stretch.

And why were Sunday games chosen as the appropriate day for the regular inclusion of "God Bless America"? Vito Vitiello, the producer of video and entertainment for the Mets, told me that Sundays are more "old-school baseball traditional, with more organ music," noting that they play more "kids programming and more old time stuff."[34] Tim Gunkel, the Mets' senior director of marketing production, added that Sundays are more geared toward "the older camp from baseball that wants to hear no popular music, that wants to go back to the days of the organ, and silence."[35] "God Bless America," which is imbued with nostalgia for a bygone era, fits in well with this nostalgic soundscape of Sunday baseball games. On a sonic level, the inclusion of "God Bless America" is also less jarring during a Sunday game, when the sound of the organ is more prevalent than hip hop and heavy metal. In addition, playing the song on a day that many Americans associate with church—a connection perhaps reinforced by the sound of the stadium organ—may have been a conscious choice, a day when a song invoking God at the ballpark may have seemed more appropriate.

BASEBALL RITUALS, INVENTED TRADITIONS, AND PUBLIC MEMORY

Many scholars have linked the experience of modern spectator sports with the experience of religion, arguing that sports follow a set of traditions and rituals, inspire faith, and take place in the bounded, sacred space of the arena.[36] These scholars often cite Emile Durkheim's notion of secular ritual in pointing out that at root, the ceremonies of sports serve to forge community allegiance.[37] In her sociological study of Brazilian soccer, Janet Lever points out that fans come not only to watch the action on the field but to watch each other: "Sport is staged in the round, in the center of a stadium, so the spectator confronts the emotion apparent on the faces of other spectators and is made even more aware of the mass of humanity sharing the event."[38] Lever also notes that sports have become one of the few acceptable sites for true group participation:

> In a time of increasing sophistication and skepticism, people seem reluctant to leave their private shells to enter the mass mood. Things that were once sacred now seem "hokey." And sporting events seem to be the last bastion of hokey. Fans will abandon so much reserve that they can scream "CHARGE" and join in songs like "Take Me out to the Ball Game."[39]

Communal singing is both a sonic manifestation of the solidarity of the fan and the epitome of a "hokey" declaration of group membership, so it makes sense that it was already imbedded within the rituals of professional baseball, long before 9/11. The singing of both the national anthem and "Take Me Out to the Ball Game" also commemorate specific moments in time, creating a ritualized space where singing is expected, thus allowing participants to bypass traditional inhibitions about singing in public.

These rituals, though peripheral to the game itself, are critical to the maintenance of the nostalgic sense of history that surrounds baseball as a cultural practice. Michael Ian Borer views this aspect of baseball as a manifestation of collective memory, which he defines as "the story, or stories, that people know and generally accept as history."[40] In addition, Eric Hobsbawm's concept of an "invented tradition"—a new ritual that implies an invented sense of continuity with the past—can certainly be applied to baseball traditions.[41] The singing of the national anthem and "Take Me Out to the Ball Game" are often assumed to be as old as baseball itself but are, in fact, products of the mid- and late-twentieth century.

In his study of commemoration in twentieth-century America, John Bodnar frames his concept of public memory and commemoration as a negotiation between the "vernacular culture" of everyday people and the "official culture" put forward by those in power.[42] These two forces can be seen at play within commemorative performances of "God Bless America," which often involve a feeling of sincere public commemoration on the one hand and a sense of imposed patriotism on the other.

THE BALLPARK AS CIVIC SPACE: SHEA STADIUM AND 9/11

Michael Ian Borer notes that baseball stadiums play an important role in civic culture by hosting a myriad of non-baseball events, including concerts, charity events, political rallies, and religious ceremonies.[43] After 9/11, this role as a public gathering place was dramatically felt in New York, where Yankee Stadium served as the venue for "Prayer for America," the first formal, large-scale memorial program for victims of the attacks.[44] Shea Stadium, the former home of the new York Mets until the construction of Citi Field in 2009, fulfilled a different kind of civic purpose after 9/11, not simply used as a gathering space for non-baseball events but requisitioned to serve as a supply center for work crews at Ground Zero.[45] As Tim Gunkel told me as we sat in the stands before a game:

Shea Stadium is a city facility, and in the immediate aftermath of 9/11, this was a transportation and supply depot, and so Mets employees and all kinds of city workers were here. It was a distribution center for donated goods. . . . And then they were running a full schedule of city buses to and from Shea so that the workers were going down to the site to do rescue. . . . Riding down and then riding back at night, they were leaving their cars parked here. So this became an emergency staging center. . . . There were gates set up with cots to house emergency workers who couldn't go home, but needed a place to sleep, and eat something. . . . They literally turned the gates of the building into dormitories, and food, and warehouses.[46]

During that time of crisis and mobilization, the stadium became much more than simply a place to watch a ball game. And baseball itself became an important symbol of a sense that life could move on in the face of the attacks. Gunkel noted that even as the stadium had taken on its new civic role,

these questions about, "Should we play a game?" were happening. So some people were saying, "You know what? We shouldn't. We should just keep doing what we're doing. It's too soon to play a game." And other people felt it's important to resume normalcy. It was important just for reasons of public morale, and of New York showing that it could continue, and it could bounce back after anything, no matter how bad.[47]

For many, baseball's return was seen as both a normalizing force and a venue for public gathering and commemoration. As Mets player Todd Zeile told a reporter about his experiences paying visits to Manhattan hospitals in the days following the attacks, "People were saying they couldn't wait to have a baseball game to go to or watch on TV. It gives you some sense of stability. People wanted to see something that felt like the normal mid-September time in their lives."[48]

When the Mets played their first home game on 21 September, the team's entertainment staff sought to construct a pre-game ceremony that somehow simultaneously honored heroes, mourned the dead, and celebrated the city's strength. The ceremonies featured a color guard representing emergency responders, a performance of "Amazing Grace" by police bagpipers, a large flag unfurled by members of the Merchant Marines, a moment of silence, a twenty-one-gun salute by the Marine Corps, and, of course, a performance of "God Bless America"—in this case sung by Diana Ross backed by two gospel choirs—followed by Marc Anthony singing the national anthem.[49] Gunkel remembered the event:

It was a moment for New York. I mean, it was the first major pro sports event after the attacks of 9/11. But it really had this feeling of catharsis, or a healing moment for the city where people felt it was okay to cheer for something. And in this case, it started out with cheering for the police and firefighters, and the EMS people and the military, and again there were representatives of all the branches that lost people in the Twin Towers. So it was very emotional. But the fans started out kind of being able to cheer for them. And that opened up something that said, "All right, it's okay for us to cheer, and for this to be a celebration of the good people and the good stuff," as opposed to a memorial ceremony. . . . Because we have the first game back. No one's done anything big to acknowledge what happened. You can see the stage for something that should be very somber. And that's not really baseball's place traditionally.[50]

"God Bless America" was one of a series of patriotic symbols that acknowledged the tragedy of 9/11 but then allowed spectators to melt into the crowd and the game.

Figure 6.2
Diana Ross sings "God Bless America" during the pre-game ceremony at Shea Stadium on 21 September 2001. Photograph by Barton Silverman/The *New York Times*/Redux.

Later in that first game, Liza Minnelli performed the song "New York, New York" during the seventh-inning stretch. Rather than reintroducing a vehicle for mourning (as "God Bless America" would have), her performance became a celebration:

> She came out with a line of firefighters. All of the police and the firefighters and the EMS that were here for the game were our guests in the picnic area. And she grabbed a bunch of them and said, "Come on out with me," and she actually sang it with them in a little kick line, and it went over huge, because she sang it with a lot of spirit and love for New York. And the firefighters were this kind of symbol of all the people who were pitching in, and trying to make things better in the aftermath. . . . It worked really beautifully, and the crowd loved it. And there was also something about the game—the game had a big home run, kind of like a big comeback. But everything about it felt like New York City is coming back now. We're coming back.[51]

For the fans, the event appeared to symbolize more than just New York's comeback, connecting to a sincere post-9/11 patriotism, as one reporter wrote: "After the final out, Ray Charles's 'America The Beautiful' serenaded the crowd from the loudspeakers. Many fans stood and sung along, waving flags and holding banners. They chanted 'U.S.A.!' as the announcer read off the statistics for the game."[52] Mike Piazza had hit a game-winning home run, and the fans had triumphed over fear of another attack just by showing up. The ballpark provided a public gathering place for commemoration that allowed space for mourning as well as the illusion of normalcy represented by a September baseball game, a temporary reprieve from the brutal reality of 9/11.

Today, the Mets follow the MLB policy to play "God Bless America" only on Sundays and holidays, even while their rivals in the Bronx continue to play the song at every game. Although they receive angry letters questioning their patriotism and arguing that the song should be played every day, Vito Vitiello explained their decision this way:

> I do relate ["God Bless America"] to post-9/11, and you don't want to forget. You never want to forget. . . . But the thing is, you come here—this is an outlet of entertainment. You don't want to be constantly reminded either. And I think that's the case with a whole lot of people where they don't mind the fact that we keep it on a limited basis with playing the song. Because we just want this to be an outlet—you know if you have troubles at home, if you have troubles at your job, you want to come here and forget all that. And that also sort of happens with 9/11, too. You don't want to forget about it, but you know what? You need something to distract you, too, every so often.[53]

THE CEREMONIES OF BASEBALL: COMMUNITY, VIRTUOSITY, AND PARTICIPATION

My interviews and observations with the Mets took place on 25 May 2008—it was Memorial Day and a Sunday, either day reason enough to play "God Bless America." Before the game, I shadowed Greg Romano, who was then the Mets' associate producer of entertainment, responsible for coordinating a dizzying sequence of military-themed, pre-game pomp. Clutching my field pass, I stood on the edge of the field behind home plate, behind a group of military personnel waiting their turn to go onto the field. A Marine Corps band was playing "Stars and Stripes Forever," and when they took up the strains of the Marine Corps anthem ("The Halls of Montezuma"), the Marines in front of me stood at attention. A local fireman (and lifelong Mets fan) officially reenlisted into the US Navy in a short ceremony on the field near home plate, and then the Marines standing near me, who would soon deploy to Iraq, stepped forward to be honored by an enthusiastic ovation from the fans. After a color guard took the field and a moment of silence was observed in honor of fallen soldiers, the Marine band played the national anthem. I watched Romano on the phone as he coordinated the timing of a military flyover, cuing the pilot so that the warplanes filled the sky above the stadium (and drowned out the sound of the band) just after the anthem's last phrase, "home of the brave"—an impressive spectacle by any measure.[54]

These pre-game ceremonies provide a venue for civic engagement, creating public space for the recognition of local community members and fostering a sense of community participation. They also are ideal venues for the celebration of civic holidays and secular rituals that can serve to unite a diverse community of fans. Different teams embrace holidays and "theme dates" to different extents, and the Mets appear to have a particularly large number of special games; that year, they included eleven "community dates" welcoming specific local neighborhoods, fifteen "health awareness dates" aimed at education about various diseases, fifteen "heritage dates" celebrating different ethnic groups, and twenty-eight other "theme dates" honoring an array of civic groups, issues, and holidays.[55] At a Red Sox game in September 2009, Dan Lyons, manager of entertainment and special event operations, told me that the pre-game ceremony participants are chosen as they relate to the theme date: "Today just happens to be Grandparents Day. So we selected a grandmother who sang the anthem. I had a one-hundred-year-old grandfather who threw out the first pitch. . . . And our 'God Bless America' singer today is an eighty-seven-year-old vet who's in a wheelchair."[56] Marty Ray, the Red Sox public affairs manager, added

that these themes "make our pre-game ceremonies and our in-game entertainment a little more meaningful, kind of serve a community purpose."

Although the emphasis on honoring the military at the Mets game was
obviously heightened because of Memorial Day, such connections to national identity and the military have been a regular presence at baseball
games since the early twentieth century.[57] During World War I, professional baseball found itself battling accusations of a lack of patriotism by
putting men on the playing field as others went to war.[58] As a result, the
1918 World Series between the Cubs and the Red Sox—the game at which
"The Star-Spangled Banner" was first played at the professional level—
became a venue for overt patriotic displays, with players marching in
military-style drills, carrying baseball bats like rifles. Today, most teams
have a military color guard take the field as the national anthem is played.
On the rare occasion that the Mets do not have a live performance of "God
Bless America," they play a recording by the Air Force band. And in a dramatic example of the link between baseball players and soldiers, the San
Diego Padres, who call themselves "the Team of the Military," play a series
of military appreciation games in which players wear a desert camouflage
version of their team uniform.[59]

In keeping with the military theme on Memorial Day at Shea Stadium in
2008, "God Bless America" was sung by a Marine from the Sixth Communications Battalion in Brooklyn, Sgt. Elizabeth Quinones.[60] An aspiring singer,
Sgt. Quinones works as a Food Service Marine when not sent out by her
battalion on performance detail. Before she took the field during the seventh-inning stretch, Greg Romano helped position a monitor in her ear;
Shea Stadium's antiquated sound system had just one speaker, and the echo
effect was so dramatic that most singers needed a monitor to hear themselves and avoid being thrown off by the delayed sound of their own voice.

Quinones stood on the field near home plate, facing the stands. Her performance was virtuosic—as virtuosic as a simple song like "God Bless
America" can be—featuring grace notes, appoggiaturas, slurs, trills, and
scoops borrowed from the performance practices of gospel, R&B, and pop.
(See fig. 6.4 for a map of the ornamentation within this performance. The
recording, complete with echo effect, is track 7 on the companion website. ◐)

Such musical embellishments have become almost standardized in the
song's live performances. This could be partly the result of the stylistic influence of the television show *American Idol* and its emphasis on "artistic
uniqueness" as a key requirement of performances.[61] *American Idol* stars are
often tapped to perform the song, especially in post-season games that are
televised on Fox (the same network that broadcasts *Idol*), thus providing
some easy cross-promotion. A brief analysis of two seventh-inning stretch

Figure 6.3
Sgt. Elizabeth Quinones at Shea Stadium in 2007. Photograph by Karim Delgado.

---

       scoop   *trill*   *octave↑* *trill*
God bless A<u>merica</u>, <u>land</u> that <u>I</u>   <u>love</u>

       slur   *trill slur APP↓*   *ANT*   *ANT*   *trill*
Stand be<u>side</u> her <u>and</u> <u>guide</u> <u>her</u>, though the <u>night</u> with a <u>light</u> from a<u>bove</u>

            APP↓   *APP↓*   *scoop*   *APP↓*
From the moun<u>tains</u>, to the prai<u>ries</u>, to the <u>oceans</u> white with <u>foam</u>

trill   *APP↓*   *APP↓*   *trill* *scoop* *2-syll scoop*
<u>God</u> <u>bless</u> Ameri<u>ca</u>,   <u>my</u>   <u>home</u> <u>sweet</u> <u>home</u>,

trill *ANT↓* *app↑*   *scoop* *ANT↓* *APP↓*   *trill scoop* *melisma trill*
<u>God</u> <u>bless</u> <u>A-</u>   <u>mer-</u> <u>i-</u>   <u>ca</u>,   <u>my</u> <u>home</u> <u>sweet</u> <u>home</u>

Lyrics with ornamentation are <u>underlined</u>
APP: appoggiatura
ANT: anticipation

Figure 6.4
Map of ornamentation in Sgt. Elizabeth Quinones's performance.

renditions of "God Bless America" by former *American Idol* stars Diana De-Garmo and Kelly Clarkson shows that some of Sgt. Quinones's embellishments have become standard within the performance practice of pop virtuosity—these include the same trill on the word "love" of "land that I love," and embellishments on the words "light" and "foam," and the final "sweet home."[62] These interpretive choices may also have been influenced by two contemporary recordings of the song: LeAnn Rimes's rendition from 1997 on her album *You Light Up My Life*, and Celine Dion's 2001 performance from the *America: A Tribute to Heroes* benefit concert. (Links to these performances are available on the companion website. ◑)

Sgt. Quinones's decision to follow Berlin's score and remain on the low octave on the song's final words sets her performance apart from other virtuosic singers (and Kate Smith herself), ending the song not with triumph but a quiet sincerity. In our interview, Quinones described her approach to this kind of public performance:

> My purpose here is to bring something to the people, and to touch their lives. So I take these songs very seriously. I mean, Marines think I'm practically crying up on stage because I—I just take it seriously. I'm in the military, of course I'm going to take it seriously. I think about all my brothers and sisters who are serving, and it does get kind of emotional. So yeah, I take it seriously, and you will hear it when I perform.[63]

In contrast to Irving Berlin's feeling that the song was not appropriate for soldiers to sing during World War I, by 2008 "God Bless America" had taken on a distinct emotional power when performed by military personnel, tapping into the song's connection to the 9/11 attacks and the sacrifices of soldiers in the ensuing wars.

The crowd cheered loudly after Sgt. Quinones's forceful, emotional rendition—and the security guard outside the green room behind home plate told her that it gave him chills—but very few fans sang along. In fact, everything about the performance positioned it as something to be listened to, from the singer's emotional intensity to the melodic embellishments that render the simple melody unpredictable for those who might otherwise join in. Quinones told me that often listeners are "just like, 'Whoa! We didn't expect all that. We can't even follow her now,' you know? 'I can't even sing the song any more!' . . . They start singing and then I start doing all this other stuff, and they're like, 'Okay, forget it.' But they appreciate it."

This question of whether "God Bless America" should serve as a vehicle for solo performance or for group singing can be seen within all of the musical performances that I observed at baseball stadiums. In discussing the

Mets' choice to use the Air Force band recording of "God Bless America" rather than a vocal track, Tim Gunkel pointed out that an instrumental version is "more conducive to having the crowd sing along. It feels more accessible. You're not competing—if you used a famous singer version, sometimes it's like, [we should] stop and listen, not try and sing with them. But having an instrumental with the lyrics, the crowd's voice can be the thing."[64] But the Mets use this instrumental version only as backup, in the rare case that the scheduled performer isn't able to sing. For the Mets, the vitality of a live performance is more important than a recording's predictable capacity to foster a sing-along.

Such performances are yet another way that teams use the public space of ballparks to connect with their communities, often showcasing local performers. Many teams recruit amateur or professional musicians to perform the national anthem, and some have extended this practice to "God Bless America." Teams often use different performers for the two songs, using the addition of "God Bless America" to expand the opportunities for participation by local performers. When I spoke with staff and executives from teams that use a live performance of the song, many emphasized that these performances offered an important link to their communities. Some teams stage public *American Idol*–style auditions, which act as further connections to the broader community. In larger markets and during high-profile post-season games, the performers tend to be more famous but often still have a connection to the local community—like Tony Bennett in San Francisco or Broadway stars at Mets games—so these performances can serve as a source of pride for home team fans.

Other teams prefer the predictability of a recording. During the 2008 and 2009 seasons, the New York Yankees, San Francisco Giants, and minor-league Pawtucket Red Sox regularly played Kate Smith's iconic rendition, substituting a live performance only on special occasions.[65] These taped renditions tend to result in a "karaoke effect," with more fans singing along because of the familiarity of the recording, rather than a solo performance where fans play the more passive role of a listening audience. A higher level of virtuosity often inhibits participation, but musicians can modify their performances to encourage participation, with a slower tempo, minimal embellishment, and a lower, more accessible key. (In fact, the low key of the Kate Smith recording likely contributes to its effectiveness as a vehicle for sing-alongs, since its alto range is generally comfortable for both men and women to sing.)

Although I observed many games at different ballparks, it is not possible to pinpoint the specific reasons behind the varying levels of participation in the singing, since so many factors are involved—the fan culture of each stadium, the quality of individual performances, even the enthusiasm of the fans as determined by the game itself. At the Red Sox game in which the eighty-seven-year-old veteran performed, people sang along once the singer was shown on the Jumbotron screen about halfway through the song, as if fans were singing out of a sense of support for the poignant image of the performer. At another Red Sox game, few people sang along when a young woman performed the song with a strong voice and relatively few embellishments; I ascribe this mainly to her chosen tempo, a quick pace that was a bit too fast for a large crowd to keep up with.

Using the same recording at every game also adds to the ritual power of "God Bless America," since it is not only the song but the specific performance that is repeated. Kate Smith's recording appears to fit easily within baseball partially because it is imbued with nostalgia, especially for older fans. As Bryan Srabian, the former director of marketing for the San Francisco Giants, told me: "I didn't understand who Kate Smith was, and that this was her song, per se. . . . But from the people I spoke to that were older than me, this is iconic. Kate Smith and 'God Bless America'—that's the only version they really knew."[66] But just as Smith's rendition of the song has been imbued with different associations over time, so the meaning of "God Bless America" at baseball stadiums has shifted in the years since 9/11, shaped in different ways by local adaptations to the new national ritual.

SHIFTING MEANINGS IN TWO MINOR LEAGUE BALLPARKS

"God Bless America" has become a "multivocal symbol," a term introduced by the anthropologist Victor Turner to describe how ritual symbols can hold many different meanings for participants.[67] Tim Gunkel explained his view of the song's multilayered meanings for Mets fans:

> If you interviewed a bunch of people in the stands, . . . different people would probably tell you it means something different to them. For some of them, it's probably flag and country, and patriotism like in the old-time sense. For others, it's probably very much tied to post-9/11 America. For others, it may be personal, like to somebody who's serving, troops."[68]

I observed these swirling meanings of "God Bless America" perhaps most vividly at Richmond County Bank Ballpark, home of the minor-league Staten Island Yankees, the Class-A Short Season affiliate of the New York Yankees.[69] Like their major-league counterpart, the Staten Island Yankees include a performance of "God Bless America" at every game. As the former team owner Stan Getzler pointed out, "Staten Island suffered a disproportionate amount of casualties on 9/11 than the other boroughs, because so many firemen and policemen live there. And people who worked on Wall Street lived on Staten Island. So the casualties were very, very high."[70] The stadium, perched along the water just down the road from the Staten Island ferry terminal in St. George, had provided a clear view of the World Trade Center towers rising high above lower Manhattan. The ballpark now overlooks the Staten Island 9/11 memorial—two white, winglike sculptures positioned along the waterfront that serve as a constant reminder of the void in the skyline across the harbor. Inside the stadium, three seats behind home plate (Section 9, Row A, Seats 9, 10, and 11) are painted red, white, and blue, and remain empty in memory of the attacks. As one season-ticket holder explained:

> Our neighborhood, which is not too far from here, had one of the highest number of people lost, percentage-wise. . . . One of the people who sits here was one of the last people to make it out of the World Trade Center. You see that monument here. So, you know, everyday you have reminders.[71]

Figure 6.5
View from Richmond County Ballpark in Staten Island. The 9/11 memorial can be seen to the left of the scoreboard. Photograph by author.

By 2008 this connection to the memory of the 9/11 attacks had become a part of the team culture, as John Davison, who was then the team's VP of community and media relations, described:

> Every year we have a new team, new players, new coaches. And we walked them out to the [9/11] memorial their first day here, . . . and said to them, "When you're standing out there, and it's time for 'God Bless America,' you know, realize that every fan in the stands is—their memories are going through their heads, and we should be respectful." And some of these players had tears in their eyes hearing about it.[72]

But the solemnity of "God Bless America" sits in stark contrast to the high jinks that are part of the experience of a Staten Island Yankees game. Perhaps because the level of play at this tier of minor-league baseball does not always warrant the full attention of fans, there tends to be a strong emphasis on fan involvement and on fun. My interviews with staff and fans at the Staten Island stadium were nearly drowned out by the constant interruption of music, between-inning contests, and wacky skits performed by a visiting entertainment company called the "Zooperstars."[73] This juxtaposition of entertainment and serious commemoration is apparent at most ballparks during seventh-inning performances of "God Bless America," which are usually followed by the lighthearted "Take Me Out to the Ball Game." The contrast was dramatic at the Staten Island Yankees game that I attended, where "God Bless America"—performed forcefully by a local amateur baritone—was immediately followed by a rendition of "Take Me Out to the Ball Game" sung by Harry Canary, a member of the Zooperstars in a bird costume imitating Harry Caray's original, off-key performance style. Mike D'Amboise, the team's director of entertainment, explained that the seriousness of "God Bless America" is "not something that we try and necessarily dwell on. We have our moment, and everybody appreciates it for what it is, and then we move on and everybody's happy again."[74]

For some, the song will always be linked directly to the experience of 9/11, as Davison told me: "That song is completely tied to [9/11] for me. It's the reason we do it, and it's a time every night that we do it, I stop and I remember my friends that—that aren't here anymore. . . . For me, it's definitely a moment of respect and a time to stop and think about it."[75] But the connection between "God Bless America" and 9/11 is not made explicit through announcements at the ballpark in Staten Island. Those who know the tradition can use the performance as a moment of remembrance—as one fan told me, gesturing to the skyline across the harbor, "There were two things standing right there that aren't there anymore." But other staffers talked about the song as a way to thank the troops in Iraq and Afghanistan, a connection that John Davison never made in my discussions with him. And in brief interviews during the game, many fans made no mention of either 9/11 or military troops in their response to the song—one said that he doesn't like it being played at baseball games simply because he is annoyed by the lyrics rhyming "home" with "foam."

At McCoy Stadium in Pawtucket, Rhode Island, the song's meaning is framed more explicitly. Before the top of the seventh inning at Paw Sox games, performances of "God Bless America" are accompanied by snapshots of local military servicemen and women shown on the scoreboard screen.[76] The photographs are submitted by family members, serving as yet another mode of engagement between the team and the community.

This simultaneous connection to patriotic militarism and to the sacrifices made by local community members echoes John Bodnar's description of the tension between vernacular and official culture within public commemoration. Bodnar notes that official culture often dominates: "Usually it is the local and personal past that is incorporated into a nationalized public

Figure 6.6
Scoreboard at McCoy Stadium in Pawtucket, Rhode Island. Photograph by Benjamin Shaykin.

memory rather than the other way around. Local, regional, class, and ethnic interests are sustained in one form or another in the final product, but
the dominant meaning is usually nationalistic."⁷⁷ At Paw Sox games, it is
difficult to determine which message resonates more strongly. On the sur-
face, being told by the announcer to rise for a song that is itself a signifier
for patriotic support for war would imply that the official culture of nationalism wins out. But as the photographs of members of the community flash
on the screen above centerfield, the weight of the sacrifices of local individ-
uals seems just as strong, if not stronger, than an official patriotism.

This post-9/11 ritual at Paw Sox games also reveals the rhetorical
strength of "God Bless America" as a new baseball tradition. "God Bless
America" is played after the sixth inning, essentially moving the seventh-
inning stretch and replacing the traditional singing of "Take Me Out to the
Ball Game" with this military tribute. In contrast with "God Bless America,"
for which fans were asked to rise, "Take Me Out to the Ball Game" was
played a half-inning later with no introduction whatsoever, almost as an
afterthought. At the games I observed during the summer of 2009, far
more people stood up and sang along with "God Bless America" than with
"Take Me Out to the Ball Game"—after all, why stand up and sing twice in
one inning? One fan who responded to my online survey lamented that
this practice at the Paw Sox means that "nobody stands up for the seventh-
inning stretch, so they have destroyed one of baseball's sacred traditions."⁷⁸

LOCAL ADAPTATIONS OF NATIONALISM
IN THE MAJOR LEAGUE

The framing of "God Bless America" differs from ballpark to ballpark, compli-
cating the notion of a unified expression of American nationalism. Such regional adaptations are a critical part of teams' ability to foster local allegiance
among fans, and music often serves as a sonic affirmation of team identity.
Most teams follow the policy set by MLB regarding the inclusion of "God
Bless America," although the Yankees have played the song at every game
since 2001. Other examples of local adaptations of this rule include the Cubs,
who play "God Bless America" before the game rather than during the stretch,
and the Los Angeles Dodgers, who added "God Bless America" to every game
beginning in 2009.⁷⁹ (I have not found reference to a major league team that
plays the song less frequently than the MLB office has recommended.)

In addition to "Take Me Out to the Ball Game" and "God Bless America,"
teams often orchestrate sing-alongs that engender regional pride and
identification. The Baltimore Orioles have made use of "Thank God I'm a

Country Boy" during the seventh-inning stretch, and in 2012, the Washington Nationals embraced the 1980s anthem "Take On Me" by A-ha as an unlikely team battle cry.[80] Another example is the Red Sox tradition of playing Neil Diamond's "Sweet Caroline" during the middle of the eighth inning, a song that I observed fans singing more boisterously than either song from the seventh-inning stretch.[81] More evidence of fan loyalty to these local musical traditions is revealed in an email survey of Mets fans conducted by the team, where 72 percent of fans ranked hearing the team song "Meet the Mets" as an important part of the game, only a few points below "Take Me Out to the Ball Game" and far above "God Bless America."[82]

Teams' regional identities are showcased within choices about how "God Bless America" is presented. At a New York Yankees game that I attended in August 2009, Kate Smith's rendition of "God Bless America" was preceded by the announcer calling for "a moment of silent prayer for people serving our country at home and abroad," while the image of an NYPD badge on a police officer's baseball cap was projected on the scoreboard screen. This introduction ties the song's performance to 9/11 through an association with the NYPD, and also links to both first responders and the military through the wording of the silent prayer introduction (though in a less overt way than displaying photographs of military personnel). The Boston Red Sox—who perform "God Bless America" only on Sundays and holidays—frame the song as a prelude to the traditional seventh-inning stretch, as the announcer proclaimed at a Sunday game I attended, "Now please rise and strrrrrretch and prepare to sing along with our in-park organist as he plays 'Take Me Out to the Ball Game,' presented by Coca Cola. But before that, here to perform this afternoon's rendition of 'God Bless America' please welcome . . ." In addition to the noteworthy downplaying of "God Bless America" here, the corporate sponsorship of the seventh-inning stretch itself reveals the tension between commercialism and honored tradition within professional baseball.[83]

At Yankee Stadium, "Take Me Out to the Ball Game" is treated as a coda to the more weighty presentation of "God Bless America," freighted as a symbol for 9/11 and the military. At Fenway Park, an old stadium steeped in tradition and lore, "God Bless America" serves almost as an opening act for the more traditional "Take Me Out to the Ball Game." The song was treated similarly at a San Francisco Giants game that I attended in July 2009: After the Kate Smith recording was played—to which few people sang along, although everyone did stand during the song and cheer afterwards—the announcer praised the crowd and seemed to almost offer a reward for good behavior: "Good job. And now it's time for the seventh-inning stretch and 'Take Me Out to the Ball Game!'"[84]

This treatment may be a reflection of the West Coast's general sense of distance from the 9/11 attacks that inspired the song's inclusion, as Bryan Srabian at the Giants told me:

> I think being so far removed from the East Coast, we didn't really understand. You know, I think we all felt what everyone had felt in the nation, but the people from New York were very emotional still. . . . Whereas we were behind it all, but we weren't as affected. It was only through the news. So I think New York—and obviously Pennsylvania and Washington, too—were touched more by it than we were. So it obviously is still very close to hitting home and a solemn situation for them.[85]

Certainly the song and its connection to 9/11 resonate differently in New York than in other cities. Jon Miller, the Giants broadcaster who has also covered many national games for ESPN, agreed that the song has always held a unique meaning in New York, as he described his experience of the song in an interview:

> The most lingering memory for me was being in New York in the post-season that year [in 2001]. Because New York—the fans there, they were on the front lines, you know? Our country had been attacked, but they personally had been attacked. . . . As time went on, we moved past that year. Every stadium was doing the "God Bless America" in the seventh-inning stretch. And there was a strong wave of patriotism that swept through the country, people rallying behind the country saying, "We've been attacked." So baseball was playing its part. . . . But I think in New York, it still had a special resonance because it wasn't just about the United States, or paying tribute to the nation, and baseball as the national pastime. In New York, I think it always brought people back to September 11th. Because it was a special, painful but poignant memory for New Yorkers, far beyond [how it felt for] anybody else in the country.[86]

Miller went on to acknowledge that while it still seems appropriate and meaningful in New York, "I think in all the ballparks, even on these Sundays, it's now just something that's been mandated, and there's no big effect to it, you know?" By 2009, the song may have lost the power of its original connection to 9/11, especially for those outside of New York.[87]

Bryan Srabian was the only baseball executive I spoke with who acknowledged that, at least in liberal-leaning San Francisco, the song elicited mixed reactions from fans. While emphasizing that "the majority of people still accept it—or don't question it," he also told me, "I think some people out here—and I can't speak for other markets—are kind of like, 'Is this being forced on us? Why are we still doing this?' We do receive email from fans, and from what I hear, some fans consider the song to be more of a political statement, and baseball fans typically don't want politics mixed with sports."[88] At the Mets, Tim Gunkel said that he hasn't heard much negative feedback about the song—if anything, they are criticized for not playing it at every game, and he said, "Here it doesn't feel like we're being forced. We're not being forced by Major League Baseball to play it, and our fans don't seem put upon to hear it. It seems like something they want."[89] "God Bless America" served a unifying purpose in the period directly after the attacks and many fans now accept its presence, but beginning with the US invasion of Iraq in 2003, some began to object to the song's coercive power.

DISSENT AND COERCION AT THE BALLPARK

The first public dissent against "God Bless America" within baseball emerged after the 2003 season, when the United States invaded Iraq and the MLB's shift in language specifically designated the song as a military tribute. Beginning that year, the Toronto Blue Jays first basemen Carlos Delgado staged "his own private protest," refusing to stand outside the team dugout when "God Bless America" was played at games.[90] Originally from Puerto Rico, Delgado was already known as a social activist for his involvement in protests against the navy's use of the island of Vieques. But Delgado did not make his protest public until July 2004, when he told a *Toronto Star* reporter, "I actually don't think people have noticed it. I don't (stand) because I don't believe it's right, I don't believe in the war."[91] That article, in which he called the Iraq conflict "the stupidest war ever," created a firestorm of controversy around Delgado—not in Toronto, but on the road. "God Bless America" was not played at Blue Jays games after the 2003 season, and the Canadian government had not joined the US-led coalition forces in Iraq. But criticism of Delgado was particularly fierce at Yankee Stadium, where he was jeered by fans and condemned on talk radio shows when the Blue Jays played there in 2004."[92] It wasn't until Delgado joined the Mets in 2006 that he suspended his protest, as he explained at a press conference announcing his trade to the Mets: "The Mets have a policy that everybody should stand for 'God Bless America' and I will be there. I will not cause any distractions to the ball club. . . . Just call me Employee Number 21."[93] For the Mets, the issue of standing for "God Bless America" was framed as a company policy that employees needed to follow—though it was a policy that did not exist until Delgado joined the team.[94]

Other forms of coercion surrounding "God Bless America" had a more extensive reach. In 2007, the Yankees came under fire for using chains to block off the aisles and prevent fans from moving while "God Bless America" was played, and in 2009 the team was successfully sued by a fan who was ejected from the stadium for getting up to use the bathroom during the song's performance.[95] One participant in my online survey protested:

> ["God Bless America"] is an advertisement for militarism and a not-so-subtle form of coercion, especially if you were one of those people, like myself, who tried to go to the men's room at the old Yankee Stadium during the singing of the song, only to be barred by uniformed guards. Did they even realize the irony of prohibiting people from going to pee during the playing of a song that ostensibly celebrates our freedom?[96]

In fact, the online survey that I conducted in 2009 indicates that some fans are ready to abandon "God Bless America" in a post–post-9/11 world. As shown in fig. 6.8, more than 60 percent of 1,830 respondents dislike the song's continued presence at baseball games, with nearly half of all survey participants indicating that they "strongly dislike" its inclusion and only 20 percent expressing positive feelings about the song (see the companion website for more detailed results from this survey ◐).

Figure 6.7
Security ropes off stands at Yankees Stadium during the singing of "God Bless America" on 19 April 2007. Photograph by Barton Silverman/The *New York Times*/Redux.

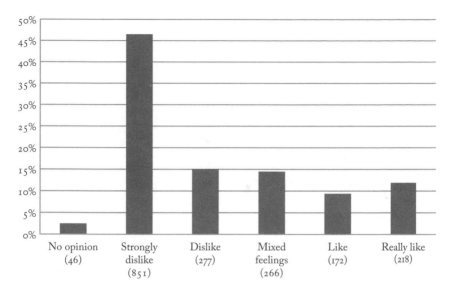

Figure 6.8
Online survey responses to the question, "What do you think of 'God Bless America' being sung at baseball games?" (1,830 responses.)

As compelling as this data may be, the demographics of my survey participants need to be taken into account. Two large-scale consumer surveys indicate that the demographics of baseball fans tend to follow those of the general population, but my survey's participants were more likely to identify themselves as politically liberal and nonreligious.[97] Analysis of the survey responses indicates that this preponderance of liberal, nonreligious participants likely had a dramatic impact on the survey results. Figure 6.9 provides a stark illustration of the extent to which liberals expressed negative feelings about the song's presence within baseball while conservatives often embrace it. Figure 6.10 shows a similar but slightly less dramatic connection between religious beliefs and approval of the song's performance within baseball, with over twice as many agnostic and atheist respondents indicating a strong dislike for the practice than did those who described themselves as religious or very religious.

Since these demographics likely represent those of Internet-savvy fans motivated to take an online survey on this topic—rather than an accurate snapshot of baseball fans more generally—I do not claim that my survey data represents the views of a true cross-section of *all* baseball fans.[98] Results from the Mets' email survey indicate nearly the mirror opposite results, with more than half of Mets fans in favor of the song's inclusion, and 42 percent indicating that it should be played at every game rather than only on Sundays.[99] This conflicting data attests to the power of "God Bless

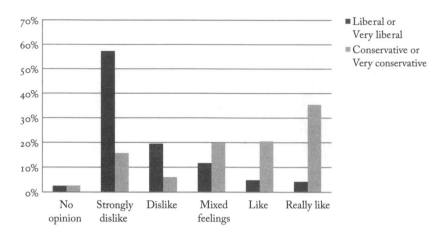

Figure 6.9
Online survey responses to the question, "What do you think of 'God Bless America' being sung at baseball games?" by political views. (888 "Liberal" or "Very liberal" respondents; 320 "Conservative" or "Very conservative" respondents.)

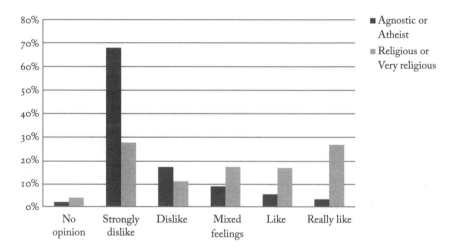

Figure 6.10
Online survey responses to the question, "What do you think of 'God Bless America' being sung at baseball games?" by religious views. (663 said they were "Agnostic" or "Atheist"; 391 respondents identified themselves as "Religious" or "Very religious")

America" as a truly multivocal symbol, one that invokes such opposing responses that it may be impossible to draw any conclusions about its reception across all fans.

The high number of responses to my survey provides a wealth of information about fans' perceptions of "God Bless America," especially among those who dislike its presence within professional baseball. One participant neatly summarized the principal reasons behind negative opinions of the song within the majority demographic of my survey:

> I am an American who is an agnostic, liberal Democrat who loves baseball and its traditions. Playing "God Bless America" at baseball games offends me in three ways: forced worship of a God I don't believe in, forced participation in a political "rally" whose views I don't share, and the extended interruption of a sport that I love.[100]

This quote touches on the main themes that I found within the responses of those who said they "strongly dislike" the song's presence at baseball games: it interferes with baseball's traditions; infuses the game with a coerced sense of religion, patriotism, and/or conservative politics; and disrupts the flow of the game itself. Other reasons given by survey participants for their dislike of the song at baseball games include (but are not limited to): aversion to the song itself; feeling that the song's seriousness does not fit within the fun diversion of baseball; that the song does not take the internationalism of the sport into account; and that it represents corporate marketing efforts to benefit from patriotism.

Complaints about the song usurping baseball's traditions took a few forms within survey responses, and most reflected loyalty to the existing musical practices of singing the national anthem and "Take Me Out to the Ball Game." Some respondents said that singing the national anthem was enough to fulfill any patriotic obligation that baseball might have to the nation—though a vocal minority also protested that the national anthem has no place in baseball, either. Others were offended by the fact that "God Bless America" is treated like the national anthem, with fans rising and removing their caps. Of course, Irving Berlin himself emphatically protested that his song was not the national anthem and should not be treated as such. In 1966, when the Chicago White Sox briefly replaced the national anthem with "God Bless America" because "The Star-Spangled Banner" was deemed too difficult to sing, Berlin said, "I'm delighted that they are using 'God Bless America,' but if they are doing it in place of 'The Star-Spangled Banner,' I don't approve of it. I think there is only one national anthem, and I certainly don't want anything else to take the place of it."[101]

Another group of fans resented that "God Bless America" interferes with the traditions of the seventh-inning stretch and upstages their beloved "Take Me Out to the Ball Game." As one survey participant complained: "People should be allowed to have a little fun and sing 'Take Me Out to the Ballgame' . . . like I did when I was a kid, and what my parents and grandparents did when they were kids."[102] These comments highlight the perceived timelessness of the game's invented traditions, since "Take Me Out to the Ball Game" became a regular part of the seventh-inning stretch only in the 1970s.

The power of tradition was also cited by some respondents who "really like" the song played at baseball games. For them, it has become a new tradition with just as much legitimacy as older rituals, as one fan wrote: "To me now, it's more part of baseball than even the opening pitch."[103] Others who support the song's presence mentioned the importance of honoring the troops or 9/11, an appreciation for the inclusion of blessings or religion within the game, or argued that the song represents a small moment to honor the sacrifices of others. In addition, some survey participants who like the song's inclusion in baseball appreciate its ability to provide unity and group cohesion ("The unity when thousands of people are singing together is uplifting"), and another response emphasized that these feelings of connection engendered by the singing itself can trump any ideological meaning that the song might carry: "It creates a sense of bonding and camaraderie, even with the Republicans I despise."[104]

On the flip side, one fan who dislikes the song's presence at baseball games warned of the dangerous power of the singing itself: "We should not have a song like that forced upon us in a public setting like this. It is almost a way of peer pressure as it makes people try to conform to nationalistic tendencies without having them think for themselves. This is done because when someone sees fifty thousand people singing a song they will want to be included and join in."[105] Another said, "I think it was a way of pressuring people to support a nationalist agenda and silencing, by the sheer numbers of attendants at a ballpark, any and all opposition to that agenda."[106] Such coercive power complicates any assumption that the only by-product of communal singing is a cozy "kumbaya" sense of togetherness. A few respondents went even farther, linking baseball's use of "God Bless America" with fascist displays of control over the populace, as one noted, "To me, it has undertones of Nazi Germany and totalitarian states like North Korea when we're forced to stand up and sing patriotic songs."[107]

Many of those who strongly support the song's new role in baseball referenced some version of the comfortable fit between "America's pastime" and a patriotic symbol like "God Bless America." Certainly, sporting events have long been venues for an affirmation of national pride through rituals like the national anthem. But the baseball historian David Voigt argues that baseball's claim to being "America's national game" was a marketing ploy by the nineteenth-century baseball entrepreneur Albert Goodwill Spaulding, which forever linked the sport with American nationalism—and thus with politics.[108] Almost every president has thrown the ceremonial first pitch on opening day since Taft first did it in 1910.[109] President George W. Bush, who played baseball in college and had been an owner of the Texas Rangers, famously threw the ceremonial first pitch during the 2001 World Series in a New York still reeling from the 9/11 attacks.[110]

So despite purist assumptions about a separation between baseball and politics, there is a long history behind the "political rally" that some fans complain of when "God Bless America" is played. In 1976 David Voigt wrote, "If being America's national game requires baseball officials to stand by while clever politicos exploit the game for image advantages or for support of military policies, surely this must alienate from baseball those fans who see this posture as pandering to superpatriots and war lovers."[111] More than thirty years later, issues of national identity and patriotism continue to be played out on the baseball diamond whenever an announcer asks fans to rise for "God Bless America."

THE RISE AND FALL OF RONAN TYNAN:
BASEBALL, ANTI-SEMITISM, AND TOLERANCE

A series of events involving the tenor Ronan Tynan, "God Bless America," and the New York Yankees acts as a bizarre bookend to the song's early connections to religious tolerance and anti-Semitic backlash. Tynan, a medical doctor, gold-medal Paralympic athlete, and former member of the Irish Tenors, first performed "God Bless America" at a Yankees game in the spring of 2000.[112] After 9/11, Tynan performed "God Bless America" at many memorials and commemorative events in New York, but he became best known for his unique renditions of the song—which always included the rarely sung verse—during the seventh-inning stretch of Yankees games. When the Yankees began to use the Kate Smith recording for most games during the season, Tynan was invited to perform the song on special occasions and during post-season games. Among respondents to my online survey who said that they associate the song with a particular performer, 20 percent identified Tynan.[113]

Tynan's long association with the Yankees came to an abrupt end in October 2009, when he was accused of making an anti-Semitic remark in his apartment building.[114] Tynan apologized to the woman he had offended, and he subsequently appeared at the annual meeting of the Anti-Defamation League (ADL) to offer a public apology and sing "God Bless America."[115] ADL's director Abraham Foxman accepted Tynan's apology, noting that "We need to give a message to people that they can be forgiven if they own up to their bigotry," but the Yankees disinvited Tynan from any future performances at Yankee Stadium.[116] This excommunication impelled Tynan to leave New York and move to Boston in 2010, where, despite a previously professed hatred of the Red Sox, he sang his well-known rendition of "God Bless America" on the Fourth of July at Fenway Park, a performance that was welcomed by a loud ovation from Boston fans.[117]

There are many historical echoes in this story, all engaging with the song's past connections to cultural and ethnic tolerance. First of all, Ronan Tynan is an immigrant like Irving Berlin; he chose to sing "God Bless America" rather than "The Star-Spangled Banner" when he first performed at Yankee Stadium because he felt that only American citizens should sing the anthem.[118] Tynan's performance of "God Bless America" at the ADL annual meeting is a strange reprise of the song's early appearance at the 1938 dinner of the National Conference of Christians and Jews, which occurred in tandem with speeches condemning bigotry (see chap. 4). This time, the song's vague lyrics, its new associations with post-9/11 unity, and the fact that Tynan's own celebrity was boosted by his connection with the song, combined to give his apology greater rhetorical power. But Tynan's performance also shows continuities with the song's past as a symbol for tolerance, even as its connections to Irving Berlin's Jewish immigrant roots—and the early anti-Semitic backlash against the song— have faded into history.

More than ten years after 9/11, it can be difficult to remember the raw emotions of the months directly after the attacks. Picture, for example, the first football game after 9/11, when the Kansas City Chiefs hosted the New York Giants. While the visiting New York team stood in the stadium tunnel before the game, some Chiefs fans reached down to the opposing players; as Giants running back Tiki Barber explained, "They wanted to hold our hands during the singing of 'God Bless America.' So we held hands."[119] This inconceivable pairing of people and activities—football players and fans of the opposing team *holding hands* as they *sang together*—somehow made sense in the direct aftermath of 9/11.

Of course, some fans felt at odds with this embrace of "God Bless America" from the beginning. In a critique that framed the song's inclusion in baseball as part of a larger post-9/11 suppression of democracy, the communications scholar Michael Butterworth argues that such "ritualized performances of nationalism" featured "a defiant and reactionary patriotism that all but eliminated the possibility for disunity."[120] But Butterworth's elision of the period from September 2001 to the fall of 2003 ignores the fact that before the song was explicitly used as a symbol for support for the Iraq War in 2003, it served as a vehicle for public mourning that allowed space for sincere commemoration. Many people *wanted* unity in the weeks after 9/11, even those who previously might not have liked the song or its many associations. Some survey respondents—even those who strongly dislike the presence of "God Bless America" within baseball—acknowledged that they thought the song was appropriate after 9/11.[121]

If "God Bless America" had only remained in place through the end of the 2001 season, or even through the 2002 season, it might have retained its direct connection to post-9/11 public mourning. But the song's coercive power took hold most strongly in 2003, when the language surrounding the playing of "God Bless America" specifically turned to support for the Iraq war, and the horror of 9/11 had begun to subside for those not directly impacted by the attacks.

Some of my survey participants agree with Ira Berkow that the song's performance could now be scaled back to holidays, and others would likely prefer to see it removed from the game altogether.[122] But any change in professional baseball's policy regarding "God Bless America" seems unlikely. When I asked MLB executive Rich Levin whether "God Bless America" would continue to be part of the game, he said that it would, "at least, for the foreseeable future."[123] Jeff Bradley, the director of community relations at the Pawtucket Red Sox, told me, "There's absolutely no talk of stopping that tradition. I don't see any need to do that, I think it's something that we're going to continue and that should continue, and it *will* continue."[124] Greg Romano at the Mets reflected on the difficulty of discontinuing such a patriotic ritual: "If they stop, then it's like, 'What am I, unpatriotic?' . . . There's no reason for them to, particularly. . . . They wouldn't get any positive press from it. All it would be is negative."[125] The national anthem was added to sporting events as part of a home-front mobilizing effort during World War II, and the practice has now remained in place for more than seventy years, in times of war and peace. Such traditions of nationalistic display, so easily invented, prove nearly impossible to remove.

Coda: As We Raise Our Voices

The Place of Communal Singing

Americans have too few opportunities to sing together. As far back as 25 years ago, the sense that singing together at summer camp was fun was giving way to the notion that singing together was for losers. Unless we avail ourselves of fairly obscure opportunities, the only chance those leading secular lives have to sing together is at the ballpark[.]

—*Encyclopedia Britannica blog, January 2007*[1]

This book has examined "God Bless America" as a vehicle for communal singing, whether sung by strangers on a midnight train, sorority members at a monthly meeting, angry counterprotestors at a peace rally, mourners at a candlelight vigil, or a crowd asked to stand and remove their caps in support of a war. At root, such singing can engender an affirmation of community ties, as well as a sense of alienation for those who feel out of step with the majority. Communal singing—and the specific song "God Bless America"—played a fundamental role after 9/11, momentarily suspending previous associations to become a principal vehicle for group mourning and a sense of unity. But this primacy of group singing was largely temporary. For many, communal singing retains its stigma as a hokey holdover from grade school and summer camp. In conducting research at baseball games, I sometimes felt that my fascination with the seventh-inning stretch was the equivalent of a study of intermission within theater or opera—many fans see it as nothing more than a break in the main attraction.

Is communal singing dead? A 1991 *New York Times* article on the loss of a "singing culture" in the United States noted that "informal, everyday singing is in a slump," and quoted one music teacher lamenting that "we have made singing the province of the select few."[2] In 2008, an article about the small subculture of organized community sings noted that the earnestness of group singing represents "a natural opposite to gold-plated pop irony and faceless file sharing—music as the American majority knows it."[3] The political scientist Robert Putnam has observed that the role of the collective in the United States overall has weakened considerably since the late 1960s, when "Americans in massive numbers began to join less, trust less, give less, vote less, and schmooze less."[4] In a culture with waning opportunities for collectivity, communal singing can serve to strengthen community ties, even if not consciously, to strangers singing together on a train, or within a group of protestors, or baseball fans, or a nation of mourners.

In his groundbreaking sociological study of religion, published in 1912, Emile Durkheim described how public collective action can serve a ritual function similar to that of religious ceremonies:

> There can be no society which does not feel the need of upholding and reaffirming at regular intervals the collective feelings and ideas that provide its coherence and its distinct individuality. This moral remaking can be achieved only through meetings, assemblies, and congregations in which the individuals, pressing close to one another, reaffirm in common their common sentiments. Such is the origin of ceremonies that, by their object, by their results, and by the techniques used, are not different in kind from ceremonies that are specifically religious.[5]

Group singing is certainly one method for affirming "common sentiments," using congregational singing typical of sacred ceremonies in nonreligious contexts. Pete Seeger, a preeminent authority on collective music-making, took note of the sacred quality of secular communal singing in a 2008 interview: "No one can prove a damn thing, but I think that singing together gives people some kind of a holy feeling. And it can happen whether they're atheists, or whoever. You feel like, 'Gee, we're all together.'"[6]

This feeling of togetherness has been called "communitas" by the anthropologist Victor Turner, who coined the term to define a bond that is created between participants during ritual events, where people feel a connection across the social structures that usually separate them.[7] Such suspension of social boundaries is often present within group singing, which can serve as a sonic acknowledgement of community ties—a fleeting sense of communitas—before returning to everyday life.

But group singing can also create a sense of alienation among those who find themselves unmoved or at odds with the singing or the message of a particular song. They may feel pressured to sing lyrics they don't believe, or questioned by those around them if they choose not to participate. The strength of the sonic declaration of community and the desire for communitas make communal singing a potent coercive force, using the feelings engendered by the singing as an instrument of control over the populace. Nazi Germany is often used as an example of music's coercive power, as Hitler is said to have declared of his use of mass music, "The audience is not being informed. It is made to perform, and its performance makes history."[8] It is easy to use the extreme example of the Nazis here, but this book has shown that the coercive power of mass singing is certainly present in the United States. These simultaneous effects of communal singing—engendering both communitas and alienation among participants—give these moments a unique power to both forge and contest community ties.

The use of "God Bless America" as a vehicle for public mourning after 9/11 is just one facet of a larger story about musical responses to crisis in modern American life. The emotional force of these moments of communal singing is partly derived from the juxtaposition of a seemingly old-fashioned mode of community declaration amid the increasingly impersonal and individualized nature of a modern, urban landscape. Jody Rosen has written that this "perennial American tension between progress and nostalgia" was particularly acute during the 1930s when "God Bless America" first became popular, as the Depression showed that "the fruits of modern, big-city individualism came at the expense of connection—the sense of security and stability that in the past had been provided by ancestral and communal ties."[9]

Earlier examples of spontaneous group singing in response to tragedy evoke the fleeting nature of the connection that was achieved through shared songs in urban settings. The composer Charles Ives described a memory that inspired his quotation of the hymn "Nearer My God to Thee" in his Fourth Symphony, recalling, "a scene one evening at Café Boulevard, New York, after McKinley's assassination in 1901. Everybody stood up and sang this hymn."[10] And Ives's experience was not an isolated incident. "Nearer My God to Thee" was sung so frequently after McKinley's death that the writer and humorist Sarah Vowell later dubbed it the assassination's "theme song."[11] The president was reported to have uttered the words to the hymn just before he died, and it became a central part of the public response to his assassination. In 1901, a *New York Times* reporter described this scene at an outdoor band concert the day after McKinley's death:

Hundreds of people were overcome with emotion as the strains of "Nearer, My God, to Thee" floated from the bandstand. Many broke down and cried and left the pier. A stylishly dressed woman accosted the bandmaster and asked him to repeat the hymn, and then slowly and softly the music again filled the air. This time everybody on the pier arose and sung the hymn—the one that the dead president loved so well—in a low tone, that was almost a chant.[12]

Another article described passersby singing the hymn with organ grinders and street bands, concluding, "Not within memory have such spontaneous bursts of reverence and affection been witnessed on the streets of New York."[13]

This use of group singing as a vehicle for public mourning would continue through the twentieth and twenty-first centuries. In 1968, mourners joined in spontaneous singing as they gathered to watch the funeral train of Robert F. Kennedy: "At Baltimore, someone started singing 'The Battle Hymn of the Republic,' and others picked it up until nearly the whole crowd was sweetly singing in slow cadence as the funeral train slid slowly by."[14] For Edward Kennedy's funeral in 2009, the official song on the memorial program was "America the Beautiful," but as one journalist noted, "remarkably, . . . the crowd spontaneously sang 'God Bless America' to send off the motorcade as it snaked, headlamps blinking out of time, to Mr. Kennedy's final resting place in Virginia."[15]

It is worth examining the specific songs that were embraced at these particular moments in history. For one, they reflect shifts in a shared repertoire of songs: a Protestant hymn was assumed to be known by most Americans in the early twentieth century, but by 2001, the hymn was replaced by a song from Tin Pan Alley, originally composed by a Jewish immigrant. In addition, the meanings associated with each song imbue the singing with added significance. The historical associations of the "Battle Hymn of the Republic"—with the death of abolitionist John Brown, with the Civil War's fight against slavery, and later with the protests of the civil rights movement—strengthened its power to memorialize Robert F. Kennedy, a twentieth-century activist for social justice.[16] And post-9/11 associations of "God Bless America" with public mourning and unity gave added resonance to the song's spontaneous use at Edward Kennedy's memorial in 2009. Describing the power of this kind of commemorative singing in the wake of the 9/11 attacks, the music critic Alex Ross wrote that "when we are all in the grip of the same emotion, music can shoulder the heaviest part of what we are feeling. A familiar tune billows above us, and we are carried along by it for a short distance."[17] The emotional power of communal singing as a vehicle for commemoration derives both from the act of singing itself and the multivocal meanings of the chosen songs.

This book has also shown that group singing serves an important function in times of celebration and protest, giving voice to feelings of solidarity. Yet recent events involving group demonstrations in public space seem to indicate a general preference for mass speech over communal singing as a form of collective expression. For example, after the killing of Osama Bin Laden in the spring of 2011, there were several accounts of crowds singing "The Star-Spangled Banner" and "God Bless America" in celebration, but the most common crowd response was not singing, but exuberantly shouting the tuneless nationalistic cheer: "U-S-A! U-S-A!"[18] One article described how a crowd at a Philadelphia Flyers game chanted "U-S-A" and cheered loudly for a performance of "God Bless America"—a song with a long history for the Flyers—but fans did not sing along.[19]

The protest music most often reported in connection with the Occupy Wall Street movement in 2011 involved performances by indie musicians like Tom Morello from Rage Against the Machine and Jeff Mangum from Neutral Milk Hotel rather than group singing—although Pete Seeger did lead protestors in singing "We Shall Overcome" and other protest songs during a march in support of the Occupy movement in October 2011.[20] As one commentator noted in November 2011, "If Occupy Wall Street has no anthem yet, it's partly due to how a new generation experiences music: through personalized iPod playlists streaming through headphones instead of communal singalongs."[21] In fact, the movement's chosen method of collective expression emerged as the "human microphone," in which crowds would repeat a speaker's words en masse in order to broadcast their message in the face of restrictions against amplification that forbid the use of a megaphone.[22] The movement also became known for its use of this collective voice—also called a "mic check"—as a way to drown out speakers with whom they disagreed, a songless version of the "*Casablanca* moments" of protest singing that this book has traced over time.[23]

These more recent examples seem to illustrate a move away from singing as a mode of collective expression. Perhaps this is partly a result of cuts to music education and an ensuing wane in arts participation, or the collapse of a general sense of collectivity in modern urban life, or the rise of the individualized soundtrack provided by the iPod. But the power of mass singing to unite and coerce will always play a role in collective expression, and particular songs will continue to be imbued with new meanings and associations over time. The waning presence of communal singing will only strengthen the poignancy and symbolic power of those rare moments when people do find themselves singing together in American public life.

NOTES

INTRODUCTION

1. Berlin quoted in Gerold Frank, "God Bless America: How It Was Written," *New York Journal and American*, 11 August 1940.
2. Tawa, *Sweet Songs for Gentle Americans*, 140; Hamm, *Yesterdays*, 165–72.
3. Crawford, *America's Musical Life*, 216–17. Also see William Austin's discussion of the song's reception in *"Susanna," "Jeanie," and "The Old Folks at Home,"* 246–47. For a larger discussion of the complex social functions and range of responses to blackface minstrelsy, see Lott, *Love and Theft*.
4. The song was a huge hit, with more than 1 million copies sold. Kimball and Emmet, *The Complete Lyrics of Irving Berlin*, 47.
5. Ibid., 90, 119, 221, 223. See Jody Rosen's discussion of Berlin and the home-song genre in *White Christmas*, 112–13.
6. Hamm, "Irving Berlin and Early Tin Pan Alley," xvi.
7. Ibid., xvii.
8. For more on Berlin's central role in Tin Pan Alley, see Hamm, *Yesterdays*, 329; Suisman, *Selling Sounds*, 53–55; and Crawford, *America's Musical Life*, 546–51.
9. For more on Cohan and patriotism, see Jones, *Our Musicals, Ourselves*, 15–24. For more on "Over There" and other songs from World War I, see Druesdow, "Popular Songs of the Great War."
10. Hamm, *Yesterdays*, 317.
11. See, for example, Arthur Bronson, "Birth of a Ballad," *Philadelphia Record*, 5 August 1940; and "Badgered Ballad," *Time*, 30 September 1940.
12. Shaw, "The Vocabulary of Tin-Pan Alley Explained," 39.
13. Ibid.
14. Bohlman, *The Music of European Nationalism*, 150.
15. Ibid.
16. Anderson, *Imagined Communities*, 145. Anderson's inclusion of "Waltzing Matilda"—a folk song considered Australia's unofficial anthem—within his discussion of national anthems provides further evidence for Bohlman's argument that state sanction is not required for such songs to wield nationalistic power. For more on "Waltzing Matilda," see National Library of Australia, "Who'll Come a Waltzing Matilda With Me?" accessed 3 July 2010, http://www.nla.gov.au/epubs/waltzingmatilda.
17. See Branham and Hartnett, *Sweet Freedom's Song*, 14–44; and Goodman's chapter on eighteenth-century songs in "American Identities in the Musical Atlantic World."
18. For histories of these songs, see Sherr, *America the Beautiful*; and Jackson, "Is This Song Your Song Anymore?"

19. Turner, *The Forest of Symbols*, 50.
20. For more on historical ethnomusicology research, see Bohlman, "Returning to the Ethnomusicological Past"; Shelemay, "Historical Ethnomusicology"; and Wiora, "Ethnomusicology and the History of Music."
21. Slobin, *Subcultural Sounds*, 29. See 27–35 for Slobin's full discussion of the superculture.
22. Hilmes, *Radio Voices*, xvii.
23. For more on Smith's "coon shouter" days, see Hayes, *Kate Smith*, 10–11. For more on coon shouters in general, see Lavitt, "First of the Red Hot Mamas"; for a perspective from the period, see Niles, "Shout, Coon, Shout!"
24. Hilmes, *Radio Voices*, 20, 21.
25. Odessa Armstrong, "Letter: Odessa Never Fails to Attend Her Church," *Chicago Defender*, 29 April 1941.

CHAPTER 1

1. Berlin quoted in S. J. Woolf, "What Makes a Song," *NYT*, 28 July 1940.
2. Don Wharton, "God Bless America," *Look*, 17 December 1940.
3. Crawford, *America's Musical Life*, xiii, 229.
4. For the history of plugging in American popular music, see Suisman, *Selling Sounds*, esp. 59, 86, 266.
5. Furia, *Irving Berlin*, 87.
6. Sanjek and Sanjek, *Pennies from Heaven*, 185. The practice did continue after this ban, but it was not standard by 1938.
7. Monson, *Freedom Sounds*, 29.
8. For biographer's accounts, see Bergreen, *As Thousands Cheer*, 155–56, 369–72; Freedland, *Irving Berlin*, 54–57, 138–39; Furia, *Irving Berlin*, 191–93; Hayes, *Kate Smith*, 52–54; Jablonski, *Irving Berlin*, 75–82, 192–93. For newspaper and magazine articles from the period, see Arthur Bronson, "Birth of a Ballad," *Philadelphia Record*, 5 August 1940; George W. Clarke, "God Bless America! The Story Behind a Song Hit," *Green Magazine*, 21 July 1940; Gerold Frank, "God Bless America: How It Was Written," *New York Journal and American*, 11 August 1940; Alvin H. Goldstein, "Irving Berlin and His 'God Bless America,'" *St. Louis Post-Dispatch*, 25 August 1940; "Story of 'God Bless America,'" *New York Herald Tribune*, 27 October 1940; Don Wharton, "God Bless America," *Look*, 17 December 1940; Ira Wolfert, "'God Bless America' Spent 22 Years Lying in Trunk," *Boston Evening Globe*, 5 August 1940; and S. J. Woolf, "What Makes a Song: A Talk with Irving Berlin," *NYT*, 28 July 1940.
9. Irving Berlin to William P. Maloney, 10 October 1940, IBC Box 259, Folder 8.
10. Rosen, *White Christmas*, 17.
11. Hayes, *Kate Smith*, 3–4.
12. Furia, *Irving Berlin*, 78–79; Kimball and Emmett, *Complete Lyrics*, xxii.
13. Press release, 11 July [1940], IBC Box 259, Folder 8.
14. Berlin's draft registration card is featured on ancestry.com, "World War I Draft Registration Cards, 1917–1918," accessed 5 May 2010, http://search.ancestry.com/iexec/?htx=List&dbid=6482. For information about World War I draft eligibility, see Oregon State Archives, "On the Home Front: The Draft Board Wants to See You," accessed 23 September 2012, http://arcweb.sos.state.or.us/pages/exhibits/war/ww1/draft.html.
15. "'Yip! Yip! Yaphank!' Makes Rousing Hit," *NYT*, 20 August 1918.

16. On the last night of the show's Broadway run, the soldiers actually marched out of the theater and down the street to board ships to France, a reminder of the stark reality behind the entertainment of Berlin's show. Berlin remained at Camp Upton for the duration of the war. Furia, *Irving Berlin*, 84.
17. Harry Ruby quoted in Wilk, *They're Playing Our Song*, 275. The two biographers' accounts can be found in Jablonski, *Irving Berlin*, 82; and Furia, *Irving Berlin*, 192.
18. For these various descriptions, see: Berlin to Chaplain John M. Hughes, 14 November 1946, IBC Box 261, Folder 8; Berlin quoted in Woolf, "What Makes a Song"; Berlin quoted in Furia, *Irving Berlin*, 192.
19. Berlin to Herbert Bayard Swope, 12 April 1956, IBC Box 258, Folder 2. For more on the relative popularity of patriotic songs during the war, see Jones, *The Songs that Fought the War*; and Smith, *God Bless America*.
20. See Gerold Frank, "God Bless America: How It Was Written," *New York Journal and American*, 11 August 1940; and Alvin H. Goldstein, "Irving Berlin and His 'God Bless America,'" *St. Louis Post-Dispatch*, 25 August 1940.
21. Ibid.
22. Goldstein, "Irving Berlin and His 'God Bless America.'"
23. "The Kate Smith Hour," which began on CBS radio in September 1937, was one of many successful variety shows undertaken by Collins and Smith beginning in 1931. For more on Smith's radio career, see Hayes, *Kate Smith*, esp. 18–51, 61, 74.
24. Although many other sources date the song's premiere to Armistice Day itself, 11 November, the radio show appears to have taken place on 10 November 1938. See Hayes, *Kate Smith*, 52–54.
25. See Saul Bornstein to Berlin, 10 February 1939, IBC Box 258, Folder 4.
26. Nick Kenny, *New York Sunday Mirror* (date and title not given, likely 11 November 1938), quoted in Hayes, *Kate Smith*, 54.
27. Ibid.
28. Moore, "The Story Behind 'God Bless America,'" *Chicago Radio Guide*, 23 August 1940.
29. Ben Gross, *I Looked and I Listened*, 140 (referenced in Hayes, *Kate Smith*, 54); Ernest Foster, "Ted Collins Man Behind That Melody," *Hollywood Citizen News*, 8 June 1943.
30. Hayes, *Kate Smith*, 55. The radio ban of ASCAP songs was the culmination of a conflict between songwriters and broadcasters over royalty fees. See Sanjek and Sanjek, *Pennies From Heaven*, 184–211; and Schultz, "Performing-Right Societies in the United States."
31. Whitburn, *Pop Memories*, 39. This resurgence in popularity in July 1940 coincides with Berlin's announcement regarding the donation of his royalties to the Boy Scouts and Girl Scouts through the God Bless America Fund, as well as the publication of many stories in the press about the song and its history.
32. Don Wharton, "God Bless America," *Look*, 17 December 1940. Crosby's recording, released by Decca in March 1939, was a modest Billboard hit, peaking at number 17 and remaining on the charts for two weeks during April 1939, the same period when Smith's recording was first popular.
33. "'God Bless America' Grips U.S.," *Cleveland News*, 8 December 1939.
34. Hayes, *Kate Smith*, 61, 72.
35. Kimball and Emmet, *Complete Lyrics*, xxiii.
36. Unfortunately, the perspectives of Tony Gale and Jack Miller cannot be adequately represented here, since no correspondence or other materials are found in the archives of either Berlin or Smith. There is a short profile on Jack

Miller in George W. Clarke, "God Bless America! The Story Behind a Song Hit," *Green Magazine* (Boston), 21 July 1940, and he appears as a regular presence in Richard Hayes's biography of Kate Smith. But Tony Gale remains a mysterious figure behind the scenes.

37. See Hayes, *Kate Smith*, 143.
38. Suisman, *Selling Sounds*, 15. Of course, many performers were active collaborators with composers and musicians. For example, Jody Rosen notes that Berlin had a "special bond" with Bing Crosby (Rosen, *White Christmas*, 103–4, 188), but Collins insured that Smith established no such ties.
39. Jack Sher, "Curiosity About Kate," *Detroit Free Press*, 2 October 1938.
40. Smith, *Upon My Lips a Song*, 8.
41. Hayes, *Kate Smith*, 15–16.
42. The agreement between Smith and Collins—famously made with no written contract—gave Collins 50 percent of all profits. Hayes notes that the share for personal managers is usually much lower, closer to 10–20 percent. See Hayes, *Kate Smith*, 17.
43. Smith, *Upon My Lips a Song*, 131.
44. "Collins' News Vital Part of Kate's Program," *Roanoke Times*, 3 October 1943.
45. For a sociological study of Smith's war bond drive, see Merton, *Mass Persuasion*.
46. Smith, *Upon My Lips a Song*, 118–19.
47. Smith, *Living in a Great Big Way*, 209.
48. Smith, *Upon My Lips a Song*, 130.
49. "Fireman Lefanchek Wins $1,000 Kate Smith Award for Heroism," *Syracuse Journal*, 15 February 1938; "Kate Smith's Talent Quest to Include Atlanta Girl," *Atlanta Georgian*, 19 May 1938; "Typical American Boy," *Radio Guide*, 22 April 1939.
50. For an example of criticism against Smith, see Joseph Mitchell, "Home Girl," *New Yorker*, 3 March 1934. Unlike Berlin, Smith and Collins did not collect negative press in Smith's scrapbooks, so the portrait painted of her there does not include such detractions. But Smith does mention these critics in her autobiography, and also mentioned being accused of using her frequent visits to veterans and gifts of dolls to hospitalized children as publicity stunts. Smith, *Living in a Great Big Way*, 36, 143.
51. *Philadelphia News*, 19 July 1938, untitled clipping in KSCS Package 9.
52. Hayes, *Kate Smith*, 148.
53. Cassidy, *What Women Watched*, 63.
54. Hayes, *Kate Smith*, 147–50.
55. Ibid., 149. For a discussion of the inevitable question of whether Smith and Collins were romantically linked, see 143–50.
56. See Smith, *Upon My Lips a Song*, esp. 8–13.
57. Hayes, *Kate Smith*, 17.
58. Radio transcript, *Kate Smith Speaks*, 10 November 1938, quoted in Hayes, *Kate Smith*, 53.
59. Ibid.
60. Kate Smith, "The Star Spangled Banner vs. God Bless America," *Pic*, 29 October 1940.
61. Berlin to Maloney, 10 October 1940, IBC Box 259, Folder 8.
62. Ibid.
63. Radio transcript, *The Kate Smith Hour*, 10 November 1938, quoted in Hayes, *Kate Smith*, 54.

64. See *Radio Daily*, 14 November 1938; *Houston Post*, 10 November 1938, 18 March 1939, all untitled clippings in KSCS Package 10. Also see "Kate the Great," *Time*, 15 May 1939.
65. Press release, 11 July [1940], IBC Box 259, Folder 8.
66. From its appearance, this press release was likely generated on one of the United Press teletype machines that Collins had installed in their offices to prepare for Smith's commentary program, *Kate Smith Speaks*, in the spring of 1938. See Smith, *Upon My Lips a Song*, 102.
67. Ted Collins to "Benny," undated (likely July 1940, in response to the 11 July press release), IBC 259, Folder 8.
68. Wharton, "God Bless America," *Look*, 17 December 1940, 12.
69. This caption is quoted in full in the epigraph of this chapter.
70. Berlin to Collins, 29 November 1940, IBC Box 259, Folder 8.
71. Collins to Berlin, 10 December 1940, IBC Box 259, Folder 8; Proof of editor's note, *Look*, 9 December 1940 (handwritten date) in IBC Box 259, Folder 8.
72. For more on the often overlooked role of arrangers in shaping American popular music, see Bañagale, "Rhapsodies in Blue"; Magee, *The Uncrowned King of Swing*, esp. 2–3, 6–9; and Suskin, *The Sound of Broadway Music*, esp. 3–8.
73. Maloney to Berlin, 6 August 1940, IBC Box 259, Folder 8.
74. Underlined copy of Woolf, "What Makes a Song," in IBC Box 259, Folder 8.
75. Berlin to Maloney, 7 August 1940, IBC Box 259, Folder 8.
76. Smith quoted in Hayes, *Kate Smith*, 54.
77. Suisman, *Selling Sounds*, 59.
78. See Berlin to Collins, undated and unsigned draft (likely 4 April 1939), IBC Box 260, Folder 8.
79. Bornstein to Berlin, 10 February 1939, IBC Box 258, Folder 4.
80. Berlin to Bornstein, 17 February 1939, IBC Box 258, Folder 4.
81. Bill Bacher to Bornstein, 20 February 1939, IBC Box 258, Folder 4.
82. Bornstein to Berlin, 21 February 1939, IBC Box 258, Folder 4.
83. Bornstein to Berlin, 28 March 1939, IBC Box 258, Folder 4.
84. Bornstein to Berlin, 4 April 1939, IBC Box 258, Folder 4.
85. Berlin to Bornstein, 4 April 1939, IBC Box 258, Folder 4.
86. Ibid., emphasis in original.
87. Collins to Berlin, 4 April 1939, IBC Box 259, Folder 8.
88. Mentioned in night telegram, Berlin to Bornstein, 5 April 1939, IBC Box 258, Folder 4.
89. Berlin to Collins, undated and unsigned draft (probably 4 April 1939), IBC Box 260, Folder 8.
90. Unsigned statement, 19 September 1940, IBC Box 260, Folder 8.
91. Ibid.
92. The strife here was not only between Berlin and Collins, since Berlin's donation of royalties was one of the main factors leading to the eventual split between Berlin and his business partner Saul Bornstein. According to Berlin's daughter Mary Ellin Barrett, the already troubled working relationship between Berlin and Bornstein became a "dogfight" over the lost publishing revenue from "God Bless America," and the strife intensified when Berlin donated the royalties from *This is the Army* to the fund as well. In 1944 the two men split, with Berlin keeping the copyright to his own songs with the new company name Irving Berlin Music Co., and the rest of the catalog of standards by other composers going to Bornstein, under the new name, Bourne, Inc. See Barrett, *Irving Berlin*, 222.

93. Bornstein to Berlin, 25 February 1939 and 13 March 1939, IBC Box 258, Folder 4. This push by Collins to publicize the donation does provide some support for those Smith detractors who felt that her obsession with veterans and sick children was a publicity grab. See Smith, *Upon My Lips a Song*, 36, 143.

94. Berlin to Bornstein, 1 March 1939, IBC Box 258, Folder 4.

95. Collins to Berlin, 4 April 1939, IBC Box 259, Folder 8.

96. Berlin to Collins, undated and unsigned draft (probably 4 April 1939), IBC Box 260, Folder 8.

97. Kate Smith to Governor Sprague (undated) in Bornstein to Berlin, 31 March 1939, IBC Box 258, Folder 4.

98. Bornstein to Berlin, 31 March 1939, IBC Box 258, Folder 4.

99. Berlin to Bornstein, postal telegraph, 3 April 1939, IBC Box 258, Folder 4.

100. Berlin to Bornstein, 4 April 1939, IBC Box 258, Folder 4. Smith was very generous with both her time and money to a multitude of charities and on-air fundraisers. I do not mean to imply a lack of generosity on her part, merely to acknowledge that her stake in donating royalties from "God Bless America" was different from Berlin's.

101. Press release, 11 July 1939, IBC 259, Folder 8; Collins to "Benny" (likely Berlin), 1939 (likely July, in response to press release), IBC 259, Folder 8.

102. For more on Berlin's role in the escapist musicals of the 1930s, see Dickstein, *Dancing in the Dark*, 357–407.

103. Furia, *Irving Berlin*, 95.

104. Ibid. Swope and Berlin have a long history, as Swope was the first reporter to mention Irving Berlin (then a singing waiter named Izzy Baline) in print, in 1905. For the story of their meeting, see Woollcott, *The Story of Irving Berlin*, 51–52; Kahn Jr., *The World of Swope*, 111–13; and Lewis, *Man of the World*, 13–14.

105. "Fireside Philosophy of Kate Smith," *Worcester (MA) Telegram*, 27 November 1938.

106. Slogan on the *New Yorker* masthead, as noted in Furia, *Irving Berlin*, 95.

107. Joseph Mitchell, "Home Girl," *New Yorker*, 3 March 1934.

108. Furia, *Irving Berlin*, 95–96.

109. Frank G. Prial, "Kate Smith, All-American Singer, Dies at 79," *NYT*, 18 June 1986.

110. Corrections, *NYT*, 21 June 1986.

111. Online survey disseminated by author, 31 March–31 August 2009: 791 out of 1,849 respondents named Smith as a performer with whom they associate the song; 433 correctly identified Berlin. (See survey information on the companion website. ◑) A large proportion of these respondents are baseball fans—and specifically fans of the Yankees, a team that has played the Kate Smith recording of "God Bless America" at nearly every home game since September 2001.

CHAPTER 2

1. Adela Rogers St. Johns, "Irving Berlin Tells Adela Rogers St. Johns: 'I'd Like to Write a Great Peace Song!'" *New York Journal and American*, 4 September 1938.

2. "The Girl All America Loves . . . And What She Can Do For You" (New York: Mutual Broadcasting System, 1 May 1947), KSC Box 3, Folder 4; CBS War Bond Drive advertisement, *Washington Post*, 21 September 1943, KSC Package 15. For more on Smith's associations with patriotism and the War Bond drive, see Merton, *Mass Persuasion*, 101–6.

3. American Institute of Public Opinion survey cited in Jonas, *Isolationism in America*, 1.
4. Kennedy, *Freedom from Fear*, 386.
5. Smith, *Living in a Great Big Way*, 147.
6. Ibid., 148.
7. See United States Department of Veterans Affairs, "History of Veterans Day," accessed 11 November 2009, http://www1.va.gov/opa/vetsday/vetdayhistory. asp. The holiday, which had been set aside to commemorate veterans directly after the First World War, retained its associations with peace until 1954, when its name was officially changed from Armistice Day to Veteran's Day.
8. St. Johns, "Irving Berlin Tells Adela Rogers St. Johns."
9. Radio transcript, *Kate Smith Speaks*, 10 November 1938, quoted in Hayes, *Kate Smith*, 53.
10. See, for example, *Hollywood Reporter*, 8 November 1938 (untitled clipping in KSCS Package 10).
11. Radio transcript, *Kate Smith Speaks*, 10 November 1938, quoted in Hayes, *Kate Smith*, 52.
12. See Jonas, *Isolationism in America*, 211–12; Kennedy, *Freedom from Fear*, 416; Wallace, *The American Axis*, 192.
13. *Fortune* magazine surveys from October 1937 and November 1938, cited in Jonas, *Isolationism in America*, 212.
14. Harry Axst sketch [n.d.] and Lyric sheet ("Original Version," [n.d.]), IBC Box 30, Folder 1.1. Axst worked for Berlin in the period after World War I. This sketch is the only known record of the 1918 version of "God Bless America." I am grateful to Ray White, curator of the Irving Berlin Collection in the Music Division of the Library of Congress, for sharing his insights about this sketch and other aspects of the song's changing musical form and lyrics. Thanks also to Ryan Bañagale for his helpful comments on the song's form.
15. The leaps and rhythmic phrasing in this original opening melody cast some doubt on Jody Rosen's argument that Berlin borrowed the opening line of "God Bless America" from an early Jewish novelty song, "When Mose with His Nose Leads the Band," written by Irish songwriters in 1906. It seems unlikely—though not impossible—that Berlin remembered this old tune in 1938, when he made these changes to "God Bless America." See Rosen, liner notes, *Jewface*, 6.
16. Charles Hamm uses the relative similarity between the 1918 and 1938 incarnations of the song as evidence for his argument that the musical style of Tin Pan Alley remained constant throughout the early and mid-twentieth century, despite drastic changes in technology. Hamm, *Yesterdays*, 338–40.
17. Lead sheet, 25 October 1938, IBC Box 30, Folder 1.2.
18. Typed lyric sheet, 25 October 1938, IBC Box 30, Folder 1.2.
19. Furia, *Ira Gershwin*, 31, quoted in Magee, "Irving Berlin's 'Blue Skies,'" 550.
20. Jones, *The Songs that Fought the War*, 58–62.
21. Proofs, IBC Box 30, Folders 1.3 and 1.4.
22. First proof, 31 October 1938, IBC Box 30, Folder 1.3.
23. Hamm, *Yesterdays*, 359.
24. Piano score (probably Helmy Kresa), 2 November 1938, IBC Box 30, Folder 1.6.
25. Administrative files ("Berlin–God Bless America [Las Vegas manuscript]"), Music Division, Library of Congress, Washington, DC. This copy was faxed to the Library of Congress in 1991 by a sheet music dealer who claimed that it was the song's

"original manuscript." In its upper righthand corner, in handwriting that is likely Irving Berlin's, a note reads, "Ted—What do you think now—I," indicating that this copy reflects final changes to the song. In this version, a line that appears on lyric sheets as "optional" ("From the green fields in Virginia / To the gold fields out in Nome") is crossed out. Since Smith sang this line when the song debuted, it is likely that this copy was exchanged after the song's premiere, though the lyrics could have been crossed out at a later date. See Lyric sheets, IBC Box 30, Folder 1.10.

26. Berlin quoted in Furia, *Irving Berlin*, 193.
27. Bornstein to Berlin, 26 November 1938, IBC Box 258, Folder 4.
28. Irving Berlin, *God Bless America* (New York: Irving Berlin Inc., 1939) in IBC Box 30, Folder 1.11.
29. Berlin to Bornstein, 1 February 1939, IBC Box 258, Folder 4. The original verse persisted in Kate Smith's performances at least through 16 February 1939.
30. Freedland, *Irving Berlin*, 144; A. C. Horn, Anti-Defamation League of B'Nai Brith, to Berlin, 31 December 1940, IBC Box 419, Folder 1.
31. Barrett, *Irving Berlin*, 186. Berlin's wife Ellin, a dedicated supporter of Roosevelt who spoke out against the Lindberghs' support of the Nazis, seems to have been a strong influence on her husband's activism.
32. Sara K. Crampton to Irving Berlin, 26 September 1939, IBC Box 261, Folder 7.
33. Berlin to Bornstein, 30 September 1939, IBC Box 261, Folder 7.
34. "Trainees Parents to Rally Tuesday," *NYT*, 18 May 1941; "Freedom Rally Cheers Demands to Erase Hitler," *Philadelphia News*, 29 May 1941; "La Guardia Warns of Aid to Enemy by Lack of Unity," *NYT*, 29 May 1941. The song was also sung at Allied Relief events. See, for example, "1400 See Stewart, Neff, Campbell Performance Last Night," *Indiana Gazette*, 14 September 1940.
35. "One Nation—Indivisible?" *Chicago Times*, 23 December 1940; and "Lindbergh Joins in Wheeler Plea to U.S. to Shun War," *NYT*, 24 May 1941. Some journalists wondered if the position against this song was part of anti-Semitic and anti-British propaganda by factions of America First affiliated with the Nazis. See also "Disreputable Camp Followers," *Waterbury Republican*, 29 May 1941.
36. Kennedy, *Freedom from Fear*, 427.
37. Jonas, *Isolationism in America*, 215.
38. Berlin quoted in S.J. Woolf, "What Makes a Song," *NYT*, 28 July 1940.
39. For another discussion of Berlin's omission of a verse to create a sense of universality, see Rosen, *White Christmas*, 28, 56.
40. Kate Smith, "God Bless America" premiere, 10 November 1938, Irving Berlin Collection of Noncommercial Sound Recordings, 1933–1989, New York Public Library for the Performing Arts.
41. Wharton, "God Bless America," *Look*, 17 December 1940, 12.
42. Gross, *I Looked and I Listened*, 140; Hayes, *Kate Smith*, 54. That Berlin wanted the song to be performed like a "ballad" is complicated by the fact that he added the tempo marking "marziale" to proofs of the song before its premiere as well as to his published sheet music. See first proof, 31 October 1938, IBC Box 30, Folder 1.3; and Berlin, *God Bless America* (sheet music), in IBC Box 30, Folder 1.11.
43. Hayes, *Kate Smith*, 54.
44. Bornstein to Berlin, 26 November 1938, IBC Box 258, Folder 4. Those in attendance seem to be Sam Katz (an MGM executive) and Max Winslow (a friend of Berlin who worked at the Ted Snyder music company). "Disney" could very well be Walt, since Berlin's music company published the music from *Snow White*, which was released in 1937. See Jablonski, *Irving Berlin*, 226.

45. Berlin to Bornstein, 13 February 1939, IBC Box 258, Folder 4.
46. Kate Smith, "God Bless America (with verse)—2/16/1939," *Kate Smith on the Radio: The Ted Straeter Collection*.
47. Without access to internal correspondence, it is impossible to know the creative source behind these changes in tempo, whether from Smith herself, her conductor Jack Miller, Tony Gale, or Ted Collins.
48. Posted by "Alan (co-founder)," 17 January 2005, accessed 4 June 2010, www. english-test.net/forum/ftopic2030.html. This posting on an ESL instructional website was in response to queries about an exam question that asked students to distinguish between the two words.
49. Kate Smith, "God Bless America," *The American Songbook Series: Irving Berlin*.
50. These include a version for MGM recorded in early 1948, one for Tops in fall 1959, and a live performance issued by RCA Victor in November 1963. See the discography in Hayes, *Kate Smith*, 247, 252, 253.
51. The album includes the title song as well as a selection of well-known songs about specific states, including "Stars Fell on Alabama," "Oklahoma," and "My Old Kentucky Home." Ibid., 252.
52. Dunn and Jones, *Embodied Voices*, 3. See also Abbate, "Opera; or, the Envoicing of Women," 254; and Cusick, "On Musical Performances of Gender and Sex," 25–33. This also resonates with Kate Smith's embodiment of "safe femininity" discussed in Cassidy, *What Women Watched*, 49–74.

CHAPTER 3

1. Quoted in S. J. Woolf, "What Makes a Song," *NYT*, 28 July 1940.
2. Don Moore, "The Story Behind 'God Bless America,'" *Chicago Radio Guide*, 23 August 1940.
3. Abel Green, "'God Bless America' a Saga," *Variety*, 17 July 1940; "Patriotic Song Boom Nearing '17 War Peak," *New York Herald Tribune*, 20 July 1940; George W. Clarke, "God Bless America! The Story Behind a Song Hit," *Green Magazine*, 21 July 1940; Woolf, "What Makes a Song a Song"; Arthur Bronson, "Birth of a Ballad," *Philadelphia Record*, 5 August 1940; Ira Wolfert, "'God Bless America' Spent 22 Years Lying in Trunk," *Boston Evening Globe*, 5 August 1940; Gerold Frank, "God Bless America: How It Was Written," *New York Journal and American*, 11 August 1940; Moore, "The Story Behind 'God Bless America'"; Alvin H. Goldstein, "Irving Berlin and His 'God Bless America,'" *St. Louis Post-Dispatch*, 25 August 1940; "Story of 'God Bless America,'" *New York Herald Tribune*, 27 October 1940.
4. Irving Berlin to E. C. Mills (ASCAP), 20 August 1940, in Barrett research folder, R&H Communications files.
5. Furia, *Irving Berlin*, 5; Rosen, *White Christmas*, 13.
6. Gerold Frank to Irving Berlin, 20 July 1940, IBC Box 261, Folder 7. Frank, a journalist at the *New York Journal American*, wrote a profile about "God Bless America" for the newspaper on 11 August 1940, perhaps inspired by this experience on the train.
7. Wm. C. Johnson, letter to the editor, *Louisville Courier-Journal*, 10 November 1940.
8. "'God Bless America' and the British," *Danville (VA) Register*, 2 December 1940.
9. See clippings from September 1940 in IBC Box 257, Folder 1. Also see Charles E. Kopp, Ritual Committee Chairman, United War Veterans to Irving Berlin, 25 July 1939, IBC Box 261, Folder 9. In many of these cases "God Bless America" was sung in addition to "The Star-Spangled Banner," "America," and other songs.

10. See, for example, "Berlin Tune Made State School Song," *Atlanta Constitution*, 1 September 1940.
11. See articles from the *Chicago Defender* (not included in the Irving Berlin Collection): "Billikens Join Safety Drive," 28 September 1940; "Sigma Gamma Rho Sorors Open Educational Week," November 30, 1940; "Railroad Firemen Gird to Protect Jobs," 12 April 1941. For more on "Lift Every Voice and Sing" and its role as an African American anthem, see Bond and Wilson, *Lift Every Voice and Sing.*
12. "Patriotic Song Boom Nearing '17 War Peak"; David A. Banks, "The Lost and Found ASCAP 'Cavalcade of Music' Recordings," The Virtual Museum of the City of San Francisco, accessed 3 June 2010, http://www.sfmuseum.org/hist5/cavalcade.html; "'God Bless America' Is Patriotic Theme," *Chicago Defender*, 20 July 1940.
13. "Patriotic Song Boom Nearing '17 War Peak"; sports clippings in IBC Box 257, Folder 1; and "Wilberforce and Florida Tie, 0–0," *Chicago Defender*, 14 December 1940.
14. *Baltimore News-Post*, 13 September 1940 and *Hastings (NY) News*, 26 September 1940, in IBC Box 257, Folder 1; "Patriotic Song Boom Nearing '17 War Peak"; Diana, "In Passing," *Chicago Defender*, 13 July 1940; and Moore, "The Story Behind 'God Bless America.'"
15. Wharton, "God Bless America."
16. "Stokowski, Here for Concert Tonight, Praises Martial, Folk Songs," clipping in IBCS 548, identified as Nashville, Tennessee, June 1941.
17. "Democrats Will Use Tune Willkie Forces Will Sing," *NYT*, 14 July 1940.
18. "'God Bless America' Is Put Into German," *NYT*, 22 September 1940; "Japanese Vow Loyalty," 22 October 1940, *Los Angeles Times*.
19. "Bund Camp Bars Hitler Pictures," *NYT*, 11 August 1940; "Nazi Bund and Ku Klux Klan Hold Joint 'Americanism' Rally," *Altamount (MO) Times*, 28 August 1940.
20. "God Bless America! We Should Sing of Our Blessings," *Los Angeles Examiner*, 27 July 1940.
21. "Audience is Invited to Sing," *New Bedford Times*, 17 July 1940; "Crowd to Sing 'Pop' Finale," *Youngstown Vindicator-Telegram*, 25 July 1940; "Sing Planned at WPA Concert," *Wilmington (DE) News*, 6 August 1940; "First Songfest Will Be Held On Wednesday Night," *Missouri Valley (IA) Daily News*, 10 August 1940. For more on the history of community sings, see Blair, *The Torchbearers*, 68–70; and Culbertson, *He Heard America Singing*, 184–86. For more about the community music projects of the WPA, see Bindas, *All of This Music Belongs to the Nation*, 17–23.
22. "Sing Planned at WPA Concert."
23. Susman, "The Culture of the Thirties," 172.
24. Bergreen, *As Thousands Cheer*, 372.
25. Wharton, "God Bless America."
26. "History Set to Music," *Pic*, 29 October 1940.
27. "Story of 'God Bless America."
28. Berlin interview with Phyllis Battelle (1968), quoted in Jablonski, *Irving Berlin*, 313.
29. "Willkie Hits Charge He's 'Aristocrat,'" *Chicago Times*, 26 September 1940.
30. Irving Berlin Inc. to Wilbert A. Hunt, 9 April 1940, IBC Box 261, Folder 8.
31. See Clarke, "The Story Behind a Song Hit"; and Green, "'God Bless America' A Saga."
32. "Remarks by 'Mike,'" *Mike Magazine*, 13 May 1939.
33. Barrett, *Irving Berlin*, 173, 187.

34. Hayes, *Kate Smith*, 55.
35. Wharton, "God Bless America."
36. For more on this phenomenon, see Jones, *The Songs that Fought the War*, 63.
37. Al Stillman, "Of Thee They Sing," *Variety*, 4 December 1940, cited in Jones, *The Songs that Fought the War*, 64.
38. "Radio Time Table," *Washington Post*, 20 September 1940.
39. Berlin quoted in Goldstein, "Irving Berlin and His 'God Bless America.'"
40. "'God Bless America' Called 'Trashy Ballad' By Prominent Singer," *Cumberland (MD) News*, 16 December 1940. Ashley's strange definition of "jazz" has roots in the 1920s, when the term was used to describe popular music of any kind. See Oja, *Making Music Modern*, 318; Evans, *Writing Jazz*, 14; Savran, *Highbrow/Lowdown*, 23.
41. "Story of 'God Bless America'"; Berlin to Mike Gold, 29 January 1941, IBC Box 260, Folder 9.
42. See, for example, *China Grove (NC) News*, 27 September 1940; and William Willard, "It's Never Too Late to Learn," unidentified clipping, 29 September 1940, all in IBC Box 257, Folder 1.
43. A summary of responses from college newspapers was included in "God Bless America," *Gonzaga Bulletin*, 27 November 1940.
44. Earl Wilson, "Harry Richman Singing Martial Tune," *New York Post*, 22 October 1940.
45. M. Matlin, untitled clipping, *San Francisco Call-Bulletin*, 11 June 1941 (in IBCS 548).
46. Klein, *Woody Guthrie*, 133.
47. Ibid., 136, quoted in Jackson, "Is This Song Your Song Anymore?" 252.
48. For more on the dueling nature of these two songs, see Jackson, "Is This Song Your Song Anymore?"; and Jody Rosen, "Two American Anthems, in Two American Voices," *NYT*, 29 July 2000.
49. Jackson, "Is This Song Your Song Anymore?" 256.
50. "This Land Is Your Land" was also under copyright when it was published in 1945, but Guthrie had a much different orientation around copyright than Berlin, apparently writing the following notice on a mimeographed songbook circulated in the late 1930s: "This song is Copyrighted in U.S., under Seal of Copyright # 154085, for a period of 28 years, and anybody caught singin' it without our permission, will be mighty good friends of ourn, cause we don't give a dern. Publish it. Write it. Sing it. Swing to it. Yodel it. We wrote it, that's all we wanted to do." The Museum of Musical Instruments, "Bound for Glory: The Life and Times of Woody Guthrie," accessed 3 June 2010, http://www.themomi.com/museum/Guthrie/index_1024.html. The copyright to "This Land Is Your Land" expired in 1973. For more on Guthrie and copyright, see Raizel Liebler, "*This Land is Your Land* belongs to you and me," LibraryLaw Blog, accessed 11 February 2010, http://blog.librarylaw.com/librarylaw/2004/08/ithis_land_is_y.html; and Katie Dean, "JibJab is Free for You and Me," *Wired*, 24 August 2004.
51. Mike Gold, "As a National Hymn, 'God Bless America' Lacks Real Dignity," *Daily Worker*, 21 January 1941.
52. Irving Berlin Inc. to Wilbert A. Hunt, 9 April 1940, IBC Box 261, Folder 8.
53. "Finds No Penalty For Use of Music," *Prescott (AZ) Courier*, 2 July 1941.
54. For more on the struggles between ASCAP and BMI, see: Sanjek and Sanjek, *Pennies From Heaven*, 184–211; and Schultz, "Performing-Right Societies in the United States." For a contemporary view, see T. R. Kennedy, Jr., "The Case of ASCAP vs. BMI," *NYT*, 15 December 1940.

55. A fascinating parallel to this battle emerged more than fifty years later in 1996, this time between ASCAP and the National Restaurant Association over site-licensing fees. The fight became public in a media war in which the restaurant lobbying group made public the fact that ASCAP was preventing Girl Scouts from singing copyrighted songs around the campfire, creating a public relations nightmare for ASCAP that ultimately moved the organization to release the Girl Scouts from paying those fees. The God Bless America Fund again served as a bulwark against criticism, since in addition to announcing that they would return fees to any Girl Scout camp that had already paid, ASCAP "added that in 1940 Irving Berlin had donated all future royalties from 'God Bless America' to the Girl Scouts and Boy Scouts." See: Elisabeth Bumiller, "Battle Hymns around Campfires," *NYT*, 17 December 1996; Lisa Bannon, "Birds Sing, but Campers Can't—Unless They Pay Up," *Wall Street Journal*, 21 August 1996; Ken Ringle, "ASCAP Changes Its Tune," *Washington Post*, 28 August 1996.
56. "Heard and Overheard," *New York City PM*, 9 January 1941.
57. James Alden Barber to Berlin, 22 July 1940, IBC Box 261, Folder 7.
58. Berlin's protection of his copyrights often meant that he did not allow his songs to be included in books or his lyrics to be quoted or excerpted. See Stephen Holden, "Accord Opens Up Irving Berlin's Musical Legacy," *NYT*, 5 June 1990.
59. Berlin to Barber, 12 August 1940, IBC Box 261, Folder 7.
60. In 1933, ASCAP released a pamphlet titled "The Murder of Music," which chronicled dwindling sheet music and recording sales. They also claimed that radio was killing music through overexposure and repetition of hits. See Schultz, "Performing-Right Societies in the United States," 516–17.
61. Suisman, *Selling Sounds*, 51.
62. Alvin H. Goldstein, "Carrying On in a Large Way," *St. Louis Post-Dispatch*, 2 July 1939.
63. Samuel H. Williamson, "Seven Ways to Compute the Relative Value of a U.S. Dollar Amount, 1774 to present," MeasuringWorth, April 2012, accessed 21 January 2013, www.measuringworth.com/uscompare.
64. See Green, "'God Bless America' A Saga." In fact, since Berlin had always planned to donate his royalties from the song to charity, the higher royalty fee was meant to maximize his donation (and limit the song's performances), rather than to increase his own profit.
65. W. Livingston Larned, "Penned at Random," *White Plains (NY) Reporter*, 12 August 1940.
66. "The Star Spangled Banner," written in 1814, did not become the United States' official national anthem until 1931. It also had a "parlor song lineage," being played in the home alongside love songs and other popular hits of the day—perhaps an early nineteenth-century equivalent to the pop song status of "God Bless America." See Crawford, *America's Musical Life*, 240–41. For more on "The Star Spangled Banner," see Mark Clague, "O Say Can You Hear: A Music History of America's Anthem," accessed 21 January 2013, http://osaycanyouhear. wordpress.com.
67. "Sales of 'God Bless America' Top National Anthem in U.S.," *Knickerbocker News*, 16 September 1940. A few examples of the song being treated as an anthem: "When the song was played at Brooklyn's Ebbets Field last Memorial Day, the crowd rose and uncovered as if for the national anthem." At the Williams County Fair in Ohio: "Although 'The Star-Spangled Banner' is still the national anthem, the entire crowd in the grandstand stood up and removed hats while Kate

Smith's 'God Bless America' was sung." See "Footnotes on Headliners," *NYT*, 14 July 1940; "Heard on the Banks of the Wabash," *Montpelier (OH) Leader Enterprise*, 19 September 1940.

68. Smith, "The Star Spangled Banner vs. God Bless America," *Pic*, 29 October 1940.
69. Berlin to E. C. Mills (ASCAP), 20 August 1940, in Barrett research folder, R&H Communications files.
70. Swope to Berlin, 19 August 1940, IBC Box 260, Folder 9. This letter was in response to "Campaign to Oust National Anthem," *Gaelic American*, 27 July 1940.
71. Berlin to Swope, 20 August 1940, IBC Box 260, Folder 9. Berlin went on to point out that the vast majority of clippings about the song were positive.
72. Constance Rittenhouse to Swope, 2 December 1940, IBC Box 358, Folder 14.
73. B. E. Sackett (Special Agent in Charge, Federal Bureau of Investigations) to Swope, 30 January 1941, IBC Box 260, Folder 9.
74. Edward Smythe to the director, Girl Scouts of America, 30 November 1940, IBC Box 358, Folder 14.
75. "Nazi Bund and Ku Klux Klan Hold Joint 'Americanism' Rally," *Altamount (MO) Times*, 28 August 1940. "Bundsmen and Klansmen Hold Love Feast in New Jersey," *Los Angeles Times*, 19 August 1940.
76. Cleve Sallendar, "G-A-W-D Bless A-M-E-R-I-K-E-R!" *Free American and Deutscher Weckruf und Beobachter*, 5 September 1940. This article was previously cited as an "unidentified news clipping" (see Furia, *Irving Berlin*, 296n195.2), but there is a reference to the publication information in a letter buried in the "miscellaneous correspondence" folders of the God Bless America files at the Library of Congress: National Blue Men of America to Irving Berlin, 4 September 1940, IBC Box 261, Folder 10.
77. Handy, *A Christian America*, 66 (quoted in Dinnerstein, *Antisemitism in America*, 105). For more on anti-Semitism during this period, see also Sarna, *American Judaism*, 214–20.
78. Kennedy, *Freedom from Fear*, 413, 415.
79. Roscoe Conkling Simmons, "The Week," *Chicago Defender*, 20 July 1940.
80. Dinnerstein, *Antisemitism in America*, 115–16, 121.
81. Ibid., 118.
82. Ibid., 116.
83. Ibid., 121.
84. Plan in "Reports and Memoranda on Anti-Semitism in America and AJC's Work to Combat It, 1939," 8, Anti-Semitism/AJC file, American Jewish Committee Subject Files, accessed 7 November 2008, http://ajcarchives.org/ajcarchive/ DigitalArchive.aspx. Reprinted with permission. New York: American Jewish Committee, © 2013. www.AJC.org. All rights reserved.
85. Quoted in Dinnerstein, *Antisemitism in America*, 123.
86. Barrett, *Irving Berlin*, 186.
87. "Badgered Ballad," *Time*, 30 September 1940.
88. "Songs Such as 'God Bless America' Scored by Dr. Romig as 'Mawkish' and as 'Doggerel,'" *NYT*, 29 July 1940.
89. Herbert Bayard Swope, "Letters to the Times: 'God Bless America' Held Real Tribute With Highly Practical Aim," *NYT*, 31 July 1940. Berlin later met with Rev. Romig as a result of intervention by the head of the National Conference of Christians and Jews, Everett Clinchy, where they came to understand and admire one another. See Everett Clinchy to Berlin, 5 November 1940, IBC Box 318, Folder 20; Rev. Edgar

Romig to Berlin, 31 October 1940, IBC Box 318, Folder 20. See chap. 4 for more on Berlin's involvement with the National Conference of Christians and Jews.

90. "Bishop Oldham Proposes 'God Purge America,'" *New York Herald Tribune*, 12 November 1940.

91. Dr. Peter Marshall, "Why Should God Bless America," sermon delivered at New York Avenue Presbyterian Church, Washington, DC, 15 September 1940, 4 (in IBC Box 261, Folder 9).

92. Berlin quoted in Wolfert, "'God Bless America' Spent 22 Years Lying in Trunk."

93. Irving Berlin, "God Bless America," *Irving Sings Berlin*. This performance occurred less than a year after the premiere of "God Bless America," at a dinner celebrating ASCAP's twenty-fifth anniversary.

94. Frank, "God Bless America: How It Was Written."

95. Barrett, *Irving Berlin*, 173–74. This recording is discussed in similar terms by Jody Rosen: "By far the most moving version of the song I've heard is a solo Berlin performance, recorded in 1939, with the great man himself plinking at the piano and croaking away in his charming, squeaky, New York–accented singing voice. . . . It's great: 'God Bless America' as a singer-songwriter's confession, not some bloated anthem. See if you don't get a lump in the ol' throat after all." Jody Rosen, comment on Carl Wilson, "It's Their Party (Gore v. Phair)," Zoilus, accessed 2 January 2011, http://www.zoilus.com/documents/general/2005/000603.php.

CHAPTER 4

1. Jody Rosen frequently remarks on this aspect of Berlin's craft in *White Christmas*, esp. 4–5, 13, 28, 56.

2. See Turino, "Signs of Imagination, Identity, and Experience"; Turino, *Music as Social Life*, esp. 8–10; Peirce, "Logic as Semiotic," esp. 107–11.

3. Elizabeth R. Duval, "New Things in City Shops," *NYT*, 29 October 1939; and "Hats Round the World," *NYT*, 26 November 1939.

4. See, for example, Classified Ad 312, *NYT*, 10 March 1940; Classified Ad 28, *NYT*, 10 June 1940; Classified Ad 297, *NYT*, 21 July 1940.

5. "Irving Berlin Inspires American Patriotism," *Variety*, 31 July 1940. Another reporter wrote, "Innumerable by-products have sprung up—'God Bless America' banners, buttons, framed mottoes, fireworks displays." Don Moore, "The Story Behind 'God Bless America,'" *Chicago Radio Guide*, 23 August 1940.

6. "Tolerance Pleas Led by Dr. Compton," *NYT*, 29 November 1938.

7. Clinchy to Berlin, 5 November 1940 and 28 November 1939, IBC Box 318, Folder 20. It is likely that this private meeting in Berlin's office took place sometime before the NCCJ's November 1938 event, and thus long before the song became popular as a result of Kate Smith's radio performances.

8. Berlin to Clinchy, 5 December 1939, IBC Box 318, Folder 20.

9. Herbert Osborne to Berlin, 14 December 1939, IBC Box 318, Folder 20. In 1947, Berlin wrote, "Help Me To Be a Neighbor" specifically for the benefit of the NCCJ. See Clinchy to Ellin Berlin, 18 January 1947 and Irving Berlin to Clinchy, 21 April 1947, both in IBC Box 318, Folder 20.

10. Barrett, *Irving Berlin*, 122.

11. Ibid, 123. As the composer of "White Christmas" and "Easter Parade," Berlin certainly showed his appreciation for the secular celebration of Christian holidays. See Rosen, *White Christmas*, esp. 36–39, 146–48, and 164–65.

12. Statement issued by the Trustees of the God Bless America Fund (Col. Theodore Roosevelt Jr, Gene Tunney, and Herbert Bayard Swope), 9 July 1940, IBC Box 260, Folder 9.

13. See Theodore S. Chapin, "Background on The God Bless America Fund," *Happy Talk: News of The Rodgers & Hammerstein Organization*, 9:2, Winter 2001. Serendipitously, a similar structure also existed among the triumvirate of Berlin, Kate Smith, and Ted Collins, who were together responsible for "God Bless America" and its legacy. (According to Smith's obituary, Collins was a Roman Catholic, and Smith was raised Presbyterian, although she began attending Catholic services in the 1940s and converted to Catholicism after Collins's death in 1965).

14. See letterhead in correspondence in IBC Box 349, Folder 7. A fourth chairperson representing the Eastern Orthodox faith was added in 1975.

15. See Silk, "Notes on the Judeo-Christian Tradition in America," 65–85; and Hutchison, *Religious Pluralism in America*, esp. 196–218. Both scholars point out that before World War II, the term "Judeo-Christianity" had been used to describe similarities between the two religions, usually in the context of Christian retention of aspects of ancient Jewish practice. Silk, 65–66; Hutchison, 197–98.

16. Silk, "Notes on the Judeo-Christian Tradition," 66.

17. Hutchison, *Religious Pluralism in America*, 197; Silk, "Notes on the Judeo-Christian Tradition," 67. Others have argued that it was the US military itself that first institutionalized the idea of shared Jewish and Christian values during World War II. See Moore, "Jewish GIs and the Creation of the Judeo-Christian Tradition," 31–53; and Rosen, *White Christmas*, 147.

18. Quoted in Silk, "Notes on the Judeo-Christian Tradition," 65; Hutchison, *Religious Pluralism in America*, 198.

19. Hutchison, *Religious Pluralism in America*, 198; Domke and Coe, *The God Strategy*, 14–15.

20. Quoted in Silk, "Notes on the Judeo-Christian Tradition," 67.

21. Ibid., 66–67.

22. "Tells of Peril of Injustice," *New York Sun*, 30 January 1941.

23. Hud Robbins, "'God Bless America': Words of Song Runs Over and Over Again Through Minds of Austrian Refugees," *Danville (IL) News*, 25 September 1940.

24. Levitin, *The World in Six Songs*, 86.

25. Furia, *Irving Berlin*, 192.

26. Savage, *Broadcasting Freedom*, 21. This interest in acceptance in the late 1930s can be contrasted with an earlier focus on using radio for assimilation purposes, as Michelle Hilmes notes, smoothing regional dialects and bringing English into American households. In the late 1930s, however, with the specters of Nazism and Fascism threatening national unity, it appears that the role of radio tilted toward celebrating differences rather than homogenization. See Hilmes, *Radio Voices*, 18–20.

27. For an overview of this program's history and a critique of its content, see Savage, *Broadcasting Freedom*, 21–62.

28. Ibid., 22

29. Ibid., 49. Other songs capitalized on this idea of tolerance and inclusion as well. "Ballad for Americans," written by Earl Robinson and John Latouche and first performed on the radio by Paul Robeson in November 1939, celebrates the same kind of multicultural America as the radio program *Americans All*. See Savage,

Broadcasting Freedom, 61–62. For more on "Ballad for Americans," see Barg, "Paul Robeson's *Ballad for Americans*." Another song of the period that specifically addressed the patriotism and contributions of African Americans was "We Are Americans, Too," written by Eubie Blake, Andy Razaf, and Charles Cooke for their 1940 musical *Tan Manhattan* and published by W. C. Handy in 1941 ("Handy's New 'America' Out," *Chicago Defender*, 24 May 1941). For more on the genesis of the song and Razaf's excised anti-lynching lyrics, see Singer, *Black and Blue*, 306–10.

30. Jacobson, *Whiteness of a Different Color*, 95–96.
31. Hall, "The Long Civil Rights Movement and the Political Uses of the Past," 1245.
32. Hugh S. Gardner, "American Negro Exposition An Inspiration To Both Races," *Pittsburgh Courier*, 13 July 1940.
33. Profile of Swope in *Trefoil*, Girl Scout Council of Greater New York, September–October 1958, vol. 13, no. 4; Boy Scouts of America, First Progress Report to the God Bless America Fund, January 1941, IBC Box 258, Folder 6.
34. Alvin H. Goldstein, "Irving Berlin and His 'God Bless America,'" *St. Louis Post-Dispatch*, 25 August 1940.
35. Boy Scouts of America, First Progress Report, IBC Box 258, Folder 6.
36. Photograph and caption in *Boys' Life*, June 1941; photograph of African American troop in 9 May 1941 folder; M. G. Boswell to James West, 2 October 1941; L. I. Alexander to God Bless America Fund, 29 May 1942 (all in IBC Box 258, Folder 6).
37. Swope to Berlin, 25 February 1941, IBC Box 260, Folder 9; Swope to Arthur Schuck, 31 January 1949, IBC Box 259, Folder 1.
38. "$500,000 Sought for Girl Scouts," *NYT*, 11 October 1950.
39. Smith quoted in Macdonald, *Don't Touch That Dial!* 354.
40. Photograph in Smith, *Upon My Lips a Song*, in photograph inserts [n.p.].
41. "The Girl All America Loves . . . And What She Can Do For You," promotional brochure (New York: Mutual Broadcasting System, 1 May 1947), in KSC Box 3, Folder 4.
42. "Outline of Work of the American Jewish Committee in Combating Anti-Semitism," *Reports and Memoranda on Anti-Semitism in America and AJC's Work to Combat It, 1939*, AJC Subject Files Collection, American Jewish Committee Archives, accessed 3 March 2009, www.ajcarchives.org. Reprinted with permission. New York: American Jewish Committee, © 2013. www.AJC.org All rights reserved.
43. According to one online article, "The Boy Scouts of America never drew the color line, but the movement stayed in step with the prevailing mores. . . . [T]here was only one integrated troop before 1954 in the Deep South compared to the frequent occurrence of integration in the North." Kurt Banas, "African Americans in the Boy Scout Movement," African American Registry, accessed 8 June 2010, http://www.aaregistry.org/historic_events/view/african-americans-boy-scout-movement.
44. Letter to the Editor (signed "A Soldier"), "Military Police," *Chicago Defender*, 6 September 1941.
45. Sue Stengel to Nancy DiTuro, 11 November 1998, God Bless America Fund folder (1998), R&H Files.
46. Andrew Rose, "Bush Worships Amid Discord of Dissent," *NYT*, 18 February 1991.
47. For a brief description of songs used by conservative activists, see Truzzi, "Folksongs on the Right," and "The 100 percent American Songbag: Conservative

Folksongs in America," both cited in Denisoff, *Songs of Protest, War & Peace*, 59. Thomas Turino discusses the Nazi's calculated use of music, but his focus is on its coercive functions rather than the silencing of dissent. Turino, *Music as Social Life*, 190–210.

48. This anti-Communist association with the phrase "God bless America" predates the song's debut, as evidenced by a letter signed by 1,500 female WPA workers in 1936, attesting to the lack of Communist influence within the Emergency Relief Bureau: "We the undersigned, are very grateful for what the government is doing for us and we do not feel it necessary for us to belong to a union to protect us from the hand that is feeding us; furthermore we feel that all Reds and agitators should be dismissed from this and all government projects. God bless America and all who love Uncle Sam" ("ERB Challenge Issued to Critics," *NYT*, 16 July 1936).

49. Louis Stark, "Auto Union Votes Censure of Soviet," *NYT*, 4 August 1940.

50. "Break Up Red Meeting With Patriotic Song," *Gastonia (NC) Gazette*, 18 April 1941. "Bridgeport War Veterans Break Up Eisler Meeting," *NYT*, 17 November 1947.

51. "2 'Peace' Meetings Jeered By Pickets" and "Waldorf War," *NYT*, 27 March 1949; "500 Leftists Miss Reds Going to Jail," *NYT*, 22 October 1949.

52. This association with anti-Communism would continue more than fifty years later. At a 2002 event to commemorate Joseph McCarthy, participants sang "God Bless America," after which one participant commented: "This song always reminds me of Joe. I still have his picture on my bedroom wall." David Oshinsky, "Graying Now, McCarthyites Keep the Faith," *NYT*, 1 June 2002.

53. "First Lady Backs Leviton Strikers," *NYT*, 6 February 1941; Stanley Levey, "74 Suspended in Subway Dispute," *NYT*, 14 November 1956.

54. Gene Blake, "Many Dissent on Riot Film," *Los Angeles Times*, 16 May 1961.

55. Harrison E. Salisbury, "350 Negro Student Demonstrators Held in South Carolina Stockade," *NYT*, 16 March 1960; "Fire Hoses Disperse Texas Negro Crowd," *NYT*, 31 May 1960.

56. "Rights Pilgrimage," *NYT*, 23 February 1962

57. Don Neff, "Belief in 'Just Cause' Prompts Tract Pickets," *Los Angeles Times*, 5 August 1963.

58. "White Minister Held in Jackson," *NYT*, 31 May 1963; "100 March in Baton Rouge," *NYT*, 1 June 1963.

59. "125,000 Rally in Detroit to Protest Discrimination," *NYT*, 24 June 1963.

60. Thomas A. Johnson, "N.A.A.C.P. Groups Across Nation Mark School Desegregation Ruling," *NYT*, 18 May 1979.

61. The few uses of "God Bless America" by antiwar activists seemed to be either genuine attempts to reclaim the song or ironic uses that drew on its associations with conservatism. In 1968, an antiwar film included what the *New York Times* called "a not altogether ironically applauded rendition of 'God Bless America.'" Renata Adler, "From 'The Split' To Revolt On the Campus," *NYT*, 20 November 1968. There are also a few instances of the song being sung by antiwar activists: by a group of protestors holding a US flag upside down at Nixon's private compound in Florida; by students at a sit-in at UC Santa Barbara; and by demonstrators outside the 1972 Republican convention. "U.S. Aides Expect Saigon To Remove Units in Cambodia," *NYT*, 17 May 1970; Tom Paegel, "Mass Arrest of 355, Tear Gas Barrage Ends Isla Vista Sit In," *Los Angeles Times*, 11 June 1970; Anthony Lewis, "The Two Nations," *NYT*, 28 August 1972.

62. Douglas Robinson, "25,000 March to Back Vietnam Policy," *NYT*, 31 October 1965; "Eggs and Fists Fly As Pacifists Stage Times Sq. Protest," *NYT*, 17 December 1965.

63. "Detective Interrupts Vietnam Read-In," *NYT*, 21 February 1966. Participants in the read-in included Normal Mailer, Alfred Kazin, Susan Sontag, Lilllian Hellman, and others. See "'God Bless America' Jolts Viet Protest," *Washington Post*, 22 February 1966.

64. Murray Schumach, "Police Keep Rein on March's Foes," *NYT*, 16 April 1967; Schumach, "70,000 Turn Out to Back U.S. Men in Vietnam War," *NYT*, 14 May 1967; "10,000 Attend Viet Parade in Monmouth," *Chicago Tribune*, 19 May 1967; John Herbers, "Backers of Nixon Policy Rally in Capital," *NYT*, 12 November 1969; Paul L. Montgomery, "Foes of War Hold Modest Protests," *NYT*, 14 December 1969; Francis X. Clines, "Workers For Nixon And Flag Come Out In Force," *NYT*, 26 May 1970; Richard Rogin, "Why the Construction Workers Holler, 'U.S.A., All the Way!'" *NYT*, 28 June 1970.

65. Homer Bigart, "9 Hurt as Police Disperse Group in Midtown After City Hall Peace Rally," *NYT*, 22 May 1970. See also: Louise Hutchinson, "2,000 Protest Viet Nam War," *Chicago Tribune*, 1 February 1967; Murray Schumach, "Police Keep Rein on March's Foes," *NYT*, 16 March 1967; "Legion Bids Congress Propose Restrictions on Supreme Court," *NYT*, 3 September 1970; "War is Protested On Inaugural Eve," *NYT*, 20 January 1973.

66. Isserman and Kazin, *America Divided*, 4.

67. For more on radio's role in creating community, see Hilmes, *Radio Voices*, esp. 6–21.

68. Robert Windeler, "Birchers Parade Without Incident," *NYT*, 31 May 1967. For more on the John Birch Society, see Schoenwald, *A Time for Choosing*, 62–99.

69. Richard Severo, "Lester Maddox, Whites-Only Restaurateur and Georgia Governor, Dies at 87," *NYT*, 26 June 2003; Robert Sherrill, "Nixon's Man in Dixie," *NYT*, 1 September 1968.

70. McGirr, *Suburban Warriors*, 5, 6, 12. Jonathan Schoenwald similarly calls the conservative mobilization a "revolution," but frames it over a longer time, from 1957 to 1972. Schoenwald, *A Time for Choosing*, 4.

71. "Brawl Breaks Out in Cairo, Ill., After a Parade by 300 Whites," *NYT*, 27 June 1969; "9 Students Hurt in Pontiac Clash," *NYT*, 9 September 1971; "Busing Foes and Backers Stage Protests in Boston," *NYT*, 1 October 1974. For more on the song's use by anti-integration activists in Boston, see Lukas, *Common Ground*, 261, 317.

72. Joseph F. Sullivan, "S.D.S. Protesters Confront Imperiale With a Swastika at Kawaida Towers," *NYT*, 3 January 1973; Joseph F. Sullivan, "Blacks See Work Resume at Kawaida Towers Site," *NYT*, 22 February 1973. For more on the rise and fall of the Kawaida Towers project, see Woodard, *A Nation Within a Nation*, 219–54.

73. Jacobson, *Whiteness of a Different Color*, esp. 188, 246–47.

74. Jacobson, *Roots, Too*, 315.

75. Anna Quindlen, "Women End Parley With Plan for Rights," *NYT*, 22 November 1977. For more on the National Women's Conference, see Rossi, *Feminists in Politics*.

76. Press, *Absolute Convictions*, 107.

77. Paul L. Montgomery, "1,600 Are Arrested in Nuclear Protests at 5 U.N. Missions," *NYT*, 15 June 1982. At a later protest, anti-nuclear activists sang "Give Peace a Chance" while counterdemonstrators sang "God Bless America" ("Battleship Iowa Attracts a Crowd of Both Sightseers and Protesters," *NYT*, 21 October 1984).

78. Turino, *Music as Social Life*, 9, 210–24.
79. Berlin to William P. Maloney, 16 July 1940, IBC 259, Folder 8.
80. William Safire, "God Bless Us," *NYT*, 28 August 1992.
81. By "associated with," I mean uttered or sung by the candidate himself, appearing in some way at a campaign or presidential event, or mentioned in connection with the politician.
82. "General 'Own Man,'" *NYT*, 31 October 1952; W.J. Lawrence, "'Party of Future,'" *NYT*, 24 July 1956.
83. Domke and Coe, *The God Strategy*, 3–8.
84. "Renewing the Compact," *NYT*, 18 July 1980, quoted and analyzed in Domke and Coe, *The God Strategy*, 3.
85. See McGirr, *Suburban Warriors*, 259–61.
86. Domke and Coe, *The God Strategy*, 61, emphasis original.
87. "Roosevelt is seen by 2,000,000 in City," *NYT*, 29 October 1940.
88. The speeches, which were given on consecutive days, were to the executive council of the AFL-CIO and the South Carolina legislature. See Philip Shabecoff, "President Plans to Seek 'Options' in Trade Talks," *NYT*, 20 February 1973; "Excerpts From President Nixon's Address to the Legislature of South Carolina," *NYT*, 21 February 1973.
89. Tom Wicker, "In The Nation: Mr. Nixon's Affirmation," *NYT*, 21 February 1968; Christopher Lydon, "Big-Name Troupe Tours New Hampshire for Nixon," *NYT*, 4 March 1972.
90. "The President Honors the POWs with a Lavish State Dinner," *National Observer*, 2 June 1973.
91. More than thirty years earlier, Jimmy Stewart had sung "God Bless America" at an Allied Relief fundraising event before the United States entered World War II. See "1400 See Stewart, Neff, Campbell Performance Last Night," *Indiana Gazette*, 14 September 1940, in IBC Box 257, Folder 1.
92. The song's association with POWs here also underscores the highly publicized use of the phrase by Captain Jeremiah Denton a few months before this event. Denton was among the first group of POWs returning to the United States, and upon their arrival he said, "We are honored to have the opportunity to serve our country under difficult circumstances. We are profoundly grateful to our Commander in Chief and to our nation for this day. God Bless America!" James P. Sterba, "First Prisoner Release is Completed," *NYT*, 13 February 1973. For more on the coverage and critique of Denton's short speech, see "Nixon Lauds Valor of Fighting Men," *NYT*, 17 February 1973; Sterba, "Managing the P.O.W.'s," *NYT*, 20 February 1973; Maurice Braddell, "Letter to the Editor: P.O.W.'s: Our Brave Men Come Home," *NYT*, 20 February 1973; Steven V. Roberts, "The P.O.W.'s: Focus of Division," *NYT*, 3 March 1973. When Denton became a senator in 1980 (R-AL), he was described as the POW who had "electrified the country" by using "God Bless America" as his first words off the plane. Steven V. Roberts, "Six of the Many New Faces That Will Be Seen in the Next Session of Congress," *NYT*, 6 November 1980.
93. Nixon to Berlin, 28 March 1973, IBC Box 349, Folder 41.
94. Nixon to Berlin, 29 May 1973 and Berlin to Nixon, 18 June 1973, in IBC Box 349, Folder 41.
95. Donnie Radcliffe, "Pearly Mae Sings While Nixon Plays," (no publication, n.d.), in IBC Box 257, Folder 9. Other songs included "Home on the Range" and "My Wild Irish Rose."

96. "Nixon Plays Piano On Wife's Birthday At Grand Ole Opry," *NYT*, 17 March 1974.
97. Russell Baker, "No Curiosity Filled the Cats," *NYT*, 19 March 1974.
98. Domke and Coe, *The God Strategy*, 18. There is an interesting parallel between this kind of signaling and James Scott's concept of a "hidden transcript," in which messages from subordinated groups are coded or hidden from those in power. Lisa McGirr argues that Christian conservatives viewed themselves as grassroots revolutionaries against the secular mainstream, and although Reagan's presidency represents their ascendancy to power, the phrase "God Bless America" may have functioned as a partially hidden transcript, a symbol of Reagan's loyalty to the Christian Right without overtly invoking the Christian faith. See Scott, *Domination and the Arts of Resistance*, 1–15, 136–82.
99. Francis X. Clines, "Reagan Appeal on Abortion is Made to Fundamentalists," *NYT*, 31 January 1984.
100. Joseph F. Sullivan, "The Man of the Hour Wears a Blue Collar," *NYT*, 12 October 1980.
101. "Remarks on Presenting the Presidential Medal of Freedom to Kate Smith in Raleigh, North Carolina, 26 October 1982," *Public Papers of the President: Ronald Reagan, 1981–1989*, Ronald Reagan Presidential Library, accessed 7 August 2009, http://www.reagan.utexas.edu/archives/speeches/1982/102682c.htm.
102. Domke and Coe, *The God Strategy*, 63–64. The drop in uses of the phrase "God Bless America" by George H. W. Bush in fig. 4.1 thus does not reflect a move away from religious rhetoric, but only the particular phrase, "God bless America."
103. Ibid., 6.
104. References to the phrase had overtaken references to the song at earlier points in its history (in 1973, and 1994–96), but never as dramatically as they did in 2000. See fig. I.1 in the introduction.
105. See the CD recording: Oscar Brand, *Presidential Campaign Songs: 1789–1996*. For more on presidential campaign songs, see Gorzelany-Mostak, "Pre-existing Music in United States Presidential Campaigns, 1960–2008."
106. Claire Suddath notes that the song wasn't considered "the hippest musical choice," but it worked nonetheless. Claire Suddath, "A Brief History of Campaign Songs," *Time.com Special Reports*, accessed 13 June 2010, http://www.time.com/time/specials/packages/article/0,28804,1840981_1840998_1840923,00.html.
107. In 2000, George W. Bush chose Tom Petty's "I Won't Back Down" in an attempt to harness the cool defiance of the pop anthem, but this tactic was foiled by a cease and desist order from Petty (see Sudath, "A Brief History of Campaign Songs"). For more on the phenomenon of pop stars refusing to allow conservative politicians to use their songs, see Eric Kleefeld, "Stop The Music! Artists Demand GOPers Quit Playing Their Hits," *Talking Points Memo DC*, 7 June 2010, accessed 13 June 2010, http://tpmdc.talkingpointsmemo.com/2010/06/stop-the-music-artists-demand-gopers-quit-playing-their-hits.php.

CHAPTER 5

1. Irving Berlin to Herbert Bayard Swope, 15 August 1952, IBC Box 261, Folder 1.
2. Survey by *Time, Cable News Network*, and *Harris Interactive*, 27 September 2001. iPOLL Databank, The Roper Center for Public Opinion Research, University of Connecticut, accessed 29 January 2009, www.ropercenter.uconn.edu/ipoll.html.
3. Of course, other songs were sung and played in response to the attacks, such as "Amazing Grace," "America, the Beautiful," "The Battle Hymn of the Republic,"

and others, but according to ASCAP, no other song attained the popularity of "God Bless America" during this period. Levitin, *The World in Six Songs*, 305n131.

4. Katharine Q. Seelye and Elisabeth Bumiller, "Bush Labels Aerial Terrorist Attacks 'Acts of War,'" *NYT*, 13 September 2001; David E. Sanger, "Bin Laden Is Wanted in Attacks, 'Dead or Alive,' President Says," *NYT*, 18 September 2001; Jennifer Steinhauer, "A Symbol of Faith Marks A City's Hallowed Ground," *NYT*, 5 October 2001.

5. David Cay Johnston and Amy Waldman, "Despite a National Rush of Emotion, Recruiting Centers Aren't Seeing a Rush to Enlist," *NYT*, 16 September 2001; Dan Barry, "Surrounded by Grief, People Around the World Pause and Turn to Prayer," *NYT*, 15 September 2001; Andrew Jacobs, "Town Sheds Its Anonymity to Comfort the Bereaved," *NYT*, 14 October 2001; Basil J. and Eunice S. Whiting, "Letter to the Editor: Homeward Bound," *NYT*, 28 October 2001.

6. Jesse McKinley, "Lights On, Broadway Dispels the Dark," *NYT*, 14 September 2001.

7. Jacob H. Fries, "Familiar Voice Lifts the Market Before the Bell," *NYT*, 18 September 2001.

8. Jack Curry, "Flags, Songs and Tears, and Heightened Security," *NYT*, 18 September 2001.

9. Laura M. Holson, "In a Rapid Evolution, Regulations for Air Travel Are Being Rewritten Almost Daily," *NYT*, 2 October 2001; Enid Nemy, "Metropolitan Diary," *NYT*, 22 October 2001.

10. James Greenwood, phone interview, 29 July 2009; Doug Ose, phone interview, 7 August 2009. There is some disagreement about the sequence of events within the retelling of this day by the former members of Congress who participated in my research. Ose credited Dennis Hastert with recognizing the necessity of holding a press conference with a large congressional presence, while Greenwood remembered that the gathering was a result of a more spontaneous resolve among members of Congress themselves.

11. See "Congress sings 'God Bless America'-2001.09.11," accessed 21 May 2010, http://www.youtube.com/watch?v=Izb459vJ-8Q.

12. Joseph Hoeffel, email survey, 26 June 2009; Terry Teachout, "On the Wings of Song," *Wall Street Journal*, 28 September 2001.

13. Daughtry, "Charting Courses through Terror's Wake: An Introduction," xx.

14. Russell Baker, "'The World Goes By' In House Song Fest," *NYT*, 5 August 1955.

15. Martin Tolchin, "Reagan and Others in G.O.P. Vow to Be Unified If They Control Congress," *NYT*, 16 September 1980.

16. Martin Tolchin and Barbara Gamarekian, "Washington Talk," *NYT*, 18 May 1988.

17. Eleven surveys were sent via email only, forty-one via both email and standard mail, and fifty-two via regular mail only. Of the completed surveys, eight were returned via email and twenty-two were print surveys sent through the mail. All surveys were completed between June and August 2009.

18. David Phelps, print survey.

19. Ken Bentsen, print survey.

20. Richard K. Armey, print survey.

21. Of the thirty survey respondents, seventeen said that they were present when the singing took place, ten were not present, and three did not indicate whether they attended. (An additional two former congressmen participated in phone interviews rather than completing surveys.) Of those not in attendance, some mentioned that they had earlier been ordered to disperse or were focused on the

needs of their constituents, one via phone from Washington and a few others who returned to their home districts.

22. Elizabeth Bumiller, "Washington Remembers 'a Sad and Terrible Day,'" *NYT*, 12 September 2003; Kate Zernike and Adam Nagourney, "A Solemn, Sad Moment to Reflect, but Politics Also Surfaces," *NYT*, 12 September 2006.

23. Anonymous survey.

24. Henry Bonilla, email survey.

25. Halbwachs, *On Collective Memory*, 40.

26. Winter, *Remembering War*, 3–4.

27. Schacter, *The Seven Sins of Memory*, 9, quoted in Winter, *Remembering War*, 4.

28. Greg Miller, "How Our Brains Make Memories," *Smithsonian Magazine*, May 2010, accessed 18 May 2010, http://smithsonianmag.com/science-nature/ How-Our-Brains-Make-Memories.html.

29. John Parkinson and Sunlen Miller, "Congress Pays Tribute to 9/11, Sings 'God Bless America' Again," *The Note* blog, ABC News, 12 September 2011, accessed 20 November 2011, http://abcnews.go.com/blogs/politics/2011/09/congress-pays-tribute-to-911-sings-god-bless-america-again/.

30. James Greenwood, phone interview, 29 July 2009.

31. Celestine Bohlen, "No. 1 Anthem: 'God Bless America,'" *NYT*, 19 September 2001; Tim Page, "'God Bless America,' The Song in A Nation's Heart," *Washington Post*, 21 September 2001; Neva Chonin, "'God Bless America' a Balm for Nation's Grief," *San Francisco Chronicle*, 14 September 2001. See also Benjamin Ivry, "Berlin's 'God Bless America' resonates anew," *Christian Science Monitor*, 21 September 2001, and César G. Soriano, "'God Bless America' roars back after tragedy," *USA Today*, 18 September 2001.

32. This point was reiterated in survey responses from Charles F. Bass, Conrad Burns, Nancy Johnson, and David Phelps.

33. Bohlen, "No. 1 Anthem: 'God Bless America.'"

34. Chonin, "'God Bless America' a Balm for Nation's Grief."

35. Page, "'God Bless America,' The Song in A Nation's Heart."

36. Ibid.

37. Regionally, the song did have some ceremonial uses prior to 9/11, such as regularly substituting for the national anthem at Philadelphia Flyers hockey games, but until 9/11 its use was not as widespread as the national anthem.

38. Alex Ross, "Requiems," *New Yorker*, 8 October 2001, accessed 16 November 2009 at "The Rest Is Noise," http://www.therestisnoise.com/2004/05/the_noise_is_br.html.

39. Charles F. Bass, print survey.

40. In 1943, Pete Seeger conducted an experiment among his fellow soldiers serving in the army, asking them to write down all of the songs they knew, and was impressed with the number of songs. He later speculated that the shared knowledge of songs across social boundaries would likely be much lower today. See Ben Ratliff, "Shared Song, Communal Memory," *NYT*, 10 February 2008. For more on the songs most Americans know, see Russell, "I (Don't) Hear America Singing."

41. David Sedaris, "Far from Home," *This American Life*, Episode 194: "Before and After," Chicago Public Radio/Public Radio International, 21 September 2001. Available online at http://www.thisamericanlife.org/radio-archives/episode/194/ before-and-after.

42. Tiryakian, "Durkheim, Solidarity, and September 11," 314, 316.

43. Solnit, *A Paradise Built in Hell*, 3.

44. Ibid., 5.

45. Rob Simmons, print survey.
46. Ross, "Requiems."
47. Henry Bonilla, email survey; Gordon H. Smith, print survey.
48. Trent Lott, print survey; Alison Mitchell and Katharine Q. Seelye, "Horror Knows No Party As Lawmakers Huddle," *NYT*, 12 September 2001.
49. Jesse McKinley, "Lights On, Broadway Dispels the Dark," *NYT*, 14 September 2001; Terry Pristin, "A Vow to Rebuild," *NYT*, 18 September 2001; Ruth La Ferla, "High Society Goes Low Key: A Hard Time for Galas," *NYT*, 23 September 2001.
50. Richard K. Armey, print survey.
51. Surveys from Conrad Burns, Gordon Smith, David Phelps, and Henry Bonilla.
52. Rabbi Yosef Kanefsky quoted in Levitin, *The World in Six Songs*, 131.
53. Connie Morella, print survey.
54. Anonymous survey.
55. Nancy Johnson, print survey.
56. H.R. 3051, a bill "to designate 'God Bless America' as the national hymn of the United States," was introduced on 5 October 2001; it died in committee. Text of bill in R&H Communications files.
57. Laurie Goodstein, "As Attacks' Impact Recedes, a Return to Religion as Usual," *NYT*, 26 November 2001; George L. Zelizer, "Quick Dose of 9–11 Religion Soothes, Doesn't Change," *USA Today*, 7 January 2002.
58. Eric Alterman, "Patriot Games: Stop the Presses," *The Nation*, 29 October 2001.
59. Jim Bessman, "Words & Music," *Billboard*, 6 October 2001.
60. Linda Angeloff Sapienza, "'God Bless America'? I Just Like the Tune," *Newsweek*, 10 December 2001.
61. "A Plague of Aftermath Theism," *New York City Atheists Newsletter*, March 2002, accessed 25 September 2012, http://www.nyc-atheists.org/newsletters/2002/Newsletter-0302.pdf.
62. Gustav Niebuhr, "Religion Journal: In Devastation's Shadow, A Landmark's Renewal," *NYT*, 3 November 2001.
63. Greg Epstein, phone interview, 2 February 2010.
64. Interview with Donna Cayot, *Hannity & Colmes*, Fox News Network, 16 November 2001, transcript accessed via www.highbeam.com, 1 February 2010.
65. The specifics of the case are outlined in Commissioner Richard P. Mills, "Appeal of Donna Cayot, Decision No. 14,786," 22 August 2002, Appeals to the Commissioner of Education, New York State Education Department, accessed 29 January 2010, www.counsel.nysed.gov/Decisions/volume42/d14786.htm.
66. Ibid.
67. Chris Morton, Letter to the Editor: "Superintendent owes boy an apology," *Journal News*, date unknown, clipping in R&H Communications files. The paper notes, "The writer is the New York state director of American Atheists, Inc."
68. American Civil Liberties Union, "ACLU Urges Supreme Court to Uphold Ruling Removing the Phrase 'Under God' From Pledge of Allegiance Recited in Public Schools," 24 March 2004, accessed 20 May 2010, http://www.aclu.org/content/aclu-urges-supreme-court-uphold-ruling-removing-phrase-under-god-pledge-allegiance-recited-p.
69. Gary Stern, "For Atheists: One Nation, Not under God," *Journal News*, 7 March 2002.
70. Interview with Donna Cayot, *Hannity & Colmes*.
71. Kathy Bonifacio, Letter to the Editor: "Parent's Request is Unreasonable," *Journal News*, date unknown, clipping in R&H Communications files.

72. Lisa Cappiello, Letter to the Editor: "Parent Ought to Be Ashamed of Herself," *Journal News*, date unknown, clipping in R&H Communications files.
73. Michael R. Richardson, Letter to the Editor: "Parent's fanaticism is misguided," *Journal News*, date unknown, clipping in R&H Communications files.
74. Interview with Donna Cayot, *Hannity & Colmes*.
75. Epstein, "Rethinking the Constitutionality of Ceremonial Deism," 2091.
76. Meizel, "A Singing Citizenry," 497; Bellah, "Civil Religion in America," 8.
77. Interview with Donna Cayot, *Hannity & Colmes*.
78. William Glaberson, "Irving Berlin Gave the Scouts a Gift of Song," *NYT*, 14 October 2001; Jen Vitale, "Patriotic tune's revival a 'ble$$ing' for Scouts," *New York Post*, 18 November 2001; Lou Carlozo, "Through the night with a light from a buck," *Chicago Tribune*, 7 November 2001.
79. Memorandum, "Regarding Irving Berlin, 'God Bless America,' and the God Bless America Fund (Status as of Fall 2002)," Irving Berlin Music Company, R&H Communications Files.
80. Victoria Traube, GBA Fund Trustee (and senior vice president and general counsel of the Rodgers & Hammerstein Organization) confirmed that the fund charged a mechanical license fee for the 9/11 tribute album. See Victoria Traube, interview, 25 June 2008.
81. Bert Fink, interview, 25 June 2008.
82. Ibid.
83. On 24 September 2001, Napster settled a suit with the recording industry, in which they paid copyright owners for the use of their music and attempted to switch their service to a subscription model. See Matt Richtel, "Songwriters and Publishers Reach a Deal with Napster," *NYT*, 25 September 2001.
84. Kate Zernike, "Scouts' Successful Ban on Gays Is Followed by Loss in Support," *NYT*, 29 August 2000.
85. Bert Fink, Memorandum to the Trustees of the GBA Fund, Irving Berlin's daughters, and executives of the Rodgers & Hammerstein Organization, 5 November 2001, in R&H Communications files.
86. Warren Hinckle, "Gay heroes, Amos Brown & the war," *San Francisco Examiner*, 25 September 2001.
87. Doug Gruse, "'America' funds children of N.Y." *Philadelphia Gay News*, 2 November 2001.
88. The Irving Berlin Music Company on behalf of The God Bless America Fund, "Statement Regarding 'God Bless America,'" 10 October 2001, in R&H God Bless America Fund files.
89. Patrick E. Tyler, "U.S. and British Troops Push into Iraq as Missiles Strike Baghdad Compound," *NYT*, 21 March 2003.
90. It is possible that this ritualized exchange of blessings had become a part of war declarations before this, but my research turned up no such earlier uses.
91. Sheryl Gay Stolberg, "On Capitol Hill, New Maneuvers Over the War," *NYT*, 11 April 2003.
92. Carl Hulse, "Lawmakers Vow to Fight Judges' Ruling On the Pledge," *NYT*, 27 June 2002.
93. For recent examples of this phenomenon see Albin Krebs and Robert McG. Thomas Jr, "Notes on People," *NYT*, 23 July 1981; Michael Norman, "Out Town," *NYT*, 28 June 1984; Jeffrey Schmalz, "Stepping Out on Shore," *NYT*, 18 May 1986; Elsa Brenner, "Changes in Laws Spur Immigrants to Citizenship," *NYT*, 24 November 1996; Edward Wong, "Swift Road for U.S. Citizen Soldiers Already Fighting in Iraq," *NYT*, 9 August 2005.

94. See Nicholas Convessore, "Thousands Rally in New York in Support of Immigrants' Rights," *NYT*, 2 April 2006; Robert D. McFadden, "Across the U.S., Protests for Immigrants Draw Thousands," *NYT*, 10 April 2006.

95. Quoted in Brian Ross and Rehab El-Buri, "Obama's Pastor: God Damn America, U.S. to Blame for 9/11," abcnews.com, 13 March 2008, accessed 7 July 2010, http://abcnews.go.com/Blotter/DemocraticDebate/story?id=4443788&page=1.

96. David Domke and Kevin Coe, "The 'God Bless America' Test," *Seattle Times*, 22 April 2008.

97. See Mike Dorning, "Obama to Give Rare Race Speech," *Chicago Tribune*, 18 March 2008 (cited in Domke and Coe, "The 'God Bless America' Test"); Jodi Kantor and Jeff Zeleny, "On Defensive, Obama Plans Talk on Race," *NYT*, 18 March 2008.

98. Mark Leibovich, "At Rallies of Faithful, Contrasts in Red and Blue," *NYT*, 30 October 2008.

99. Alessandra Stanley, "Cheers, Tears and a Sense Of the Historic Moment," *NYT*, 6 November 2008.

100. Mark Leibovich, "From a Festive Crowd Come Chants and Tears," *NYT*, 21 January 2009.

101. Dirk Johnson, "Carl Stokes, 68, Dies," *NYT*, 4 April 1996. This sentiment was similarly expressed by the newly elected mayor of Miami, a Cuban immigrant, in 2001. See Dana Canedy, "Lawyer for Cuban Boy's Relatives Is Elected Miami Mayor," *NYT*, 14 November 2001.

102. Alex Ross, "The Rest is Noise: Union Square, 11/5/08, 1 a.m.," accessed 8 July 2010, http://www.therestisnoise.com/2008/11/union-square-11.html.

103. Momar G. Visaya, "Charice Rocks Obama Pre-Inaugural Balls," *Asian Journal*, 21 January 2009, accessed 8 July 2010, http://www.asianjournal.com/dateline-usa/15-dateline-usa/1110-charice-rocks-obama-pre-inaugural-balls.html.

104. At Obama's second inauguration in 2013, the songs in the main program included "The Battle Hymn of the Republic," "America the Beautiful," "My Country 'Tis of Thee," and "The Star Spangled Banner." A choir from Lee University sang "God Bless America" before the official ceremonies began, but this performance was not mentioned in the timeline of inauguration events used by most media outlets. See: "Factbox: Timeline for Obama Inauguration Events," reuters.com, accessed 25 January 2013, http://www.reuters.com/article/2013/01/21/us-usa-inauguration-events-idUSBRE90K06520130121. For the full schedule of events, see "Guide for Producers and Correspondents to the Inaugural Ceremonies and Capitol Hill Events," January 2013, accessed 25 January 2013, http://www.inaugural.senate.gov/docs/doc-011713-press-guide.pdf.

105. Jeff Zeleny, "Thousands Attend Broad Protest of Government," *NYT*, 13 September 2009; Kate Zernike, "Palin Assails Obama at Tea Party Meeting," *NYT*, 7 February 2010; Kathleen Hennessey, "Tax day 'tea parties' draw thousands across U.S.," *Los Angeles Times*, 16 April 2010.

106. Right-wing activist Glenn Beck's 9/12 Project typifies this appropriation of the rhetoric of post-9/11 unity to advance a conservative agenda: "The 9/12 Project is designed to bring us all back to the place we were on 12 September 2001. The day after America was attacked we were not obsessed with Red States, Blue States or political parties. We were united as Americans, standing together to protect the greatest nation ever created. That same feeling—that commitment to country is what we are hoping to foster with this idea." The 9/12 Project, "Mission Statement," accessed 8 July 2010, http://www.the912project.com/the-912-2/mission-statement/.

107. Winter, *Remembering War*, 6.

108. Assman, *Moses the Egyptian*, 9.
109. Meyer Berger, "First City-Wide Blackout Darkens 320 Square Miles," *NYT*, 6 June 1942.

CHAPTER 6

1. Excerpted in Dawidoff, *Baseball: A Literary Anthology*, 50, 52.
2. Red Sox owner Larry Lucchino was mentioned as the originator of the idea to play the song in two interviews that I conducted (Rich Levin, phone interview, 2 March 2009; and Marty Ray, interview 13 September 2009). However, the full story behind the song's inclusion, which appears to have originated with a San Diego Padres staff member, is told in Bill Ladson, "After 9/11, 'God Bless America' a Mainstay," mlb.com, 10 September 2011, http://mlb.mlb.com/news/article. jsp?ymd=20110910&content_id=24486076&vkey=09112011.
3. The League of American Theatres and Producers asked shows to perform "God Bless America" through the end of the first weekend after 9/11, although many continued through the end of the year. At the Super Bowl in 2002, the pre-game ceremony featured "America the Beautiful," Barry Manilow's "Let Freedom Ring," and Paul McCartney's post-9/11 song, "Freedom," followed by the national anthem. Jed Bernstein, email correspondence, 30 November 2009; "'Bless is More," *Entertainment Weekly*, 21–28 December 2001.
4. Memorandum from commissioner Bud Selig to all MLB clubs, 14 September 2001. Heather Flock, email correspondence to author, 11 January 2010. I did not review these memos directly, but instead received transcriptions of their contents via email from the MLB corporate office. For an overview of baseball's response to 9/11, see Kraus, "A Shelter in the Storm," 88–101.
5. Memorandum from the office of Bob DuPuy, MLB president, to all MLB clubs, 15 April 2002, in Flock, email correspondence, 11 January 2010.
6. Memorandum from DuPuy, 6 April 2002, in Flock, email correspondence, 11 January 2010. Since 2006, the policy of playing "God Bless America" during the postseason has been as follows: for the Division Series, at the discretion of the home club; for the League Championship Series, during the seventh-inning stretch of Game One in each city; and at all World Series games during the seventh-inning stretch. Memo from the Broadcasting and Special Events Departments, 27 September 2006, in Flock, email correspondence, 11 January 2010.
7. Lipsky, *How We Play the Game*, 5. The journalist David Greenberg noted that the ruling is now acknowledged as flawed and has not been extended to other professional sports, yet the exemption remains in place for MLB. David Greenberg, "Baseball's Con Game," *Slate*, 19 July 2002, accessed 2 June 2010, http://www.slate.com/id/2068290. For a more positive spin on the Supreme Court's long-standing affection for baseball, see Adam Liptak, "This Bench Belongs in a Dugout," *NYT*, 1 June 2010.
8. Zirin, *What's My Name, Fool?* 222–27.
9. Borer, *Faithful to Fenway*, 73.
10. The executives I spoke with took pains to frame these memos from MLB as *recommendations* rather than corporate mandates, but while the language of the first memo was indeed framed as a request from the commissioner ("I am asking all clubs . . ."), by 2004 the wording had solidified into a policy that all teams "should" follow.

11. "Plus: Baseball," *NYT*, 29 March 2003. The content of the MLB's 2003 memo to teams was not included among the materials provided to me by MLB headquarters, so I do not know whether the teams were explicitly told to use this language of military tribute in announcing the song that year.

12. Ira Berkow, "Eager to See the Return of Peanuts," *NYT*, 11 October 2001.

13. Gersh Kuntzman, "Play Ball, Not Prayers," *Newsweek* Online, 14 July 2003, accessed 5 May 2010, http://gershkuntzman.homestead.com/files/Play_Ball__Not_Prayers__7_14_.htm.

14. Berkow, "The Return of Peanuts," in Strasberg, Thompson, and Wiles, *Baseball's Greatest Hit*, 5.

15. There are fascinating connections between the music played at baseball games and issues of race, ethnicity, and masculinity, but unfortunately a full analysis is beyond the scope of this chapter. For more on music and sports, see Garrett, "Struggling to Define a Nation," 241–42; Porcello "Soundscapes of Contemporary Major League Baseball"; and Mihalka, "From the Hammond Organ to 'Sweet Caroline.'"

16. Crepeau, "Sport and the National Anthem (21 March 1996)," 70.

17. Strasberg, Thompson, and Wiles, *Baseball's Greatest Hit*, 63.

18. See George Vecsey, "The New Sounds of Music in the Ball Parks," *NYT*, 30 June 1980; and Mike Gibbons, "Baltimore's Seventh-Inning Tradition Within a Tradition," *Press Box*, 5 July 2007, accessed 16 June 2010, http://www.pressboxonline.com/story.cfm?id=2189. Brian Cashen, general manager of the Orioles and then the Mets, pioneered the use of recorded pop music at the stadiums of both teams.

19. For a history of the song's creation and early reception, see Sonneck, *"The Star Spangled Banner."* For a social history of the anthem, see Mark Clague, "O Say Can You Hear: A Music History of America's Anthem," accessed 25 January 2013, http://osaycanyouhear.wordpress.com.

20. "Out Door Sports," *Brooklyn Eagle*, 16 May 1862, in Anthems file, Hall of Fame.

21. Crepeau, "Sport and the National Anthem," 69–70. This idea that the song was played spontaneously by the band has an intriguing parallel to spontaneous renditions of "God Bless America" after 9/11.

22. Ibid., 71.

23. Ibid.

24. Joseph M. Sheehan, "2 Black Power Advocates Ousted From Olympics," *NYT*, 19 October 1968. Also see Gerald Eskenazi, "Garden Track Meet Will Drop U.S. Anthem to Avoid Incidents," *NYT* 16 January 1973; Neil Amdur, "Garden to Hear Anthem at Track Meet, After All," *NYT*, 17 January 1973; "About Star-Spangled Manners," *NYT*, 21 January 1973. In a more recent protest, a college women's basketball player made news in 2003 by turning her back on the flag during the anthem in protest over the Iraq War. Janet Paskin, "A Silent Protest on the Basketball Court," *Journal News*, 21 February 2003.

25. For more on the anthem's role in sports, see Garrett, "Struggling to Define a Nation," 214–21.

26. "Patriotic Song Boom Nearing '17 War Peak," *New York Herald Tribune*, 20 July 1940; Roscoe McGowen, "42,822 Tickets Sold for Contest, but Attendance Is Put at 34,000," *NYT*, 9 May 1942; Arthur Gorlick, "Sox Should Play Anthem, Not My Song, Says Berlin," *Chicago Daily News*, 20 April 1966.

27. Parton Keese, "Rangers Defeat Flyers, 8–3," *NYT*, 25 April 1978.

28. For more on the Flyers' use of "God Bless America," see Gerald Eskinazi, "Flyers Spurred by Fans in Helmets," *NYT*, 24 April 1974; Parton Keese, "Kate Smith Calls the Tune for Islanders' Swan Song," *NYT*, 14 May 1975; "Scouting: Melody Lingers," *NYT*, 18 June 1987.

29. Joe Sharkey, "It's Over When It's Over, Until We Meet Again," *NYT*, 29 March 1998.

30. Strasberg, Thomson, and Wiles, *Baseball's Greatest Hit*, 13, 22–23. For a discussion of the song's early popularity and gender politics of the time, see Boziwick, "Take Me Out to the Ball Game."

31. Strasberg, Thomson, and Wiles, *Baseball's Greatest Hit*, 62–65.

32. William C. Rhoden, "Yankees' Seventh-Inning Stretch Shouldn't Be So Stretched Out," *NYT*, 4 October 2003; Tyler Kepner, "All's Fair During a Foul Night for the Yankees," *NYT*, 9 October 2003.

33. Staff members responsible for coordinating these performances at the New York Mets and Boston Red Sox both took note of this limitation, and contrasted it with the national anthem, which can accommodate large performing groups like bands or choirs because it happens before the game. Greg Romano, interview, 25 May 2008; Marty Ray, interview, 13 September 2009.

34. Vito Vitiello, interview, 25 May 2008.

35. I do not know whether this convention is upheld across all major league teams, but it did seem to be generally true across ballparks at the games I observed.

36. See Guttmann, *Sports Spectators*, 177–78; Lever, *Soccer Madness*, 15; Lipsky, *How We Play the Game*, 18–19; and Novak, *The Joy of Sports*, 125. For discussions of the intersection of religion and baseball specifically, see Borer, *Faithful to Fenway*; and Price, *Rounding the Bases*.

37. Borer, *Faithful to Fenway*, 98, 109–111; Lever, *Soccer Madness*, 14–16; Lipsky, *How We Play the Game*, 60.

38. Lever, *Soccer Madness*, 16; also quoted in Ehrenreich, *Dancing in the Streets*, 226.

39. Lever, *Soccer Madness*, 16. Given these observations, it is surprising that Lever pays little attention to the songs that Brazilian fans sing during games.

40. Borer, *Faithful to Fenway*, 39. Borer drew on the formulation of collective memory in Barry Schwartz, *Abraham Lincoln and the Forge of National Memory* (Chicago, University of Chicago Press, 2000), 1–25.

41. Hobsbawm, "Inventing Traditions," 1–2, 12. Terence Ranger later suggested the term "imagined tradition" rather than "invented" to acknowledge that these traditions are not necessarily the top-down creations of one person in power, but are instead influenced by many people over the course of time. See Ranger, "The Invented Tradition Revisited," 81–2.

42. Bodnar, *Remaking America*, 15–20, 257n8.

43. Borer, *Faithful to Fenway*, 70, 86–94.

44. Porter Anderson, "Prayer Service: 'We Shall Not Be Moved,'" CNN.com, 23 September 2001, accessed 5 April 2010, http://archives.cnn.com/2001/US/09/23/vic.yankee.service.report/index.html.

45. A darker form of the new civic role of sports stadiums was the disastrous use of the Superdome as an emergency shelter after Hurricane Katrina. See Zirin, *Welcome to the Terrordome*, 16–22.

46. Tim Gunkel, interview, 25 May 2008.

47. Ibid.

48. Tyler Kepner, "Mets are Ready for Return from Reality," *NYT*, 17 September 2001.

49. Kepner, "Emotional Return Home for the Mets," *NYT*, 21 September 2001.

50. Tim Gunkel, interview, 25 May 2008.
51. Ibid. Trailing in the eighth inning, Mets catcher Mike Piazza hit a home run that eventually won them the game.
52. Kepner, "Mets' Magic Heralds Homecoming," *NYT*, 22 September 2001.
53. Vitiello, interview, 25 May 2008.
54. I actually found the impact of this flyover to be a bit muted by the fact that Shea Stadium lies in the flight path of LaGuardia airport, so airplanes were constantly—and loudly—flying above us. The sound of the planes served as a steady punctuation to the interview I conducted with Tim Gunkel and Vito Vitiello, which took place before the pre-game ceremonies in a set of box seats high above the first base line, and provided a kind of immediacy to our discussion about the period directly after the 9/11 attacks, when airplanes in flight took on an aura of menace.
55. New York Mets, "Theme Dates," accessed 25 April 2010, http://newyork.mets. mlb.com/nym/schedule/themedates.jsp.
56. Dan Lyons, interview, 13 September 2009.
57. For a discussion of music's role in this confluence of sports, the military, and national identity within the context of American football, see Garrett, "Struggling to Define a Nation," 214–21.
58. Crepeau, "Sport and the National Anthem," 69–70.
59. San Diego Padres, "Military Programs," accessed 29 April 2010, http://sandiego. padres.mlb.com/sd/ticketing/military.jsp; Chief Mass Communication Specialist Daniel Sanford, "San Diego Padres Host Military Opening Night," US Navy, accessed 29 April 2010, http://www.navy.mil/search/display.asp?story_ id=52654.
60. Sgt. Elizabeth Quinones, interview, 25 May 2008.
61. See Meizel, *Idolized*, 63–79.
62. See Diana DeGarmo's performance at Shea Stadium during the Mets-Dodgers playoffs in October 2006, accessed 27 September 2012, http://www.youtube. com/watch?v=E0NdDW5KVpA; and Kelly Clarkson's rendition during a World Series game in 2004, accessed 27 September 2012, http://www.youtube.com/ watch?v=iislPWcCkZo.
63. Sgt. Quinones, interview, 25 May 2008.
64. Tim Gunkel, interview, 25 May 2008. This was in addition to logistical reasons for this choice, since Vito Viticllo mentioned in the same interview that instrumental recordings sounded better on the stadium's antiquated sound system than vocals.
65. Initially, the Yankees achieved this ritualized sense by the repeated use of the same live performers (Irish tenor Ronan Tynan and police officer Daniel Rodriguez, known as the "singing cop"), but they now regularly play the Kate Smith recording. The Paw Sox switched to using live performances in 2012.
66. Bryan Srabian, interview, 17 October 2007.
67. Turner, *The Forest of Symbols*, 50.
68. Tim Gunkel, interview, 25 May 2008.
69. The minor leagues of professional baseball are divided into hierarchical classes based on level of play: AAA (just below the major leagues), AA, Class-A Advanced, Class-A, Class-A Short Season, and Rookie.
70. Stan Getzler, phone interview, 29 June 2008. For more on this aspect of Staten Island's relationship to 9/11, see "Staten Island September 11 Memorial," Office of Borough President James Molinaro, accessed 17 June 2010, http://www. statenislandusa.com/pages/memorial.html.

71. Staten Island Yankees fan interview, 3 July 2008.
72. John Davison, interview, 3 July 2008.
73. The recordings of my interviews with the team's entertainment staff are punctuated by long silences followed by laughter, as we paused to watch and appreciate the between-inning entertainment.
74. Michael D'Ambroise, interview, 3 July 2008.
75. John Davison, interview, 3 July 2008.
76. Rather than a localized tradition originating in Pawtucket, this practice of displaying photographs of military personnel during "God Bless America" appears to be a convention within the North division of the International League, the AAA minor-league division in which the Paw Sox play. Jeff Bradley, phone interview, 3 June 2009; Jim Mandelaro, "The Song Debate: Keep It Or Drop It?" Extra Bases blog, *Rochester Democrat & Chronicle*, 23 June 2009, accessed 27 September 2012, http://blogs.democratandchronicle.com/extrabases/?p=724.
77. Bodnar, *Remaking America*, 17.
78. Online survey respondent #231, submitted 23 July 2009.
79. William C. Rhoden, "Yankees' Seventh-Inning Stretch Shouldn't Be So Stretched Out," *NYT*, 4 October 2003; Bill Plaschke, "We should feel blessed for patriotic display at Dodger Stadium," *Los Angeles Times*, 6 September 2011.
80. Mike Gibbons, "Baltimore's Seventh-Inning Tradition Within a Tradition," *Press Box*, 5 July 2007, accessed 16 June 2010, http://www.pressboxonline.com/story.cfm?id=2189); Chris Richards, "'Take On Me' Becomes a Nationals Battle Cry," *Washington Post*, 9 October 2012.
81. Stephanie Vosk, "Another Mystery of the Diamond, Explained at Last," *Boston Globe*, 29 May 2005; Susan Orlean, "The Mystery of 'Sweet Caroline' and the Sox," *National Public Radio*, 30 September 2005, accessed 18 June 2010, http://www.npr.org/templates/story/story.php?storyId=4930465.
82. "'God Bless America' Survey Recap" (Survey data gathered from 1,601 respondents via e-mail, 10–12 January 2009), New York Mets, courtesy of Tim Gunkel. The percentages for the songs are as follows: 86 percent for the National Anthem; 75 percent for "Take Me Out to the Ball Game"; 72 percent for "Meet the Mets"; 51 percent for "God Bless America"; and 33 percent for "New York, New York."
83. From observations at a Red Sox game on 18 April 2010. Another example of this kind of sponsorship is the Yankees' use of the electronics retailer PC Richards's whistling jingle every time an opposing batter strikes out. But even here, the "vernacular" culture of the local community is also invoked, since only residents of the New York area familiar with the jingle from local radio can understand the whistle's commercial significance—an advertisement that subtly references regional allegiance. (I would have missed it completely had I not attended the game with a native New Yorker.)
84. From observations at a Giants game on 5 July 2009.
85. Bryan Srabian, interview, 17 October 2007.
86. Jon Miller, interview, 8 July 2009.
87. For a perspective from those near the attack on the Pentagon, I contacted the Washington Nationals to determine how the song functions there, but I was not successful in speaking with anyone about it. Online research of YouTube videos indicate that the song may be performed only on Sundays and holidays. One survey respondent noted that the Nationals do play the song at every game, though this remains unconfirmed. Survey #576, submitted 23 July 2009.

88. Bryan Srabian, interview, 17 October 2007.
89. Tim Gunkel, interview, 25 May 2008. Gunkel's impressions are supported by the survey undertaken by the Mets showing that a majority of the team's fans approve of the song's continued inclusion in games.
90. For more on the history of dissent among athletes, see Zirin, *What's My Name, Fool?*
91. Geoff Baker, "Citizen Carlos," *Toronto Star*, 3 July 2004. The communications scholar Michael Butterworth criticized the silent nature of Delgado's protest, lamenting that it was "easy to dismiss and ignore" and "incapable of challenging the dominant narrative offered by the game." Butterworth, "Ritual in the 'Church of Baseball,'" 122. However, this protest was given a large share of media attention in New York as a result of Delgado's appearance at Yankee Stadium and the possibility of being traded to a New York team in 2004 and 2005. See William C. Rhoden, "Delgado Makes a Stand by Taking a Seat," *NYT*, 21 July 2004; Lee Jenkins, "Delgado Interests Yankees," *NYT*, 16 November 2004; Murray Chass, "The Real Jeffrey Loria Steps Forward for Florida," *NYT*, 30 January 2005.
92. Dave Feschuk, "Politicos Silent; Delgado's Bat Speaks," *Toronto Star*, 7 July 2004; William C. Rhoden, "Delgado Has the Pop and the Principle," *NYT*, 20 December 2004.
93. Dave Zirin, "The Silencing of Carlos Delgado," *The Nation*, 3 December 2005.
94. Selena Roberts, "'New York, New York,' Queens Style," *NYT*, 29 November 2005. Some noted that by 2006 public support for the war had waned and that Delgado's protest had thus run its course; see Murray Chass, "On Baseball," *NYT*, 4 December 2005.
95. Michael S. Schmidt, "At the Stadium, Stay Put When the Music Plays," *NYT*, 10 May 2007; Clyde Haberman, "In the 7th Inning, Stretch, but Don't Move," *NYT*, 9 July 2009.
96. Survey respondent #101, submitted 22 July 2009.
97. The two consumer surveys are: Experian Simmons Winter 2010 full-year National Consumer Study, which was conducted from February 2009 through March 2010 and includes 8,327 baseball fans; and the 2009 ESPN Sports Poll, a service of TNS, which includes 13,994 baseball fans. Just over half of my respondents identified themselves as liberal or very liberal, with only 15 percent reporting conservative or very conservative views; a major consumer study of all baseball fans by Experian Simmons included more than twice the number of conservatives and one-third as many liberals as in my study. Similarly, 37 percent of respondents in my sample reported agnostic or atheistic views, which was twice as many as in the Experian survey.
98. As mentioned earlier in this chapter, nearly half of all survey respondents self-identified as Yankees fans. These Yankee fans are responding to their team's tradition of playing "God Bless America" at every game—not its occasional inclusion on Sundays and holidays. The Yankees' practice of playing the song at every game seems to have forged strong opinions among fans, but if anything, the high percentage of Yankee fans skewed the findings toward those who *like* the song's inclusion in baseball, since Yankee fans as a group tended to view the song more favorably, as shown in the graphs included on the companion website. 🔊
99. "'God Bless America' Survey Recap," New York Mets. In contrast, within my small sample of seventy-four Mets fans, fewer than 10 percent supported the song's presence in baseball.

100. Survey respondent #648, submitted 24 July 2009.
101. Arthur Gorlick, "Sox Should Play Anthem, Not My Song, Says Berlin," *Chicago Daily News*, 20 April 1966.
102. Survey respondent #321, 23 July 2009.
103. Survey respondent #347, 23 July 2009.
104. Survey respondent #1355, 24 July 2009; Survey respondent #42, 21 July 2009.
105. Survey respondent #1157, 24 July 2009.
106. Online survey respondent #31, 21 July 2009.
107. Survey respondent #632, 24 July 2009.
108. Voigt, *America through Baseball*, 82–83.
109. Tyler Kepner, "From Taft to Obama, Ceremonial First Pitches," *NYT*, 5 April 2010; Voigt, *America through Baseball*, 85.
110. Bush later told his senior staff that that pitch was "one of the highlights of his presidency." Elizabeth Bumiller, "Measuring the Bush Family History, and the President's Political Career, in Innings," *NYT*, 18 April 2005.
111. Voigt, *America through Baseball*, 90.
112. Charles McGrath, "A Tenor as Irish as Baseball and 'God Bless America,'" *NYT*, 12 July 2004; Alan Schwarz, "With Ronan Tynan, Yankee Stadium Soundtrack," *NYT*, 27 July 2008. Also see Tynan's official biography at ronantynan.net.
113. 204 respondents named Tynan, out of 1,016 who said they associated the song with a performer.
114. At first, it was reported that Tynan told a real estate agent selling a neighboring apartment that he didn't care if they were Red Sox fans, "as long as they're not Jewish." Later, Tynan said that his remark was misconstrued by a woman accompanying the agent. In Tynan's version, the agent had previously referred to two women who had looked at the apartment as "two Jewish ladies"—not a slur, solely for identification purposes—and Tynan invoked the phrase by saying, "as long as it's not the Jewish ladies," since he had worried that they wouldn't like living adjacent to a noisy tenor. See David Waldstein, "Yanks Discipline Tenor For Anti-Semitic Joke," *NYT*, 17 October 2009; and Corey Kilgannon, "Tenor Adopted and Disowned by Yankees Leaves Town," *NYT*, 6 March 2010.
115. Kilgannon, "Tenor Adopted and Disowned."
116. Anti-Defamation League, press release, "Acclaimed Irish Tenor Ronan Tynan Tells ADL: 'I Will Be A Foot Soldier In Your Mission,'" 30 October 2009, accessed 8 July 2010, http://www.adl.org/PresRele/ASUS_12/5639_12.htm.
117. McGrath, "A Tenor as Irish as Baseball and 'God Bless America'"; Peter Abraham, "Buchholz will be latest to go on DL," *Boston Globe*, 5 July 2010.
118. Tynan, phone interview, 3 July 2009; Schwarz, "With Ronan Tynan, Yankee Stadium Soundtrack."
119. Bill Pennington, "Chiefs' Fans Add Red and White To Giants' Blue," *NYT*, 24 September 2001.
120. Butterworth, "Ritual in the 'Church of Baseball,'" 122.
121. Although I did not ask this question outright, many survey participants who strongly dislike the song's presence in baseball mentioned that they thought it was appropriate after 9/11, including respondents #317, 449, 474, 781, 783, 852, 907, 911, 921, 945, 969, 1082, 1218, 1561, 1661, 1709, and 1802.
122. See Berkow, "The Return of Peanuts," quoted on page 00. Those who noted that the song's occasional use at holidays would be appropriate include respondents #159, 250, 299, 431, 452, 870, 982, 1032, 1060, 1218, 1219, 1333, 1464, 1735, 1760, and 1831.

123. Rich Levin, phone interview, 2 March 2009.
124. Jeff Bradley, phone interview 3 June 2009.
125. Greg Romano, interview, 25 May 2008.

CODA

1. Susana Darwin, Encyclopedia Britannica Blog, "I Heard the Americans Sing (The Lost Art of the Sing-Along)," 22 January 2007, accessed 25 June 2010, http://www. britannica.com/blogs/2007/01/i-heard-the-americans-sing-the-lost-art-of-the-sing-along/.
2. Marialisa Calta, "For Many, Singing is an Untried Art," *NYT*, 24 April 1991. Also see Russell, "I (Don't) Hear America Singing," 2–3.
3. Ben Ratliff, "Shared Song, Communal Memory," *NYT*, 10 February 2008.
4. Putnam and Feldstein, *Better Together*, 4.
5. Durkheim, *The Elementary Forms of Religious Life*, 429. For more on secular ritual, see Bird, "The Contemporary Ritual Milieu," 19–24; and Bell, *Ritual*, 138–69.
6. Seeger quoted in Ratliff, "Shared Song, Communal Memory."
7. Turner, *The Ritual Process*, 96, 132–40; Turner, *Drams, Fields, and Metaphors*, 202.
8. McNeill, *Keeping Together in Time*, 149. For more on the Nazi's use of music, see Turino, *Music as Social Life*, 190–210.
9. Rosen, *White Christmas*, 51.
10. Ives, *Memos*, 66. For more on the many connections between Ives and spontaneous communal singing, see Kaskowitz, "'The Voice of the People Again Arose.'"
11. Vowell, *Assassination Vacation*, 243.
12. "Sorrow on Recreation Pier," *NYT*, 15 September 1901.
13. "Street Tributes to Dead President," *NYT*, 22 September 1901.
14. Edward C. Burks, "City-Bound Train Kills 2 Mourners," *NYT*, 9 June 1968.
15. Sarah Wheaton, "Kennedy's Papal Correspondence and a Spontaneous Sing-Along," *NYT*, 30 August 2009.
16. For more on the history of "The Battle Hymn of the Republic," see Randall, "A Censorship of Forgetting."
17. Alex Ross, "Requiems," *New Yorker*, 8 October 2001, accessed at *The Rest Is Noise*, 16 November 2009, http://www.therestisnoise.com/2004/05/the_noise_is_br.html. Ross links this singing with the story behind a Charles Ives piece, *From Hanover Square North, at the End of a Tragic Day, the Voice of the People Again Arose*, which Ives said was inspired by his experience of New Yorkers on a subway platform singing "In the Sweet Bye and Bye" on the day the *Lusitania* sank in 1915. See Ives, *Memos*, 92–93.
18. See, for example: Elizabeth A. Harris, "Amid Cheers, a Message: 'They Will Be Caught,'" *NYT*, 2 May 2011; Jess Bidgood and Phillip Martin, "On the Common, Revelers Celebrate Bin Laden's Death," wgbh.org, 2 May 2011, accessed 13 April 2012, http://www.wgbh.org/articles/index.cfm?tempid=2818; "Bin Laden killing caps decade-long manhunt," cnn.com, 2 May 2011, accessed 13 April 2012, http://www.cnn.com/2011/WORLD/asiapcf/05/02/bin.laden.dead/index.html.
19. Mike Morreale, "Fans in Philly Roar Approval of 'God Bless America,'" foxnews.com, accessed 13 April 2012, http://www.foxnews.com/sports/2011/05/02/fans-philly-roar-approval-god-bless-america/.
20. David Bauder, "Occupy Wall Street: Music Central To Protest," *Associated Press/Huffington Post*, 13 November 2011, accessed 20 April 2012, http://www.huffingtonpost.com/2011/11/13/occupy-wall-street-music_n_1091176.html;

"Pete Seeger Marches in Support of Occupy Wall Street, *Rolling Stone*, 22 October 2011.

21. Bauder, "Occupy Wall Street: Music Central to Protest."

22. Zach Williams, "Mic Check! Occupy Wall Street Is Now Part of Popular Culture," *Villager*, 1 December 2011; Michael Kimmelman, "In Protest, the Power of Place," *NYT*, 15 October 2011; Sara Wanenchak, "'Mic check!' #occupy, technology & the amplified voice," *Society Pages*, accessed 13 April 2012, http://thesocietypages.org/cyborgology/2011/10/06/mic-check-occupy-technology-the-amplified-voice/.

23. PJ Rey, "Why We Disrupt," *Inside Higher Ed*, 3 January 2012, accessed 13 April 2012, http://www.insidehighered.com/views/2012/01/03/essay-why-occupy-movement-disrupts-speakers-campus; Fernando Alfonso III, "Occupy protestors mic-check politicians," *Daily Dot*, 17 November 2011, accessed 13 April 2012, http://www.dailydot.com/politics/mic-check-occupy-protest-speeches/.

BIBLIOGRAPHY

Articles in newspapers and lay magazines are listed only in the notes section, not in the bibliography. Examples include the *New York Times* (*NYT*), *Look* magazine, and *Variety*.

ARCHIVAL SOURCES

A. Bartlett Giamatti Research Center, National Baseball Hall of Fame and Museum, Cooperstown, NY (abbreviated to "Hall of Fame").

God Bless America Fund files, Rodgers & Hammerstein Organization, New York, NY (abbreviated to "R&H").

Irving Berlin Collection of Noncommercial Sound Recordings, 1933–1989, New York Public Library for the Performing Arts, New York, NY.

Irving Berlin Collection, Performing Arts Division, Library of Congress, Washington, DC (abbreviated to "IBC"; scrapbooks are "IBCS").

Kate Smith Collection, Howard Gotlieb Research Center, Boston University, Boston, MA (abbreviated to "KSC"; scrapbooks are "KSCS").

BOOKS AND ARTICLES

Abbate, Carolyn. "Opera; or, the Envoicing of Women." In *Musicology and Difference: Gender and Sexuality in Music Scholarship*, edited by Ruth A. Solie, 225–58. Berkeley: University of California Press, 1993.

Anderson, Alan. *The Songwriter Goes to War: The Story of Irving Berlin's World War II All-Army Production of This Is the Army*. Pompton Plains, NJ: Limelight Editions, 2004.

Anderson, Benedict. *Imagined Communities: Reflections on the Origins and Spread of Nationalism*. New York: Verso, 1991.

Assman, Jan. *Moses the Egyptian: The Memory of Egypt in Western Monotheism*. Cambridge, MA: Harvard University Press, 1997.

Austin, William W. *"Susanna," "Jeannie," and "The Old Folks at Home": The Songs of Stephen C. Foster from His Time to Ours*. 2nd ed. Urbana: University of Illinois Press, 1987.

Bañagale, Ryan. "Rhapsodies in Blue: Alternative Interpretations of an Iconic American 'Composition.'" PhD diss., Harvard University, 2011.

Barg, Lisa. "Paul Robeson's Ballad for Americans: Race and the Cultural Politics of 'People's Music." *Journal of the Society for American Music* 2, no. 1 (2008): 27–70.

Barrett, Mary Ellin. *Irving Berlin: A Daughter's Memoir*. New York: Simon and Schuster, 1994.

Bell, Catherine. *Ritual: Perspectives and Dimensions*. New York: Oxford University Press, 1997.

Bellah, Robert. "Civil Religion in America." *Daedalus: Journal of the American Academy of Arts and Sciences* 96, no. 1 (1967): 1–21.

Bergreen, Laurence. *As Thousands Cheer: The Life of Irving Berlin*. New York: Viking, 1990.

Bindas, Kenneth J. *All of This Music Belongs to the Nation: The WPA's Federal Music Project and American Society*. Knoxville: University of Tennessee Press, 1995.

Bird, Frederick. "The Contemporary Ritual Milieu." In *Rituals and Ceremonies in Popular Culture*, edited by Ray B. Browne, 19–35. Bowling Green, OH: Bowling Green University Popular Press, 1980.

Blair, Karen J. *The Torchbearers: Women and Their Amateur Arts Associations in America, 1890–1930*. Bloomington: Indiana University Press, 1994.

Bodnar, John. *Remaking America: Public Memory, Commemoration, and Patriotism in the Twentieth Century*. Princeton, NJ: Princeton University Press, 1991.

Bohlman, Philip V. *The Music of European Nationalism: Cultural Identity and Modern History*. Santa Barbara, CA: ABC-CLIO, 2004.

Bohlman, Philip V. "Returning to the Ethnomusicological Past." In *Shadows in the Field: New Perspectives for Fieldwork in Ethnomusicology*, edited by Timothy J. Cooley and Gregory Barz, 246–70. New York: Oxford University Press, 2008.

Bond, Julian, and Sondra Kathryn Wilson, eds. *Lift Every Voice and Sing: A Celebration of the Negro National Anthem*. New York: Random House, 2000.

Borer, Michael Ian. *Faithful to Fenway: Believing in Boston, Baseball, and America's Most Beloved Ballpark*. New York: New York University Press, 2008

Boziwick, George. "Take Me Out to the Ball Game: A Reluctant Signifier for Reform." Paper given at the Twenty-first Cooperstown Symposium on Baseball and American Culture, Cooperstown, NY, 4 June 2009.

Branham, Robert James, and Stephen J. Hartnett. *Sweet Freedom's Song: "My Country 'Tis of Thee" and Democracy in America*. New York: Oxford University Press, 2002.

Butterworth, Michael L. "Ritual in the 'Church of Baseball': Suppressing the Discourse of Democracy after 9/11." *Communication and Critical/Cultural Studies* 2, no. 2 (2005): 107–29.

Cassidy, Marsha Francis. *What Women Watched: Daytime Television in the 1950s*. Austin: University of Texas Press, 2005.

Chambers, John Whiteclay. *The Tyranny of Change: America in the Progressive Era, 1890–1920*. New Brunswick, NJ: Rutgers University Press, 2000.

Crawford, Richard. *America's Musical Life: A History*. New York: Norton, 2001.

Crepeau, Richard. "Sport and the National Anthem (21 March 1996)." *Aethlon: The Journal of Sports Literature* 20, no. 1 (2002): 69–71.

Culbertson, Evelyn Davis. *He Heard America Singing: Arthur Farwell, Composer and Crusading Music Educator*. Metuchen, NJ: Scarecrow Press, 1992.

Cusick, Suzanne G. "On Musical Performances of Gender and Sex." In *Audible Traces: Gender, Identity, and Music*, edited by Elaine Barkin and Lydia Hamessley, 25–49. Zurich: Carciofoli Verlagshaus, 1999.

Daughtry, J. Martin. "Charting Courses through Terror's Wake: An Introduction." In *Music in the Post-9/11 World*, edited by Jonathan Ritter and J. Martin Daughtry. New York: Routledge, 2007.

Denisoff, R. Serge. *Songs of Protest, War & Peace: A Bibliography & Discography*. Santa Barbara, CA: ABC-CLIO, 1973.

Dickstein, Morris. *Dancing in the Dark: A Cultural History of the Great Depression*. New York: W. W. Norton, 2009.

Dinnerstein, Leonard. *Antisemitism in America*. New York: Oxford University Press, 1994.

Domke, David, and Kevin Coe. *The God Strategy: How Religion Became a Political Weapon in America*. New York: Oxford University Press, 2008.

Druesdow, John. "Popular Songs of the Great War: Background and Audio Resources." *Notes* 65, no. 2 (December 2008): 364–78.

Dunn, Leslie C., and Nancy A. Jones, eds. *Embodied Voices: Representing Female Vocality in Western Culture*. New York: Cambridge University Press, 1994.

Durkheim, Emile. *The Elementary Forms of Religious Life*. Translated by Karen E. Fields. New York: Free Press, 1995.

Ehrenreich, Barbara. *Dancing in the Streets: A History of Collective Joy*. New York: Metropolitan Books, 2006.

Epstein, Steven B. "Rethinking the Constitutionality of Ceremonial Deism." *Columbia Law Review* 96, no. 8 (1996): 2083–174.

Evans, Nicholas M. *Writing Jazz: Race, Nationalism, and Modern Culture in the 1920s*. New York: Garland, 2000.

Freedland, Michael. *Irving Berlin*. New York: Stein and Day, 1974.

Furia, Philip. *Ira Gershwin: The Art of the Lyricist*. New York: Oxford University Press, 1996.

Furia, Philip. *Irving Berlin: A Life in Song*. New York: Schirmer Books, 1998.

Garrett, Charles Hiroshi. "Struggling to Define a Nation: American Music in the Twentieth Century." PhD diss., University of California, Los Angeles, 2004.

Goodman, Glenda. "American Identities in the Musical Atlantic World." PhD diss., Harvard University, 2012.

Gorzelany-Mostak, Dana C. "Pre-existing Music in United States Presidential Campaigns, 1960–2008." PhD diss., McGill University, forthcoming.

Gross, Ben. *I Looked and I Listened: Informal Recollections of Radio and TV*. New York: Random House, 1954.

Guttmann, Allen. *Sports Spectators*. New York: Columbia University Press, 1986.

Halbwachs, Maurice. *On Collective Memory*. Translated by Lewis A. Coser. Chicago: University of Chicago Press, 1992.

Hall, Jacqueline Dowd. "The Long Civil Rights Movement and the Political Uses of the Past." *Journal of American History* 91, no. 4 (March 2005): 1233–63.

Hamm, Charles. "Irving Berlin and Early Tin Pan Alley." In *Irving Berlin: Early Songs, Part 1, 1907–1911*, edited by Charles Hamm. Madison, WI: Published for the American Musicological Society by A-R Editions, 1994.

Hamm, Charles. *Yesterdays: Popular Song in America*. New York: W. W. Norton, 1983.

Handy, Robert T. *A Christian America: Protestant Hopes and Historical Realities*. New York: Oxford University Press, 1971.

Hayes, Richard K. *Kate Smith: A Biography, with a Discography, Filmography and List of Stage Appearances*. Jefferson, NC: McFarland and Co., 1995.

Hilmes, Michelle. *Radio Voices: American Broadcasting, 1922–1952*. Minneapolis: University of Minnesota Press, 1997.

Hobsbawm, Eric. "Introduction: Inventing Traditions." In *The Invention of Tradition*, edited by Eric Hobsbawm and Terence Ranger, 1–14. New York: Cambridge University Press, 1983.

Hutchison, William R. *Religious Pluralism in America: The Contentious History of a Founding Ideal*. New Haven, CT: Yale University Press, 2003.

Isserman, Maurice, and Michael Kazin. *America Divided: The Civil War of the 1960s*. New York: Oxford University Press, 2000.

Ives, Charles. *Memos*. Edited by John Kirkpatrick. New York: W. W. Norton, 1991.

Jablonski, Edward. *Irving Berlin: American Troubadour*. New York: Henry Holt and Co., 1999.

Jackson, Mark Allan. "Is This Song Your Song Anymore? Revisioning Woody Guthrie's 'This Land Is Your Land.'" *American Music* 20, no. 3 (2002): 249–76.

Jacobson, Matthew Frye. *Roots, Too: White Ethnic Revival in Post-Civil Rights America*. Cambridge, MA: Harvard University Press, 2006.

Jacobson, Matthew Frye. *Whiteness of a Different Color: European Immigrants and the Alchemy of Race*. Cambridge, MA: Harvard University Press, 1999.

Jonas, Manfred. *Isolationism in America, 1935–1941*. 2nd ed. Chicago: Imprint Publications, 1990.

Jones, John Bush. *Our Musicals, Ourselves: A Social History of the American Musical Theater*. Hanover, NH: Brandeis University Press, 2003.

Jones, John Bush. *The Songs That Fought the War: Popular Music and the Home Front, 1939–1945*. Hanover, NH: Brandeis University Press, 2006.

Kahn, E. J., Jr. *The World of Swope*. New York: Simon and Schuster, 1965.

Kaskowitz, Sheryl. "'The Voice of the People Again Arose': Charles Ives, Communal Singing, and Ritual in American Public Life." Paper presented at the Annual Conference of the Society for American Music, Chicago, 17 March 2006.

Kennedy, David M. *Freedom from Fear: The American People in Depression and War, 1929–1945*. New York: Oxford University Press, 1999.

Kimball, Robert, and Linda Emmet, eds. *The Complete Lyrics of Irving Berlin*. New York: Alfred A. Knopf, 2001.

Klein, Joe. *Woody Guthrie: A Life*. New York: Knopf, 1980.

Kraus, Rebecca S. *Minor League Baseball: Community Building Through Hometown Sports*. New York: Haworth Press, 2003.

Kraus, Rebecca S. "A Shelter in the Storm: Baseball Responds to 9/11." *Nine: A Journal of Baseball History and Culture* 12, no. 1 (2003): 88–101.

Lavitt, Pamela Brown. "First of the Red Hot Mamas: 'Coon Shouting' and the Jewish Ziegfeld Girl." *American Jewish History* 87, no. 4 (1999): 253–90.

Lever, Janet. *Soccer Madness*. Chicago: The University of Chicago Press, 1983.

Levitin, Daniel J. *The World in Six Songs: How the Musical Brain Created Human Nature*. New York: Dutton, 2008.

Lewis, Alfred Allan. *Man of the World: Herbert Bayard Swope*. New York: Bobbs-Merrill Co., 1978.

Lipsky, Richard. *How We Play the Game: Why Sports Dominate American Life*. Boston: Beacon Press, 1981.

Lott, Eric. *Love and Theft: Blackface Minstrelsy and the American Working Class*. New York: Oxford University Press, 1995.

Lukas, J. Anthony. *Common Ground: A Turbulent Decade in the Lives of Three American Families*. New York: Vintage Books, 1985.

MacDonald, J. Fred. *Don't Touch That Dial! Radio Programming in American Life, 1920–1960*. Chicago: Nelson Hall, 1979.

Magee, Jeffrey. *Irving Berlin's American Musical Theater*. New York: Oxford University Press, 2012.

Magee, Jeffrey. "Irving Berlin's 'Blue Skies': Ethnic Affiliations and Musical Transformations." *Musical Quarterly* 84, no. 4 (2000): 537–80.

Magee, Jeffrey. *The Uncrowned King of Swing: Fletcher Henderson and Big Band Jazz*. New York: Oxford University Press, 2005.

McGirr, Lisa. *Suburban Warriors: The Origins of the New American Right*. Princeton, NJ: Princeton University Press, 2001.

McNeill, William Hardy. *Keeping Together in Time: Dance and Drill in Human History*. Cambridge, MA: Harvard University Press, 1995.

Meizel, Katherine L. *Idolized: Music, Media, and Identity in American Idol*. Bloomington: Indiana University Press, 2011.

Meizel, Katherine L. "A Singing Citizenry: Popular Music and Civil Religion in America." *Journal for the Scientific Study of Religion* 45, no. 4 (2006): 497–503

Merton, Robert K. *Mass Persuasion: The Social Psychology of a War Bond Drive*. New York: Harper and Brothers, 1946.

Mihalka, Matthew. "From the Hammond Organ to 'Sweet Caroline': The Historical Evolution of Baseball's Sonic Environment." PhD diss., University of Minnesota, 2012.

Monson, Ingrid. *Freedom Sounds: Civil Rights Call Out to Jazz and Africa*. New York: Oxford University Press, 2007.

Moore, Deborah Dash. "Jewish GIs and the Creation of the Judeo-Christian Tradition." *Religion and American Culture: A Journal of Interpretation* 8, no. 1 (1998): 31–53.

Niles, John J. "Shout, Coon, Shout!" *Musical Quarterly* 16, no. 4 (1930): 516–30.

Novak, Michael. *The Joy of Sports: End Zones, Bases, Baskets, Balls, and the Consecration of the American Spirit*. New York: Basic Books, 1976.

Oja, Carol J. *Making Music Modern: New York in the 1920s*. New York: Oxford University Press, 2000.

Peirce, Charles Sanders. "Logic as Semiotic: The Theory of Signs." In *Philosophical Writings of Peirce*, edited by Justus Buchler, 98–119. New York: Dover, 1955.

Porcello, Thomas. "Soundscapes of Contemporary Major League Baseball." Paper given at the Twenty-second Cooperstown Symposium on Baseball and American Culture, Cooperstown, NY, 2 June 2010.

Price, Joseph L. *Rounding the Bases: Baseball and Religion in America*. Macon, GA: Mercer University Press, 2006.

Press, Eyal. *Absolute Convictions: My Father, A City and the Conflict That Divided America*. New York: Henry Holt and Co., 2006.

Putnam, Robert D., and Lewis M. Feldstein. *Better Together: Restoring the American Community*. New York: Simon and Schuster, 2003.

Randall, Annie J. "A Censorship of Forgetting: Origins and Origin Myths of 'Battle Hymn of the Republic.'" In *Music, Power, and Politics*, edited by Annie J. Randall, 5–24. New York: Routledge, 2005.

Ranger, Terence. "The Invented Tradition Revisited." In *Legitimacy and the State in Twentieth-Century Africa: Essays in Honour of A. H. M. Kirk-Greene*, edited by Terence Ranger and Olufemi Vaughan, 62–111. London: McMillan Press, 1993.

Rosen, Jody. *Jewface*. Reboot Stereophonic RSR 006, 2006, liner notes.

Rosen, Jody. *White Christmas: The Story of an American Song*. New York: Scribner, 2002.

Rossi, Alice S. *Feminists in Politics: A Panel Analysis of the First National Women's Conference*. New York: Academic Press, 1982.

Roth, Philip. *The Plot Against America*. New York: Houghton Mifflin, 2004.

Russell, Melinda. "I (Don't) Hear America Singing: The List of Songs Americans Should Know and Sing." *European Journal of American Studies* 2 (2011): 1–12. Accessed 21 March 2013. doi:10.4000/ejas.8962

Sanjek, Russell, and David Sanjek. *Pennies from Heaven: The American Popular Music Business in the Twentieth Century*. New York: Da Capo Press, 1996.

Sarna, Jonathan D. *American Judaism: A History*. New Haven, CT: Yale University Press, 2004.

Savage, Barbara. *Broadcasting Freedom: Radio, War, and the Politics of Race, 1938–1948*. Chapel Hill: University of North Carolina Press, 1999.

Savran, David. *Highbrow/Lowdown: Theatre, Jazz, and the Making of a New Middle Class*. Ann Arbor: University of Michigan Press, 2009.

Schacter, Daniel L. *The Seven Sins of Memory: How the Mind Forgets and Remembers*. Boston: Houghton Mifflin, 2000.

Schoenwald, Jonathan. *A Time for Choosing: The Rise of Modern American Conservatism*. New York: Oxford University Press, 2003.

Schultz, Lucia S. "Performing-Right Societies in the United States." *Notes* 35, no. 3 (1979): 511–36.

Scott, James C. *Domination and the Arts of Resistance: Hidden Transcripts*. New Haven, CT: Yale University Press, 1990.

Shaw, Arnold. "The Vocabulary of Tin-Pan Alley Explained." *Notes* 7, no. 1 (1949): 33–53.

Shelemay, Kay Kaufman. "'Historical Ethnomusicology': Reconstructing Falasha Liturgical History." *Ethnomusicology* 24, no. 2 (1980): 233–58.

Shelemay, Kay Kaufman. *Let Jasmine Rain Down: Song and Remembrance among Syrian Jews*. Chicago: University of Chicago Press, 1998.

Sherr, Lynn. *America the Beautiful: The Stirring True Story Behind Our Nation's Favorite Song*. New York: PublicAffairs, 2001.

Silk, Mark. "Notes on the Judeo-Christian Tradition in America." *American Quarterly* 36, no. 1 (1984): 65–85.

Singer, Barry. *Black and Blue: The Life and Lyrics of Andy Razaf*. New York: Schirmer Books, 1992.

Slobin, Mark. *Subcultural Sounds: Micromusics of the West*. Middletown, CT: Wesleyan University Press, 1993.

Smith, Kate. *Living in a Great Big Way*. New York: Blue Ribbon Books, 1938.

Smith, Kate. *Upon My Lips a Song*. New York: Funk and Wagnalls, 1960.

Smith, Kathleen E.R. *God Bless America: Tin Pan Alley Goes to War*. Lexington: University Press of Kentucky, 2003.

Solnit, Rebecca, *A Paradise Built in Hell: The Extraordinary Communities that Arise in Disaster*. New York: Viking, 2009.

Sonneck, Oscar G. *"The Star Spangled Banner"* (Revised and enlarged from the "Report" on the above and other airs, issued in 1909). Washington, DC: Government Printing Office, 1914.

Spaulding, Albert G. "America's National Game." Excerpted in *Baseball: A Literary Anthology*, edited by Nicholas Dawidoff. New York: Library of America, 2002.

Strasberg, Andy, Bob Thompson, and Tim Wiles. *Baseball's Greatest Hit: The Story of Take Me Out to the Ball Game*. New York: Hal Leonard, 2008.

Suisman, David. *Selling Sounds: The Commercial Revolution in American Music*. Cambridge, MA: Harvard University Press, 2009.

Suskin, Steven. *The Sound of Broadway Music: A Book of Orchestrators and Orchestrations*. New York: Oxford University Press, 2009.

Susman, Warren I. "The Culture of the Thirties." In *Culture as History: The Transformation of American Society in the Twentieth Century*, 150–83. New York: Pantheon Books, 1984.

Tawa, Nicholas E. *Sweet Songs for Gentle Americans: The Parlor Song in America, 1790–1860*. Bowling Green, OH: Bowling Green University Popular Press, 1980.

Tiryakian, Edward A. "Durkheim, Solidarity, and September 11." In *The Cambridge Companion to Durkheim*, edited by Jeffrey C. Alexander and Philip Smith, 305–21. New York: Cambridge University Press, 2005.

Truzzi, Marcello. "Folksongs on the Right." *Sing Out!* 13 (1963): 51–53.

Truzzi, Marcello. "The 100 percent American Songbag: Conservative Folksongs in America." *Western Folklore* 28 (1969): 27–40.

Turino, Thomas. *Music as Social Life: The Politics of Participation*. Chicago: University of Chicago Press, 2008.

Turino, Thomas. "Signs of Imagination, Identity, and Experience: A Peircian Semiotic Theory for Music." *Ethnomusicology* 43, no. 2 (1999): 221–55.

Turner, Victor W. *Dramas, Fields, and Metaphors: Symbolic Action in Human Society*. Ithaca, NY: Cornell University Press, 1974.

Turner, Victor W. *The Forest of Symbols: Aspects of Ndembu Ritual*. Ithaca, NY: Cornell University Press, 1967.

Turner, Victor W. *The Ritual Process: Structure and Anti-Structure*. New York: Aldine Publishing, 1969.

Voigt, David Q. *America through Baseball*. Chicago: Nelson-Hall, 1976.

Vowell, Sarah. *Assassination Vacation*. New York: Simon and Schuster, 2005.

Wallace, Max. *The American Axis: Henry Ford, Charles Lindbergh, and the Rise of the Third Reich*. New York: St. Martin's Press, 2003.

Whitburn, Joel. *Pop Memories 1890–1954: The History of American Popular Music*. Menomonee Falls, WI: Record Research Inc., 1986.

Wilk, Max. *They're Playing Our Song*. New York: Da Capo Press, 1991.

Winter, Jay. *Remembering War: The Great War between Memory and History in the Twentieth Century*. New Haven, CT: Yale University Press, 2006.

Wiora, Walter. "Ethnomusicology and the History of Music." In *Garland Library of Readings in Ethnomusicology*. Vol. 1, *History, Definitions, and Scope*, edited by Kay Kaufman Shelemay, 127–33. New York: Garland, 1990. Originally published in *Studia Musicologica* 7 (1965): 187–93.

Woodard, Komozi. *A Nation Within a Nation: Amiri Baraka (LeRoi Jones) and Black Power Politics*. Chapel Hill: University of North Carolina Press, 1999.

Woollcott, Alexander. *The Story of Irving Berlin*. New York: G. P. Putnam's Sons, 1925.

Zirin, Dave. *What's My Name, Fool?: Sports and Resistance in the United States*. Chicago: Haymarket Books, 2005.

Zirin, Dave. *Welcome to the Terrordome: The Pain, Politics, and Promise of Sports*. Chicago: Haymarket Books, 2007.

DISCOGRAPHY

Berlin, Irving. *Irving Sings Berlin*. Koch International Classics 3-7510-2 HI, 2001, compact disc.

Brand, Oscar. *Presidential Campaign Songs: 1789–1996*. Smithsonian Folkways SFW CD 45051, 1999, compact disc.

Rimes, LeAnn. *You Light Up My Life: Inspirational Songs*. Curb Records D2–77885, 1997, compact disc.

Rodriguez, Daniel. *The Spirit of America*. Manhattan Records, 2002, compact disc.

Smith, Kate. *Kate Smith on the Radio: The Ted Straeter Collection*. Kate Smith Commemorative Society, 2007, compact disc.

Smith, Kate. *Kate Smith Sings "God Bless America" and Other American Favorites*. Legacy International CD 500, 2006, compact disc.

Smith, Kate. Program excerpt, *The Kate Smith Hour*, 10 November 1938. Courtesy of the Irving Berlin Collection of Noncommercial Sound Recordings, 1933–1989. New York Public Library for the Performing Arts.

Tynan, Ronan. *The Yankees Tenor*. Bravo Tenore Productions, 2009, compact disc.

Various artists. *American Songbook Series: Irving Berlin*. Smithsonian Collection of Recordings, 1994, compact disc.

Various artists. *God Bless America: For the Benefit of the Twin Towers Fund*. Columbia CK 86300, 2001, compact disc.

CREDITS

INDEX

The abbreviation "GBA" stands for "God Bless America." Page numbers written in italics denote illustrations.